To Roy
Best wishes
Stan Cranston

Stan Anderson

Stan Anderson

Captain of the North

SPORTS
BOOKS

Published in Great Britain by
SportsBooks Limited
1 Evelyn Court
Malvern Road
Cheltenham
GL50 2JR

Cover designed by Alan Hunns.

A catalogue record for this book is available from
the British Library.

ISBN 9781899807 98 7

Printed and bound in England by TJ International.

For Sue
thanks for all the encouragement which
led to the writing of this book

Acknowledgements

To Gill and George Armitage for their kindness and help and the use of their computer skills in compiling this book – true friendship.

I would also like to thank Pop Robson, Jimmy Montgomery and Jimmy Greaves for the forewords they provided, Mark Metcalf for helping me write it, John Harvey for taking some of the photographs that appear within, Alex Zaphiropoulos, Paul Days, Paul Joannou and Gordon Sharrock

Contents

Forewords

Jimmy Montgomery

I didn't really know get to know Stan until I became a regular in the Sunderland first team towards the end of the 1961–62 season and as such didn't know he had been pushing Alan Brown to select me much earlier. Stan was constantly encouraging you to do your best and if I made a mistake he'd remind me about the earlier good saves I had made as a way of helping to maintain my confidence.

On the pitch Stan had a calming authority. He never seemed flustered and could create space in which to deliver a perfectly weighted pass. Stan was one of those players 'who could make things happen'. He wouldn't shout and bawl at other players and gained respect through his willingness to always put the needs of the side above his own. Off the field I have always enjoyed Stan's company, probably more so when playing golf than watching a football match when he can get very frustrated if a pass goes astray.

Jimmy Greaves

The England players nicknamed Stan 'Boeing' after the original 707 airplane that is generally credited with ushering in the Jet Age. This is because he cruised around the football field, and while he was never in a hurry he always got there smoothly at the right time.

I always enjoyed Stan's company greatly and got on very well with him. We had good lives although the clubs had too much control over the players until the 1960s.

I thought Stan was one of the players who could have easily got quite a number of caps, and there were a lot of those, as the gap between those who played and didn't was often very marginal, with a manager preferring one over the other because he'd got a system in mind and the player didn't quite fit into it.

Bryan Robson

Living just round the corner from Roker Park, I first started to watch Sunderland just as Stan was beginning to establish himself in the first team. In an era when Len Shackleton was the crowd's favourite, I was more drawn, because of his great passing ability, to the young, dark haired wing half. I particularly recall the FA Cup game against Arsenal in 1961 when Stan scored two goals and largely ran the show. Like a lot of young lads I would wait to collect autographs and Stan was always happy to sign.

I hadn't played a first-team match at Newcastle when Stan arrived but I can recall that he quickly made an impression in the practice games by showing what a good player he was. Eventually I ended up playing alongside him. I was wearing number seven and he was playing right midfield and he was always advising me about how to improve my game, including the need to constantly work hard.

After a match when we were travelling home on the coach or train he would make it his business to talk through the game with the younger lads like myself, Dave Craig, Frank Clark and Bobby Moncur. He had the ability to talk to the senior players and also help out the younger ones, which made him the perfect captain. I believe Stan was instrumental in me getting started in the first team, as I feel Joe Harvey might have preferred to play more experienced players such as Trevor Hockey. Stan thought if you were good enough then you were old enough. Having said all this he didn't want to pay £15,000 for me in the summer of 1968 when Joe told him I was available! I worked really hard during the break and the following season I knocked home thirty goals for Newcastle and we won the Fairs Cup!

Chapter 1

No family ties to football

There is no particular reason why I should have made football my career. Certainly there was no precedent within my family, although no one brought up in the north-east can be immune from the passion of its people for the game, as I was to discover in my own unique way by going on to play for – and captain – Sunderland, Newcastle and Middlesbrough.

However, until I came along the nearest most of my family ever got to a football pitch was when they went on Saturday afternoons as spectators to Horden Colliery Welfare's ground, which nestled little more than a mile from the North Sea with its winds and rain.

As a kid I used to go with my dad, and occasionally some pals. My favourite player was an inside forward named Jackie Price. Today he'd be called a midfield player. What I liked about him was that he was really good on the ball, was a good passer and could score goals. He also had the knack of being able to create space for himself. His presence on the ball always lifted the crowd.

Others liked the hard men, the storming centre-forwards or the wingers who took on opposing full-backs, but Price had the qualities I have nurtured all my footballing life. I liked watching Jackie Price just as in later years I liked watching, playing with and competing against players who were a step up in class; men such as Len Shackleton, Charlie Hurley, Bobby Charlton, Duncan Edwards, Billy Wright, Denis Law and Bobby Moore and, as you will discover, a whole lot more.

There was an additional pleasure when watching Horden Colliery Welfare. Beforehand, at half-time and after the match, we used to kick our own ball around in the goalmouth. It made us feel big to be treading the same soccer pitch as grown-ups.

More often than not, however, our football 'pitches' were the back streets of Horden. We spent hours and hours playing 'kicky in', defending with our lives our own back gates in Tenth Street. This was built as one of a job lot of thirteen streets when the colliery opened in 1900, and homes were needed to house those who wanted to work there. My father, James Hall Anderson, was one such, having moved the twenty miles down the coast from South Shields, where he was born in 1901. My mother, a wonderful woman, was Elizabeth Carling from Wheatley Hill. She was also born in 1901 and married my father in 1920 before they moved to Horden.

My gate was number 39 Tenth Street, and when I was born I was one of five brothers. You couldn't describe our house as luxurious. There was no inside toilet and we had to make do with a tin bath, which was filled from a hot water boiler kept hot by a coal fire below it. Sadly, when I was around two or three my sister Shirley, who'd been born a year after me, fell into the boiler and scalded herself to death. There's not a day goes by when I don't think of her – she was a bubbly little thing and seventy years later I still miss her.

This tragedy, coupled with the death of my other sister Marjorie, who passed away before I was born, almost broke my mother's heart. It left five boys – Bob the oldest, Tom, Jim who is still around, Frank and myself. My mother loved us but really wanted a little girl to bring up as well.

Our football games in the back streets never seemed to end properly. Either the ball would go through someone's kitchen window or neighbours, whose gates we were using, would come out and chase us away, complaining that we were knocking their paintwork to pieces. Today we'd probably each have ended up with an ASBO!

When I got into the school team, our house was always the meeting point for most of the players before the match. Maybe my pals, Harry Dobson, Jackie Richardson, Louis Keighley and Frankie Aston thought the best 'pitch' in the alley was behind Tenth Street, and adopted it and our house as the headquarters.

Whatever the reason, I know my mother never complained. She just made tea, or told us off when the occasion warranted it. Because it was wartime when I was in junior school, we rarely had the facilities for a proper game. Not that we suffered too badly; a small place like Horden was never going to be a major target for the German bombers, although on one occasion they did deposit unused bombs from a raid on Liverpool just as they crossed the North Sea coast and a number of residents in the Grants Houses area, which was about three miles away, were killed. Once, though, we could see buildings on fire in Hartlepool about eight miles away.

It might have been this remoteness from the war that gave my parents the idea it would be fine for me to go to London for a week at the start of 1944. My mother's great friend Ivy Williams had relatives there and offered to take me with her when she visited. The Germans had bombed London in 1940 and 1941 but when Britain retaliated the attacks had ended, only to restart in the last days of 1943.

But off I went with Ivy by train and when we emerged from King's Cross Station I couldn't believe my eyes. Buildings had been flattened and there were large craters everywhere. We walked to where we were staying but any chances of a good night's sleep to recover were swiftly ended when the air raid siren went off and everyone scrambled into the shelter that had been dug out under the road. There must have been around a hundred people crowded inside; you could sit down but sleeping was impossible.

In the daytime I found myself with dozens of other lads and lasses searching on bombsites for shrapnel, shell casings and barrage balloons. We'd clamber over the rubble, in and out of areas that were out of bounds – which brought wardens to chase you away – to find these precious objects. I never, of course, saw anything of London. After a week of this it was time for home, and so we walked back to the station with our suitcases only to discover the authorities had decided to evacuate women, children and old people from the city as quickly as possible. Trains had been requisitioned to take them to Devon and Cornwall. We walked back to Ivy's relatives' house and it wasn't until four days later that we finally left London for the north.

Back in Horden during the war much of my spare time outside of football was spent playing cowboys and Indians, and Tarzans in Horden Dene. Aged nine, and a member of Donkey Collins's gang, I broke my right arm trying to show off. We were swinging on a branch overhanging a bank and I was the smallest and youngest and the last to try. I couldn't keep a grip and I dropped right on to my arm. I didn't tell my mam but she found out when I had to help her with the washing up and couldn't hold the plates. It meant a trip to the hospital and a large plaster on my arm, which prevented me playing on any such swings for a while. It didn't stop me going to the pictures, though. In those days Horden, despite its size, had three cinemas – there are none now. We lads would go together. Being only young we'd get to sit in the first six rows and it wouldn't be long before we'd be pushing and shoving each other. This didn't bother the courting couples in the back rows, but soon annoyed those in the middle who wanted to see the action on the big screen, on which Charlie Chaplin and Laurel and Hardy were the big stars. Often we'd end up being thrown out even though we were just messing around.

Although we lived less than a mile from the sea I rarely ventured down to the beach. Waste from the pit was dumped little more than a few hundred yards out to sea by overhead tubs and as a consequence the beach was black. There'd be a line of men from the water's edge scouring for coal – the larger operators would employ men with shovels and once they'd filled a truck it would roar up a steep bank. One- or two-man bands also worked the beach and I have never seen harder toil in my life. After filling a couple of bags with coal they would haul them on to rickety old bikes and push the load across the sandy beach before straining every muscle, fighting against a steep bank. They would then drain every ounce of remaining energy going door to door selling what they had collected.

Because it was wartime, matches against other schools had been suspended but we did manage, courtesy of one of the teachers, Mr Parkin, to play organised games within the school, class against class. It was because of these games that I got my first deep liking for the game. My interest was encouraged enormously by another teacher, Jim Cole. I was bigger than the average junior, and I must have shown some sort of promise as Mr Cole was invariably advising me.

I generally enjoyed junior school and did well at the tests. So I was very disappointed when I found out that I had failed the 11-plus as a pass would have seen me go to Henry Smith's Grammar School in Hartlepool. Even today I am mystified how I didn't pass. I was sure I'd done well.

I would have been the first in the family to go to a grammar school and my mother was in tears when she found out. She and my dad made it their business to go and see the headmaster at the junior school. They were told I'd done fairly well but it was in my interest to go to Horden Secondary Modern because, the headmaster explained, 'They don't play football at Henry Smith's but they do at the secondary school.' Which seems to suggest the junior school teachers already thought I'd go on to do well as a footballer.

I hadn't been long in my new school when, wandering out at the end of the day, I glanced up at the notice board. Pinned there was the school's football team for the forthcoming match against Shotton Colliery at Horden Colliery Welfare.

I had to look again after I saw the name Anderson, and then I almost swallowed my tongue when I saw the initial 'S' alongside. This caused me to work out frantically if there was another 'S. Anderson' in the school. I couldn't think of any – but I was only eleven, while the rest of the team were all at least fourteen.

When I got home I told my dad, on night shift that week and resting between shifts. He thought I must be mistaken. 'You're crackers' were his exact words, and he asked me more than once if I was really in the side. I don't think he was fully convinced but he did agree to take me and my boots to the ground, and I suppose he thought the worst that could happen would be that I would get to kick the ball around before and after the match. He needn't have worried, and anyway I was already worrying enough for both of us at the thought of playing against lads much bigger and stronger than me.

My teammates had no idea who I was. I got to enter the dressing rooms, which was great. They had a shower and a bath, which was amazing. We won 2-1 or 3-1 – I can't remember for sure. There was a crowd of around a hundred, mainly family and friends. They were not to know, of course, but two of those they were watching were on their way to doing well as professional footballers. Ken Hawkes was playing for Shotton and he was at left back for Luton in the 1959 FA Cup final against Nottingham Forest.

I later found out that the teacher who looked after the football team, Joe Herron, had, after listening to Mr Cole, decided to give me a chance, reasoning that I'd quickly adapt and become worth my place in time even if I wasn't quite up to the mark at that stage. Anyway, they were good enough to 'carry' me for a while. I'd like to think I learned quickly and was playing well enough to deserve my place by the end of the season. At that time most of the boys went off to find a job, mostly at the pit, where one of the major topic of conversations would have been football – and particularly Sunderland, who at the time could rightly claim to be the north-east's most successful club with six league titles and one FA Cup success to their name.

My brother Bob was a big Sunderland fan, going to Roker Park for home matches. He also took the train from Horden – this was long before the station was closed under the Beeching cuts of the 1960s – to Middlesbrough to watch a 'Boro side which contained Wilf Mannion, one of his favourite footballers. George Hardwick, the England captain, was another player Bob enjoyed seeing.

It was Bob who was responsible for my first taste of big-time football. As part of the end of war celebrations the three north-east sides played each other and Bob took me to see the 'Boro–Newcastle game. We took the bus to Billingham – cheaper than the train as there were two of us – hopped on another to the Transporter Bridge and walked from there. People were in a jubilant mood, and it was reflected on the pitch where the home side won 5-3 with 'Boro centre-forward Mickey Fenton striking a hat-trick.

Bob later took me to my first professional league games, at Ayresome Park and Roker Park, during the 1947–48 season and I was captivated by the performance of Johnny Mapson in goal for Sunderland. Out wide on the left, Eddie Burbanks was in the twilight of his career at Roker Park but you could catch glimpses of what a good player he must have been, able to beat players and shoot accurately. He'd been part of the Sunderland side which had won the 1937 FA Cup final, scoring the third goal as they beat Preston

North End 3-1. Eddie had also scored Sunderland's last goal before the war started in 1939 and the club's first after it ended.

On the other wing, Len Duns, also a member of the 1937 cup-winning team, was very quick, had good control of the ball and crossed it accurately. I played reserve football with Len at Sunderland. But for the war Len could well have ended up making a record number of outfield appearances for the club. By the time he retired in 1952 his total was 244, yet he lost six years. Len Ashurst, of course, holds the record with 452 starts, plus six substitute appearances. That's five more than me, and Len never mentions it – except every time he sees me!

Of course Jimmy Montgomery tops everyone. He played 627 times in the Sunderland first team, but goalkeepers go on for ever.

It's interesting what stays in the mind of the young. I remember that the following season Barney Ramsden played ten first-team games for Sunderland and every time there was a free kick in his area of the field he would be cheered as he ran to give the ball a big whack up the field. Fred Hall was at centre-half. I would later play alongside him at Roker Park.

In those days just after the war Roker Park was always packed – most grounds were. People were hungry for entertainment. We would go in the Roker End, which was massive, and aim to get a spot in front of a barrier so that when the crowd swayed forward we wouldn't get crushed.

Thirty-three spectators were killed during a cup-tie at Bolton in 1946 and looking back it is clear that too many people were allowed into most grounds – Roker Park was not unique in this respect. But the packed crowds certainly created a magnificent atmosphere, and while people would shout and bawl they certainly never lost their temper and hurled obscenities the way some spectators do today. In fact, if someone was swearing a lot people would turn on them, and if they didn't stop they would be made to. It was very much a case of the crowd policing itself and there were very few bobbies at the games. People wore flat caps; most had finished work at 12.30pm or 1.00pm and headed straight to the ground to try and get the best spot.

At the end of the game supporters' first thoughts weren't necessarily about the result – it was more a case of whether they'd enjoyed it. After the rigours of war many people had a more relaxed attitude to results – after all, it wasn't a matter of life or death. That had been all too close in the recent years. In addition the players didn't earn much more than the average wage, so no one was jealous of their great wealth. They didn't feel 'cheated' like they do today if someone doesn't play well.

Bob and I also occasionally went to Hartlepool as well and each time we went home we'd have agitated conversations about key moments and players. Going to the match was always a great day out.

Bob was to work all his life in the pit and, typically, was dead within a year of retiring in 1980. He was a football man to the end, with a season ticket at Roker Park and a healthy respect for good footballers of any team.

In my second year at senior school I was a regular member of the team, playing in my usual position of centre-half. It was when I was thirteen that I first played right half – the berth I later regarded as my own. In those days every team lined up in the same way. In defence there was the goalkeeper and two full backs flanking a central defender in a back three. In midfield were two half backs – one attacked more than the other – and two inside forwards, also with one pushed forward; two wingers played in attack with a centre-forward. My switch to right half happened after I had been selected to represent East Durham schoolboys – Ken Hawkes was also in the team. We were losing 3-0 at half-time when a man came into the dressing room saying he was a Mr Errington, one of the Durham County selectors.

He said he was looking for a right half and asked whether I could play there in the second half. As the game was virtually sewn up, I was switched. And although we lost 5-1 I must have made a good impression as I was chosen for Durham County's next game against a touring Kent side at Darlington. It was hardly an auspicious debut. The match was abandoned after seventeen minutes because of torrential rain. Sadly that was that for season.

The following year I was in luck. I was selected at right half for the county's game against Northumberland – invariably our 'bogey' team. I played well in a 2-1 victory.

One of my most abiding memories of that time was after one game when I was given the East Durham kit to take to the lady who laundered it. Instead of taking it to her house immediately, I left it in the shed in our back yard. I totally forgot about it and went to play more football the following day. Walking back from the Recreation Ground someone told me there had been a fire at my house. I had visions of blackened, gutted rooms and horrible disasters and ran like mad. It wasn't, thankfully, nearly as bad as what I had imagined but I soon spotted the smouldering remains of the shed with the kit in it. As I ran into the yard, I saw my mother picking up tattered, burnt pieces of cloth. She looked at me and said, 'Your football stuff.'

It was a catastrophe and I was inconsolable. I didn't dare tell the teachers what had happened. So Mam went to the school and told them she would make a mat as a competition prize. That was her hobby; she made a huge mat, raffled it and bought a whole new set of outfits. My face was saved thanks to her.

In my final year at school we won the local league – the second time when I was there – and I was selected for the North trials, the first step to playing for England. The match, at Brunton Park, Carlisle United's ground, finished

3-3 with Dennis Viollet, who was to play for Manchester United as a 'Busby Babe', scoring one of the goals.

I must have done pretty well as the next step was turning out the North against the South. This was played at Barnsley's Oakwell ground on March 19 1949 with the following teams:

North: Taylor (Bolton); Eden (Prescott), Whitefoot (Stockport); Anderson (East Durham), Jackson (East Northumberland), Mitchell (Doncaster); Birkett (Newton-le-Willows), Viollet (Manchester), Levitt (Barnsley), Lydon (Sunderland), Luke (Newcastle).

South: Matthews (Aldershot); Bassham (Ealing), Bryan (Birmingham); Stevens (Finchley), Daniel (Edmonton), Devlin (Luton); Tracey (Gillingham), Charsley (Mitcham), Ames (Wareham), Bennett (SW Middlesex), Curtis (Swindon).

It proved to be a mismatch; three of our side had played for the full England team the previous season and the South defence were given a very hard time. Matthews was great in goal and I felt he was really unlucky when the first all-England schoolboys' trial match was staged at Ashton Gate, home of Bristol City, on April 2 and he was part of 'the rest' against an England side containing Stanley Anderson at right half.

There was a crowd of 8,000, and of the South team only Tosh Chamberlain, later to play for Fulham, made the England side, although playing at inside left for the rest was Johnny Haynes, later to play 658 games for Fulham and fifty-six for England.

The score was 0-0 at half-time but two goals from Sunderland's Michael Lydon settled it. Even though I was pleased with my performance and optimistic I would be picked for the match with Wales at Vetch Field, Swansea, the following Saturday it was still a special thrill when, after prayers at school assembly, the news was announced that I was in the team.

At that time there were only three teams in the Victory Shield; Northern Ireland did not take part because their school leaving age had not yet risen to fifteen to bring it into line with the rest of Britain. Everyone clapped and cheered when my name was read out. It was a really wonderful moment.

So I joined a select band that included greats such as Arsenal's Cliff Bastin and Sunderland's Raich Carter. Not that selection guaranteed a future in the game; hundreds of schoolboy internationals had failed to make it.

I travelled down on the train with my dad. We met up with Jimmy Jackson and his dad. They were from Ashington and although that was only about forty miles north of Horden we could hardly understand them, their accents were so strong.

The team were put up in a fantastic hotel in Mumbles Bay. For many it was the first time away from home without parents and of course such freedom was to be exploited. Frankie Levitt, from Barnsley, asked me if I fancied going to a party in his room. Once there he asked, 'Fancy a fag, Stan?' I didn't, in truth.

The Welsh side were not a bad outfit. They included Len Allchurch, brother of the legendary Ivor, up front and Johnny King in goal. King made more than 350 appearances for Swansea and although he was a goalkeeper once played centre-forward in a league match. He was to prove a stumbling block for me and Sunderland in a few years. But England had only lost three times in thirty-six matches against Wales, the last defeat coming a quarter of a century before, and we were confident. The teams were:

Wales: King (Ferndale); Thomas (Aberdare), Lloyd (Swansea); Samuel (Swansea), Williams (Merthyr),

Chard (Swansea); Griffiths (Arvon), Denham (Flint), Davies (Newport), Jones (Mountain Ash), L Allchurch (Swansea)

England: Taylor (Bolton); Eden (Prescott), Whitefoot (Stockport); Anderson, Jackson (East Northumberland), Mitchell (Doncaster); Birkett (Newton le Willows), Viollet (Manchester), Levitt (Barnsley), Lydon (Sunderland), Chamberlain (Islington)

There was a big crowd – Wales had selected four Swansea lads. But they but should have gone a goal down in the first few minutes when Dennis Viollet shot wide after a fine ball from Cliff Birkett. We did, however, take the lead with a great shot by Tosh Chamberlain and I felt we were well on the way to winning.

My direct opponent at inside left was Derek Jones, who the papers said was a 'vigorous whole-hearted player'. It was a fitting description: he was a right roughhouse and he scored the equaliser when Jimmy Taylor misjudged his long, dropping shot. Jones then showed he could play a bit as well when he darted past the England defence to make it 2-1 just before half-time. He ended up with a hat-trick and despite a late Birkett goal we couldn't grab an equaliser and lost 4-3.

I hadn't played well and as we came off Micky Lydon said 'Well, we'll be out next time'. He was right – we were both dropped for the match with the Republic of Ireland.

So you can imagine my mixed feelings as I watched from the Upton Park stands as England won 7-0. It seemed hardly likely that I would get back.

But Lady Luck was on my side. The next international was at St James' Park, Newcastle, against Scotland. Presumably, the selectors considered the 'local boy' appeal to the football fans and both Jimmy Jackson and I were selected to play, although Michael Lydon was left out.

England had not beaten Scotland for twenty-two years and with special railway excursions from all over the north set to bring thousands to the match I was as excited as I had ever been. Around 19,000 tickets had been sold in advance and there was even talk of a 60,000 crowd – four times the number of people who lived in Horden! The teams were:

England: Matthews (Aldershot); Bassham (Ealing), Whitefoot (Stockport); Anderson, Jackson (East Northumberland), Young (Derby); Birkett (Newton le Willows), Vickers (Rotherham), Ames (Wareham), Viollet (Manchester), Chamberlain (Islington)

Scotland: Prasher (North Ayr); Ogilvie (Aberdeen), Bowman (Wemyss); Raeburn (Bategate), J Patterson (Edinburgh), Miller (East Ayr); Lennox (North Ayr), C Patterson (Glasgow), Anderson (Kilmarnock), Martin (Edinburgh)

As it transpired the crowd was 43,700, still, by far, the biggest I had played before. We again took the lead. It was slightly lucky, with referee W Lauder deciding the Scottish 'keeper George Hume had stepped over the goal-line when collecting Cliff Birkett's centre. Thirteen years later I was to be on the receiving end of a dubious refereeing decision in an England v Scotland game.

We ended up easy winners, 4-0. Tosh Chamberlain got two although Jeff Whitefoot was the star of the show. He was a right half but was switched to left back to accommodate me. He was a very good right half but he fitted in just as easily at left back. He won two league championship medals with Manchester United and when he made his debut for them was their youngest ever player at sixteen years and 105 days.

It was a fine team performance and thrilling to play before such a large crowd. That should have been the end of my involvement at schoolboy level but England decided that for the first time ever they would play Wales for a second time in a season. The England team was the same as had played at St James' Park while the Welsh fielded the team which had beaten us at Swansea.

The game was at Manchester City's Maine Road and I really wanted revenge. There was another huge crowd – 52,000 – as people were still desperate for entertainment even though the war had been over for four years. It was at the time the largest attendance at a boys' soccer match in England. Wales again took the lead just before half-time.

Just after the interval I hit a twenty-yard shot that Johnny King saved superbly and I was also disappointed when my well-placed free-kick was put wide by Dennis Viollet. Fortunately Ken Ames made it 1-1 on the hour mark, although four minutes later Griffiths put Wales back in the lead. Then, on sixty-seven minutes, Peter Vickers drove home the equaliser and five minutes after that England were in the lead when Cliff Birkett fired a powerful shot past King.

I nearly made it four near the end when I hit a left-foot shot that seemed certain to hit the net before Johnny King came from nowhere to tip the ball over – something he was to repeat thirteen years later to deny Sunderland promotion. We had avenged our earlier defeat and were given a real ovation as we left the field.

That England side had some wonderful players who went on to do very well in the professional game. As well as his medals with Manchester United, Whitefoot won a cup winner's medal with Nottingham Forest in 1959; Jimmy Jackson played for Aldershot; Ron Archer for Barnsley; Cliff Birkett for Manchester United; Peter Vickers for Leeds; Geoff Ames for Portsmouth; Tosh Chamberlain for Fulham; and Dennis Viollet for Manchester United.

It was said that this was the best team to represent England schoolboys. What cheered me was reading a report afterwards that stated that, while it was clear that Viollet, Whitefoot and Birkett were going to 'make it' professionally, I had the best chance of the rest.

Chapter 2

Signing for Sunderland

It might seem strange but, despite my success at schoolboy level, I never thought about making football my full-time career. I suppose at the age of fifteen you don't really envisage what the future has in store for you.

At the time most people were just happy to have seen things get better after the end of the war and to welcome home loved ones. People didn't have that much. In our case, with my dad working there was always plenty on the table and we'd get extra treats at Christmas when we all tried to find the biggest stocking in the world in the hope our parents would fill it with fruit and nuts.

But there was rarely enough money for presents, so it was a big moment when my father found enough to buy me a football, which in those days contained a bladder that needed blowing up and laces which needed tying.

I loved that present so much that when my older brother Jim burst the bladder I went crazy and walloped him with the coal shovel. He didn't mind – well, not much. He only kept reminding me about it for the next forty or fifty years!

Like all families we had our ups and downs. My parents had a good marriage but my dad did like to get drunk at the weekends, which could cause tension. He took the attitude that as he worked hard during the week he was going to get as much ale down him as possible on Fridays and Saturdays. A lot of miners felt the same.

I received several offers to join clubs as an amateur, but although I was flattered I took little notice. Blackpool asked, as did Leeds United and Queens Park Rangers and several Third Division sides. But the only offer I was interested in came from Sheffield Wednesday. For some reason I rather fancied going to Sheffield. They were a large club with a big reputation and with my schoolboy thinking I considered it would be 'nice' there.

The club that tried hardest to sign me, at least at first, were Middlesbrough. Shortly before the end of my school days my father took a knock at the door to find a scout from 'Boro. He explained the club were interested in me and we were invited to their next match. This was against Newcastle and it was arranged that my dad and I would meet the manager David Jack after the game in his office.

Every young lad of my era knew who David Jack was. An England inside forward from the 1920s, he was famous for scoring the first goal at Wembley in 1923, when Bolton Wanderers beat West Ham United to win the FA Cup. He won another FA Cup winner's medal with Arsenal as well as two league champions' medals. I was very excited and hardly slept the two nights beforehand.

On the day of the match, Easter Tuesday 1949, the scout turned up in his car. That caused quite a stir in our road as very few people had cars in those days. We were made very welcome and had great seats in the directors' box to watch a match in which Middlesbrough came from a goal down at half-time to win 3-2.

As the boisterous crowd of 44,000 poured out of the ground I waited anxiously to meet the manager.

When we did get to meet him his breath reeked of alcohol. He didn't have a clue who I was. These were the days when clubs had dozens of players on their books, some of whom never got anywhere near the first team.

Jack didn't even look at me. He asked my father, 'About your son – what position?'

'Right half,' said my dad, nothing more.

'We've got loads of right halves here,' was the reply.

My dad was having none of that. He might just have been a pitman but he was a proud one, and he wanted his kids to do their best, even if he didn't necessarily show it at times.

Quick as a flash he said, 'Well if that's the case, you won't be interested in my son.' With that he turned on his heels and we walked back out of the room. I never did see Jack's face. I was naturally disappointed but trusted my dad. The embarrassed scout drove us home.

It didn't take long for my disappointment to fade. Mr Herron called me over one day and said that Sunderland were interested. Now if the story is true, and I have no reason to believe otherwise, I had at the tender age of three paraded a large flower vase, pretending it was the FA Cup, around the street following Sunderland's 1937 3-1 victory over Preston North End. That seems to have been the first time I showed a real interest in the game that has been a large part of my life.

But despite this very youthful enthusiasm it would be stretching things to say that at fifteen I was a Sunderland fanatic. I liked Sunderland because they were our nearest big club. But of course I was thrilled when it became clear they were interested.

I have heard of youngsters today being given a lot of money just for signing for a club. It wasn't like that in those days, and while the wages of a professional footballer were better than average it wasn't that much better.

It was agreed that I would sign as an amateur simply because Mr Herron convinced my parents and me that it was the best thing. He argued that because I was only fifteen I should not leave home to take what was, after all, a risky step. He said there were hundreds of promising schoolboy players who never developed into successful seniors. Physique, personal circumstances and lots of other things change during adolescence. Mr Herron suggested I should stay at home, and enjoy my mother's cooking and family life until I was seventeen. By then I should have a better idea whether I would to make the grade. If I was any good Sunderland would take me on.

And so I stayed in Horden, and after leaving school without qualifications I got a job with a Sunderland building firm, L.W. Evans. This was very much at my dad's instigation. Like many miners he didn't want his son following him down the pit. He had been unable to prevent Bob becoming a miner, so he was extra keen that I shouldn't follow him. Being a pitman was a dangerous occupation, with injuries and fatalities a fact of life. Two years later at nearby Easington Colliery an explosion resulted in the deaths of eighty-one miners and two rescuers. It was a very sad day.

Other miners died more slowly, killed by breathing in the coal dust, and my father was one of them. The rewards for working down a black hole miles under the sea weren't too great either. Once I was sent to collect my father's pay, and although I knew little about the cost of many goods it was clear that with a family to support it wouldn't go too far. Send me down the pit? Not likely. And I am ever so grateful to him. Of my other brothers, Jim did work for the colliery but as a blacksmith, while Tom went in the army and Frank became a tiler after leaving the army.

My ability with a football was working in my favour as the company I joined was owned by the Sunderland director Laurie Evans and the job came after I'd signed as an amateur.

I started as an apprentice joiner earning £1 35s a week, from which I had to give my mother 85d for my digs and spend 25d a week on travelling. I didn't like the work. So I tried my hand at plastering, and hated that. It was bad enough that at the end of the day my dark hair was beginning to look like Raich Carter's greying locks but worse, much worse, was the monotony. There was only one tool to use, the trowel, and I was soon bored.

Third time lucky I started plumbing, and served my time at that trade. I have to say I thoroughly enjoyed it. Indeed, if I hadn't made it as a footballer I'd have been happy to be a plumber. During my training I helped to fit the individual baths at Roker Park and did an odd job or two in the treatment room. My chargehand at that time was Les Burns, a wonderful craftsman.

At the time my football education with Sunderland was confined to two training sessions a week, Tuesday and Thursday evenings, and it was just as well I enjoyed plumbing – to a fifteen-year-old my footballing career appeared to be going nowhere fast.

I was disappointed to discover that Sunderland didn't run a junior team. Fortunately a chap called Tom Jones asked me to play for the works team, Springwell United. They played in the South Shields and District League and, while playing against older and stronger players was difficult, I did well enough to ensure that I got a place in the Sunderland 'B' side that operated in the Houghton and District League.

The 'B' team was Sunderland's fourth team and my debut was at Chester-le-Street just before Christmas 1949. It was my first taste of real football. The Houghton League was full of experienced players who knew all the tricks of the trade. It was not long before I discovered that my youthful outlook on the game was slightly awry and every Saturday night and Sunday morning I nursed giant-sized bruises. It was a tough class of football. Some games frightened the life out of me. There were miners, dockers, butchers – Uncle Tom Cobley and all – who played for the teams in the East Durham area. They knew they were playing against semi-pros and they'd say to themselves, 'I'll show them.'

You could not afford to be careless or lose your concentration for a single moment. Otherwise, there were tricks, not all legal, which could bring about your downfall. One thing I soon learned was to be just as hard as my opponents in order to show my skill. I felt I wasn't doing too badly, yet only once that season did I step up to the 'A' team.

It was a big help that I had a great relationship with the coach Tommy Urwin, at that time the only man to have played for Sunderland, Newcastle and Middlesbrough. Tom would say, 'This bloke's after you so get the ball away quickly and go for the return; pass it and link up with the right winger and inside right – you're quicker than your opponent.' His enthusiasm was a big help in convincing me I could make it as a professional footballer.

Other players were not so fortunate. It often happens at a big League club that there were a lot of players from the 'B' team who never made the grade – players like Tommy Beech, Tommy Fairley, Tommy Bell, Jackie Rowell, Jack Webb, Ian Quinn, Gerry Crosby and my England schools teammate Mick Lydon. Mick went to Leeds United from Roker and finished with Gateshead; the rest finished on what is quaintly termed the 'football scrapheap'.

During my second year as an amateur I felt I might well be following them. Despite my best efforts I seemed stuck in the Houghton and District League.

It was all very depressing. It seemed that the rest of the boys who had played with me for England Schools were making much faster progress.

Cliff Birkett, an outside right, became one of the original Busby Babes and was actually in the Manchester United first team while I was still watching Sunderland seniors. He played for United at Roker Park after I'd signed for the club, and when he went past the Sunderland full back and crossed for United to score I started cheering. He was a friend but I suddenly remembered where I was as people began to look around!

Dennis Viollet had established himself as a regular reserve at Old Trafford before his seventeenth birthday;

Jimmy Jackson, a centre-half or full back, was in and out of the reserve team at St James' Park.

Tommy Urwin, however, was constantly stressing in training the need to work hard to stay fit. Tommy and Jimmy Teasdale, a former master in charge of Sunderland schoolboys, who was now in charge of the Sunderland 'B' team, would encourage me to play my natural passing game at right half at all times. I enjoyed the position because it meant being involved in the game all the time.

Although I didn't know it, both men must have been giving me good reports for as soon as I reached seventeen the Sunderland manager Bill Murray – of course I called him Mr – asked me to sign professional terms. I couldn't wait and it was arranged that I meet the club secretary, George Crow.

Usually the younger players started on professional terms at £3 a week but Tommy told me not to accept anything less than £5 because I was worth it. My dad said I should listen to his advice, so when I turned up on the Tuesday night for training and to sign my contract I asked for £5. How I managed to blurt out I was worth the money I still don't know. George Crow said I'd never get that much. I asked if my dad could come into the meeting and when George Crow agreed my dad said he felt I was worth £5. It was the best thing he ever did for me. Time seemed to stand still, but eventually George Crow said they'd be happy to pay me £5 during the season and £4 in the summer. I agreed and the contract was signed.

I still don't know who made the best deal but I was very glad to become a professional footballer for Sunderland on February 27 1951 – my seventeenth birthday. It was now up to me to get into the reserves and play well enough to make the first team and be offered full-time professional terms. I was on my way.

Chapter 3

Being paid to play

Having turned professional I was pleasantly surprised when the various team-sheets were posted the next Friday to see that I had skipped the 'A' team and was playing for the reserves against Crook Town in a cup match. They were not a bad side, and went on to win the FA Amateur Cup twice during the 1950s.

I was to spend a season and a half in the reserves, joining players such as Jackie Pigg, a left half. As you can imagine, with a surname like that and a dressing room full of young footballers Jackie had the mickey taken out of him. One day he came in and said he'd changed his name to Rowell. He never made the grade; he was a big lad who never quickened but his son went on to become a Sunderland legend. Gary Rowell played at Roker Park in the '70s and '80s. Michael Lydon also signed professionally around the same time as me, but, as I have mentioned, although he was a big schoolboy star Mick struggled in the professional game.

When I moved up to the reserves the trainer was Hughie Ross. He was a great guy and his promptings had a lot to do with my progress. He would defend his players to the hilt – often at the expense of injury from an umbrella or other missile thrown from the crowd!

I was also grateful for the help of players like Billy Walsh, the centre-half who also from Horden Colliery, although he was a few years older than me. His professional career had started at 23 because of the war. He had made his first-team debut in September 1946. But the first-team centre-half spot was monopolised by Fred Hall and Bill was restricted to just over a hundred first team appearances in his seven years at the club.

The first team's loss was my gain, and I was also lucky to be able to draw on the experience and skill of Albert Snell. In the 1950s Sunderland had a professional staff of around fifty and Albert, a left half, played only nine times in six years.

The reserves played in the North-eastern League and you'd get good crowds at places such as Consett, Eppleton Colliery Welfare and North Shields, who had the ex-Newcastle favourite Frank Brennan as manager. Two or three thousand was by no means unusual and although we had some really hard games they were fortunately not nearly as rough or dirty as in the Houghton and District League. We ended up winning the league in 1951–52. I still have the medal I won and I was very proud to win it.

I really enjoyed playing for the second team. I felt I was improving all the time, getting stronger, which was helping me to hold on to the ball when challenged and giving me time to pass it. I was also confident enough to take the penalties.

Yet never at any time did I think I would be playing for the first team the next year. I was happy to train two evenings a week, work hard at my plumbing apprenticeship and enjoy the matches at the weekend. Life was great and I was lucky in that I managed to avoid serious injury. Football is littered with potential stars who are dealt the wrong cards. One of these was Albert Quinn. I honestly thought Albert, from Middlesbrough, was going to be a big star for Sunderland and even England. Yet one day when we were playing at Chester-le-Street, Albert, running to collect a loose ball for a throw-in, tried to jump over a rope round the pitch. Misjudging it, he caught his boot on the rope, broke his foot and never played again.

Even when the 1952–53 season started and I was more than happy with my form I still didn't consider I was a serious prospect for the first team. Sunderland had a wealth of experienced halfbacks to call on in Willie Watson, Arthur Wright and George Aitken. Also, the club were not known for launching young players at that time. They didn't have a youth policy. I think they found out about me only because I'd played for England schools.

The only youngster who struck it rich was Harry Kirtley. Bill Murray thought the world of him. He was two or three seasons ahead of me and he was a powerful runner with an accurate pass and a knack of scoring goals.

Harry was in the 'big' team when I made my debut against Portsmouth at Roker Park in the First Division on October 4 1952. Needless to say, I was overwhelmed at the thought of playing before more than 40,000.

I had an inkling I would be in the team against Portsmouth because Willie Watson had been selected as the travelling reserve for England against Northern Ireland and George Aitken was injured. Nothing was said to me, but when I looked at the team-sheet there was my name at number 4. Murray hadn't said anything but later he told me that I would be in for one game only.

I could hardly wait to get back to Horden and let my parents know the news, which took time to sink in.

The teams were:

Sunderland: Threadgold, Stelling, Hedley, Anderson, Hall,
    A Wright, T Wright, Kirtley, Ford, Shackleton, Toseland.
Portsmouth: Butler, Stephen, Thompson, Scoular, Flewin,
    Pickett, Harris, Gordon, Reid, Phillips, Dale.

I was in the same team as my heroes. I was playing with the great Len Shackleton and against players like Jimmy Scoular and Peter Harris. It didn't seem possible. I'd started training with players like Shack and Trevor Ford, but I hadn't had much to do with them. I was in awe of Shack – he was a class act; you thought he could make the ball talk – and in those days youngsters didn't speak to their elders unless they spoke to you. Later I got to know him well but at the start there wasn't much interaction between the players. The dressing room wasn't split – apart from some feeling between Shack and Trevor Ford – but we tended to keep to our own age groups. For instance we didn't discuss tactics. I knew Harry Kirtley and stuck with him.

I stripped next to Fred Hall and, gulping, held out my hand: 'Stan Anderson.'

'I know who you are, son,' said our centre-half.

He only ever called me 'son' and I think he looked upon me that way. Certainly he was like a second father to me. Most of them, sitting around the dressing room that day, looked as old as my dad and when Fred, who must have been fifteen stone, took his shirt off he had a big gut. I wondered how he could play football like that. He could and he found time to look after me as well, guiding me through games.

Against Portsmouth we scored first with a penalty from Trevor Ford after five minutes. Although we were top of the league at the time it was only the twelfth goal we'd scored in ten matches – that might not be unusual today, when some top teams can't even average a goal a game, but in 1952 two goals a game was commonplace. Crowds expected to see goals and as a result the entertainment was greater than it is today. No club in the First Division had scored fewer goals than Sunderland; in fact only two teams in all four leagues had scored fewer. And Trevor Ford had scored five of the dozen.

I'd first seen Trevor play for Wales against England at Roker Park shortly after his big money move from Aston Villa two years before. He scored twice, but two goals from Tottenham's Eddie Baily and efforts from Wilf Mannion and Newcastle's Jackie Milburn were enough to secure a

4-2 win. I was one of those packed together in the Roker End and had great fun as the huge crowd swayed from side to side.

Trevor Ford averaged more than a goal every game for his country, with twenty-three in thirty-eight games (making him equal with Ivor Allchurch as the top scorer) and exceeded that with seventy goals in 117 appearances for Sunderland.

Portsmouth had won the League Championship in consecutive seasons as the end of the 1940s. This Pompey team had a great halfback line of Scoular, Jack Froggatt and Jimmy Dickinson, but only Scoular was playing on the day I made my debut. The absence of two key players was mitigated by a recall for the stylish Reg Flewin at centre-half. Flewin, an England wartime international, had captained Portsmouth in their championship-winning seasons so was no mean deputy. But he went off after half an hour.

Disappointingly, Portsmouth, even with ten men, managed to equalise when Fred Hall diverted a speculative shot from Jimmy Scoular past Harry Threadgold soon after half-time.

Len Phillips, a future England wing-half, was at inside forward and he certainly taught me a few things that day. Phillips was not particularly nippy, and looking back I'd say he was an average First Division player with above-average distribution.

Yet he had good control. He showed me just how good when I went into my first tackle. The next moment I was sitting on my backside and Phillips was surging through the middle. Fortunately the danger was averted but, determined to make amends, I again lunged at him the next time he collected the ball. The result was the same as he left me trailing in his wake.

I had always been a firm believer in 'getting stuck in' and the value of sliding tackles. Running back, I spotted the left back Jack Hedley in a tussle with the Portsmouth right winger Peter Harris. It dawned on me that he was not throwing himself straight at the ball. He was holding off, 'kidding' the winger so that the rest of the defence – Stan Anderson in particular – could get back into position.

Jack had not touched the ball but nonetheless he had wrecked the attacking movement. Sliding tackles at this level I soon learned were to be kept as a desperate last-ditch method of trying to foil an opponent. If you were beaten you were out of the game and your defence was one man short.

For my money Jack Hedley was one of the greatest and most underrated players in the game. I would class him as the best of Sunderland's buys during the period when they became known as the 'Bank of England' club, signing the likes of Ray Daniel, Len Shackleton, Billy Bingham and Don Revie.

Jack was plagued with injuries. He got arthritis in a knee and I reckoned this stopped him playing for England. But to me he was unbeatable in his positional play and his fantastic ability to jockey an opponent into mistakes.

Jack helped me a lot in my early years and I am convinced that, had he been a little more flashy, he would have played for England, especially as he was equally comfortable at right or left back.

Despite this difficult start I was able to recover my confidence and was pleased to be able to get control of the ball and pass it to Tommy Wright on the wing or Harry Kirtley at inside right. But it was the other Wright, Arthur (no relation to Tommy), who showed me what passing was – he was controlling the ball and using his wonderful left foot to ping it to his namesake Tommy at outside right. When he did it the first time I thought 'you lucky so and so', but after he'd done it five or six times I knew there was no luck involved.

At the end I made a mental note to practise so I could do the same, only in my case from right half to the outside left. It took me some time, with more than a few mistakes on the training ground and pitch, before it came off, but eventually I mastered the technique and it was a ball I used effectively in the subsequent matches I appeared in for Sunderland, Newcastle, Middlesbrough and England.

I was pleased to see that the press said I had done reasonably well and although I was back in the reserves the following weekend I felt that, as long as I kept training hard and showed form in the reserves, I would get another opportunity.

However, when it arrived it was something of a surprise. In those days professional footballers were used to playing twice over Christmas, occasionally on Christmas Day itself. In 1952 on Boxing Day Sunderland had drawn 1-1 with Wolves at Molineux and afterwards the teams travelled north for the return fixture the following day.

Having no idea that I might be called upon, I was persuaded by my mother to have a full dinner before she, my dad and I took the train from Horden to Sunderland to watch the match. As always I was at the ground in good time and when I went in the players' entrance Bert Johnston, then a trainer at the club after serving Sunderland on the pitch in the 1920s and '30s, said that the manager wanted me upstairs in his office. Worrying about what I might have done wrong, I knocked gingerly on Bill Murray's door to be told that Willie Watson was injured and I was to fill in. My only thought was how on earth I was going to play having had so much food. Fortunately by the time kick-off arrived I was feeling fine.

So it was just as well that I had the habit of turning up early at the ground. It became part of my pre-match ritual. Like most players I tended to stick to a routine. I would get there an hour and a half before kick-off; I would polish my boots – there were no groundstaff boys in those days to look after them – put them on, tie the laces, take them off, put on my street shoes, put on the boots again and retie them. I'd put on my boots about three times to make sure the laces weren't too tight. I think it stemmed from when I was at school and someone stood on my toe. It became swollen and my boots were too tight.

Wolves were building a great side under Stan Cullis that was to rival Manchester United as the best in English football in the 1950s with title wins in 1953–54, 1957–58 and 1958–59.

Cullis adopted a style of football that was based on an extraordinary level of fitness. He even employed a fitness trainer and made use of Olympic athletes to give his players sprint training – employing speed and athleticism rather than skill on the ball. It was very effective and they scored a lot of goals but I am not sure it was that attractive to watch. Peter Broadbent was perhaps the exception as he could beat players, but he got very few England caps because England were well served when he was at his peak by Johnny Haynes. Wolves' best player was Billy Wright, who became the first player to play 100 times for England. He read the game very well.

Wolves arrived at Roker Park at the top of the league; Sunderland, in sixth with a game in hand, were only three points worse off. The teams were:

Sunderland: Mapson, Hedley, Hudgell, Anderson, Aitken, A Wright, Bingham, Davis, Ford, Kirtley, Reynolds.
Wolverhampton Wanderers: Williams, Short, Pritchard, Baxter, Chatham, Wright, Smith, Broadbent, Swinborne, Wilshaw, Mullen.

Wolves' keeper Bert Williams was top class and he showed his full value that day, as even though Fred Hall, Len Shackleton and Tommy Wright were out injured, as well as Watson, we played ever so well. We were one up within six minutes and two goals apiece from Billy Bingham and Dickie Davis and one from Harry Kirtley meant we received a standing ovation for a 5-2 victory that saw the team shoot up to third.

On a personal level, despite the extra helpings, I found boundless energy, having a game which a young player usually dreams about. Everything went right and the older players in the team kept me right. Jack Hedley was very good in this respect. He gave me constant encouragement and I was given inch-perfect passes from Arthur Wright playing at left half.

Early in the game, Billy Wright, England captain at the time, and I went for the same ball and he hit me right in the middle of my chest, knocking me to the floor.

I was slightly injured but in those days it was felt you should never show it and with a quiet word from George Aitken I was soon back on my feet without the need for the trainer to rush on with the wet sponge.

'Next time he comes through, push him on the inside,' said George, which I duly did, and all I heard was this great big crunch and I turned round to see Wright, a truly great player, lying on the floor. Anyway, it seemed to do the trick as he rarely came over the halfway line after that!

I knew I had played a lot better than in my first match, which was also the view of the press with the *Journal* report on the Monday stating: '18-year-old Anderson showed a brightness of promise that was in no way dimmed by the proximity of such half back stars as Aitken and Arthur and Billy Wright. Anderson took some hard knocks without flinching and following the lead of all his colleagues he ran himself almost into the ground in the biggest effort any Sunderland team has put in for many a long day.'

I was on my way, or so I hoped, and I was delighted to keep my place for the New Year's Day match at home to Aston Villa.

We took an early lead through Trevor Ford but against a struggling Villa side we were slightly fortunate to grab a late equaliser in a 2-2 draw. The *Journal* match report was nothing like as complimentary, saying simply that 'Anderson, after another good opening, tired in the later stages.' I was left out for the following game with Arsenal, when a 3-1 victory took us to the top of the league, and two FA Cup games with Scunthorpe.

But Murray must have been pleased with me because I was soon back. We played Blackpool when, as usual, thousands packed Roker Park to see the legendary Stanley Matthews. Then I made my FA Cup debut at Burnley and just how big the tournament was at the time can be gauged by the fact that the crowd at Turf Moor was 53,231. During the 2008–09 season, when Burnley played QPR at Turf Moor in the same competition the crowd for the replayed fourth round tie was just over 3,000!

Sadly my first experience of the world's oldest competition, like many that followed, proved to be a disappointment. We were not very good and let down a good number of travelling supporters by losing 2-0. Indeed that marked the start of some very bad results, with only two league wins from fifteen matches, one of which was in the final league game of the season at home to Cardiff City that 'attracted' a crowd of just 7,469.

I played in three of the matches, including a 5-1 thrashing back at Turf Moor. More happily my performance during the 1-1 draw at The Hawthorns encouraged me to believe I might win a regular first-team place and my confidence was given a big boost when I read the following in the *Journal*: 'Especially pleasing were the contributions made by Anderson, Walsh and Smith, players it is not unfair to describe as reserves. The brilliant Anderson, just turned 19, will surely not remain in that category much longer.'

In the other game I played against Middlesbrough and England legend Wilf Mannion. He was coming towards the end of his career but he seemed to pop up all over the field with the ball at his feet in yards of space. He had a very low trajectory and was a smashing passer of the ball.

He could dribble up to you and beat you and although he was mainly right-footed, his left wasn't just for standing on – a cracking player and similar in style to Raich Carter. He was head and shoulders above any Middlesbrough player that day at Roker Park and helped his side to a 1-1 draw, vital to a club desperate to avoid relegation.

A poor second half of the season proved fatal to our chances of winning the league and we finished ninth with forty-three points, eleven adrift of the champions, Arsenal.

This was the year Blackpool won the FA Cup with the great Stanley Matthews at last winning a medal and I was there. It was dubbed 'the Matthews final', which seemed harsh on Stan Mortensen, who hit a hat-trick, the last to be scored in an FA Cup final. Mortensen was another great player to come from the north-east. He was born in South Shields and was very strong and mobile. He had a bullet of a shot and was as brave as a lion. I later got to know him very well during my time as Middlesbrough manager as he was in charge at Blackpool.

Ernie Taylor was another Blackpool star that day and when he joined us at Roker Park he used to grumble: 'Matthews final? What about me?'

Chapter 4

Establishing myself in the team

After sampling first-team football I could hardly wait for the next season. However, during the summer break I didn't know whether to laugh or cry, as each week brought news of another major signing as Sunderland attempted to assemble a side good enough to capture the club's first post-war title.

Nine players were bought, including 'keeper Jimmy Cowan, from Morton, Welsh international centre-half Ray Daniel from Arsenal for the then massive sum of £27,000, Joe McDonald from Falkirk, Billy Elliott from Burnley and, once the season was under way, Ken Chisholm from Cardiff. The amount spent earned the club the title of 'the Bank of England Club.'

Each new signing added to the excitement felt by the Sunderland fans and the anxiety experienced by the existing playing staff. I found myself torn by the prospect of playing alongside such talent and the fear that the club would spend heavily on a right half, leaving me with an uncertain future.

I was determined to give myself as good a chance as anybody of making the first team and I worked hard in pre-season training. I was always lucky that I never put on a lot of weight during the summer. That wasn't the case with lots of players, and in an age when players were nowhere near as fit as they are today some really suffered in pre-season training as they worked to remove excess poundage. In particular, Tommy Wright would usually return at least a stone and a half overweight. Pre-season training really hurt him.

Despite my efforts, when the season kicked off at Charlton Athletic it wasn't a new man keeping me out of the side but George Aitken. I always got on very well with George, and with Willie Watson, with whom I was also competing for the number four shirt. We trained together and when the team-sheet went up on Friday there was no animosity if you were left out. George played the first four matches of the season.

I made my return to first team football at Molineux and was delighted when I played a part in creating the opening goal for Tommy Wright, now at centre-forward. But despite our best efforts we lost a thrilling game 3-1.

In spite of a return of just three points from the first six matches the Sunderland side, with me in it, ran out before a near 60,000 crowd at Roker Park against Arsenal. The Gunners had surprisingly started the season very poorly and were bottom.

It was some occasion. We scored seven times against a solitary goal from Arsenal, although that had put them into the lead. But Trevor Ford, back leading the attack, scored three times and Tommy Wright notched a couple.

It must have been one of Arsenal's worst displays ever but despite his obvious disappointment I will always remember Joe Mercer coming over at the end to shake my hand warmly and say, 'Well played, kid.'

He was a good player, Joe; he had an art of being able to take the ball away from a player and he could then pass it on quickly and accurately. He was a good captain, too, as you could see him encouraging his teammates, and he must have kept himself fit because in an age when many players retired not too long after they reached their early thirties he played on into his forties. After winning three league championship and two FA Cup winners' medals with Everton and Arsenal he later became, which didn't surprise me, a top-class manager with Manchester City, capturing all three domestic trophies and the now long gone European Cup Winners' Cup.

When I became manager at Middlesbrough, Joe would be one of the people I would ring if I was considering buying a player from a First Division club. I knew he would give an honest assessment and also let me know about the player's attitude and desire for the game.

Considering the money that had been spent, most Sunderland fans thought the victory over Arsenal would be the start of their side's rush towards the top of the table – but it wasn't.

Still, there were more than 60,000 fans at Roker Park when Blackpool next visited. When you were playing Blackpool you always had to account for the appearance of Stanley Matthews. He was knighted later and to gauge the position he held in the minds of football supporters you can only compare George Best in the '60s and '70s and David Beckham today. We won 3-2 and I felt I had done well. As always I was grateful for the advice given to me by the man behind me at right back, Jack Hedley. He kept telling me to stay tight on my opponent, not to get out of position and to play on the defensive side of the inside forward.

Fortunately I was not in the team when they went down heavily at Preston in late October, but after that I missed only two further league games till right at the end of the season when I was left out of the final couple.

Yet if I was a regular the manager never let me know. In fact, Bill Murray hardly said a word to me. He might say, 'Keep tight on this player' but in terms of tactics or telling me anything about the players I would be facing, their strengths and weaknesses, nothing. I wasn't, I am sure, any different from any of the other players. He didn't really speak to them either. As for seeing him at training, forget it.

We trained at Roker Park by running round the track and he could see us from a little window in his office. But he never came down to supervise or get us to practise a particular move or even discuss the team we would be facing that weekend.

I never saw Bill Murray in anything other than a suit and, despite the fact he was the manager for most of the time I was at Roker Park, I cannot say I ever really knew him.

He did have a go at me once after we'd played Huddersfield and Tommy Cavanagh went past me, had a shot and just missed.

'What about him?' I protested, pointing at Len Shackleton. 'I didn't get any cover.'

Len looked over and muttered, 'We're even getting told how to play by youngsters now.'

I decided I'd keep my mouth shut after that.

Bill Murray once gave me a lift to the ground. I'd changed buses in Sunderland and was waiting for one to take me to Roker Park when he pulled up in his big expensive car.

'Get in, Stan,' he said.

'Good morning, boss,' I said.

And that was that. Not another word was exchanged during the ten-minute journey.

I also have my doubts that Murray bought any of the players. I'd guess he might have been consulted along the lines of 'We are thinking of signing so and so, what do you think?' and he'd say yes or no. I am not sure, however, that had he said no the directors would have reconsidered.

That expensive collection of players never really gelled. In their own way they were all characters and but they didn't blend together. As I've written, we never discussed tactics and the ball was a stranger to our training sessions. They were never the most exciting. They generally involved running and more running. 'Stan, you do three laps; Fred, you do two as a warm-up.' Then we'd do relay races in which you'd jog, run and sprint.

Ludicrously, the idea was that if you didn't see that much of the ball during the week you'd want more of it on a match day. Everybody disagreed with this. Ray Daniel pleaded with Jack Jones, one of the trainers, for a ball, but to no avail.

But we did often get hold of one, even if the staff tried to keep us and the ball apart. Under the terracing at the Roker End there was a gymnasium and we'd sneak down after training, pinch a football and play tennis – 'keepy up' – using every part of our bodies to get the ball over the net in no more than two touches. Ray Daniel was excellent at it but Len Shackleton was head and shoulders above everybody.

It was Len who was mostly responsible for finding the locked-away balls and he'd win money with side bets although he'd lose out close to the end of a game when Arthur Wright, who had moved on to the training staff, would find out what we were up to and try to take the ball away.

I was never any better than average but I enjoyed competing with some extremely talented players.

Talent, of course, will only get a player so far. I'm sure there were more talented players than me who never made it. What I lacked in talent I tried to make up for by learning as much about the game as possible. I was a big reader of football books and magazines and I'd constantly be on the lookout for ideas to improve my game. I'd watch other players and teams and I'd practise and practise my passing. After a game I would analyse how many times I had misplaced a pass, and if it was more than six or seven I would set out to ensure I did better in the following game. I'd also listen to other players talking about the game to pick up tips.

I would also like to think I always acted in the best interests of the team, rather than myself. I enjoyed being recognised by the crowd for my efforts, I enjoyed being cheered for a particularly good piece of play or goal but I never lost sight of the fact that football is largely a team game. After a game when I arrived home or travelled back on the coach I would take the time to think about events on the field. Of particular importance was how my side of the field – which for ninety-nine per cent of my career was the right side – had worked together as a unit. How had the right full back, myself at right half and the outside right and inside right performed together? To this mix would be added the role of the centre-half, and how we five had blended as a unit.

My first goal for the senior team was extra special. Imagine opening the scoring for Sunderland against Newcastle at Roker Park. It was six days before Christmas 1953 and there were nearly 50,000 there. It gave us the lead and resulted from me following up a shot from Billy Elliott. Although Newcastle came back to snatch a draw I was still thrilled.

Less exciting was having to play on Christmas Day. We drew 1-1 at Roker Park with Huddersfield Town, then changed as quickly as we could before boarding the waiting coach and heading down to Yorkshire for the return game on Boxing Day. We lost 2-1.

Also, to my intense disappointment, we lost at home to Doncaster Rovers in the FA Cup. Two goals from Eddie McMorran gave the Yorkshire side a deserved victory, but the defeat has to be laid at the door of Jimmy Cowan. When Jimmy signed for Sunderland he had already won twenty-five Scottish caps, and his display at Wembley in 1949 had inspired a 3-1 win in a game afterwards referred to as 'Cowan's match'.

Sadly, Jimmy never played anything like as well when he was with us. He had been poor in the first half of the season and after a 6-2 defeat at Preston in late October he was dropped. By January he had won his place back but he gifted Doncaster their second, allowing a simple shot to slip out of his hands and into the net. It was Jimmy's only FA Cup game for Sunderland and he played just twenty-nine times for us before joining Third Lanark in the November.

Fortunately we bounced back straight away with a 5-0 defeat of Cardiff City at home, with new boy Ted Purdon scoring twice on his debut. When he then knocked home a hat-trick at Highbury in a 4-1 victory and another goal at home to Portsmouth as we won 3-1, there was a real hope that Ted would go on to lead the side to glory.

He'd been signed for £15,000 from Birmingham City after Sunderland had let Trevor Ford go to Cardiff for £30,000 in November. To outsiders that must have been a shock but it wasn't to us. There was generally a good spirit in our dressing room with one exception: the relationship between Fordie and Shack. This was a shame. They were the mainstays of the side: Shack was the provider and Ford the scorer. If they'd played together, as they should have, we would have won the league.

One of the problems was that Ford was very friendly with a director, W.S. Martin, and I think Shack took umbrage, thinking, 'Does he think he's better than the other lads?' It became an issue.

Also Ford would stand in front of the dressing room mirror, combing his hair, and say: 'You must be the best-looking player in the game' – it was only partly in jest! Shack used to cringe. He'd say, 'Look at that silly bastard'.

So Shack didn't like him; if he liked you he'd tell you. He didn't like Ford and the feeling was mutual. There wasn't really room for both of them in the same dressing room. I have nothing against Ted Purdon but he was nowhere near as good as Trevor Ford.

Shack played his finest game that season in a 4-1 victory at Highbury. Shack was brilliant. Typically, he couldn't keep himself from taking the mickey out of the Arsenal defenders. If only he had played like that every week away from home. In fact Len's attitude in away games was very different to when he played at Roker Park, and he wasn't the only one. Many of the more experienced players had the attitude that as long as you did well in front of your own spectators then that was good enough.

In the Highbury win he had the ball on the wing with the Arsenal and Wales full back Walley Barnes twenty-five yards away. Shack kept moving the ball halfway over the touchline and then back. He did it a few times as the linesman watched intently to see if the whole of the ball had gone over the line. Finally an exasperated Barnes decided to attempt to win the ball and Shack just waltzed past him and ran away up the wing. What made it better in Shack's eyes was that this took place in front of the main stand, so the Arsenal management and dignitaries were closest to the action. He enjoyed that because he was always angry that the Londoners had turned him down as a schoolboy in the spring of 1939, only months before the start of the war.

He joined Bradofrd Park Avenue, his home town club, before signing for Newcastle United at the start of the 1946–47 season, scoring six on his debut in the Magpies' club record victory of 13-0 over Newport County. But he was always at odds with the directors, who he felt treated the players like servants, and although the crowd at St James' Park wanted him to stay he was allowed to move to Roker Park in February 1948 for £20,500. That was then a record fee, and it was money well spent.

Len was always very vocal about our wages, or rather the lack of them. He'd say things like: 'Oh I see so and so's playing at the Palladium in London on Saturday. How many do you think might be there?' When you'd reply 'A couple of thousand' he'd come back with 'I wonder how much he'll get for that?' Eventually, one way or another, an answer of at least a few hundred pounds would be arrived at.

A minute or so later he'd say, 'We're playing at Highbury in London this weekend. How many do you think might be there?' and when the reply of fifty or sixty thousand came back he'd ask, 'How much will we get?' knowing fine well it would be fifteen pounds or so. Then he'd make comparisons between our wages and someone like Archie Taylor, who would be playing at Halifax before a crowd of around one tenth the size of Sunderland's. Just to hammer home the point he'd remind us that the same player at Halifax would end up with more money in his pay packet if Halifax won and Sunderland lost because of the £2 win bonus he'd receive.

Len, of course, had a very valid argument and although he lost out badly – he'd retired from playing by the time the maximum wage was scrapped – I know that he was glad to see players earn much better rewards as a result.

I think Len's anger at how poorly rewarded we were affected his performances away from home. He would say he wasn't bothered about what the crowd thought at an away match because 'There's none of our spectators here'. He was largely right as at some games even 200 travelling was a lot. Today there are much larger numbers of away fans at games, as travelling is much easier. In those days there were no motorways and very few people had cars. And there wasn't much spare cash either.

In any walk of life if you feel you're underpaid you tend not to put in 100 per cent. I think most of the experienced professionals I played with at Sunderland in the 1950s had this attitude. They also knew that they were unlikely to be looked after if they suffered a career-ending injury. They thought it was best to take things a little easier and ensure they played for as many years as possible.

This approach, I feel, was responsible for Sunderland not winning the First Division title in 1954–55. And in this respect Len should share much of the blame, and before anyone suggests that I wouldn't be writing this if he was still alive I can assure you I told him my views on many occasions.

In February 1955 Sunderland were in with a chance of winning both the League and the FA Cup after being drawn to play Swansea Town in the fifth round.

Len made it clear that he supported the view that the double wasn't possible; that you couldn't win the League and the Cup in the same season. It was true no club had managed it in the twentieth century but, perhaps because I was only twenty in 1955, I felt it could be done. Spurs showed I was right when they won both in 1961. But Len was adamant, and because he was right on so many other issues the players listened to him and I am convinced his argument had an effect on them.

I'd have been happy to have won either competition, of course, but Len would say, 'Let's get to Wembley and win the FA Cup, it will be fantastic.' He didn't say 'Let's lose the league,' but the implication was pretty clear and we did lose it by putting in some terrible performances between the fifth-round draw and our semi-final knockout. Nowadays clubs and players would swap an FA Cup winners' medal for a place in the top four of the Premier League and a chance to play in the Champions League, but then the European Cup was in its infancy and the FA was attempting to stop English teams from playing in it. But of course we didn't even make it to Wembley.

Len did play at Wembley that season, scoring a beauty as England beat the World Champions West Germany 3-1. When we next met at training I congratulated him on his achievement, only to be left speechless when he told me that it had been 'a waste of time'.

I know he felt the national team was badly run. It was his fifth and final match in England's colours. He should have won far more caps but it doesn't take a genius to work out why he didn't. Quite simply he was far too outspoken for the powers that be and to prove it the following year he released his autobiography, *Clown Prince of Soccer*.

This famously had a chapter entitled 'The Average Director's Knowledge of Football' followed by a page containing only a note at the bottom which read: 'This Chapter has deliberately been left blank in accordance with the author's wishes.'

There is something in Len's book that I have never seen mentioned but which I think is worth raising. It concerns a part of the book in which Len praises two of the Sunderland directors, Bill Ditchburn and W.S. Martin, for their 'progressive approach'. I am convinced that Len was in fact having a laugh at them, and Ditchburn in particular.

In 1953–54, when the side was playing so desperately badly despite the big-money signings, Bill Murray said that Ditchburn wanted to speak to us. This was very unusual. Directors speaking to players – never!

We trooped through to the away dressing room where Ditchburn said, 'Well, I don't know what's gannin on. It's a poor show, but I think I know what's the problem. It's yer boots. I've had a look at them, and you've hammered doon the toes.'

Amazingly, this was true. In those days you'd get a pair of boots two sizes too small for you, put them on and sit in a hot bath to soften the leather. Then you'd hammer down the tin toecaps.

'But Mr Chairman, you don't kick the ball with your toes,' replied Len.

'Oh, aye, I see. Well I just think it's a queer thing, that's all I thought,' said the now somewhat bemused chairman.

Len couldn't possibly have forgotten that incident when he wrote the book. Neither would he have forgotten that Martin had been very close to Trevor Ford. Len wasn't daft – he didn't name anyone in his book!

Len's size was a great encouragement to me when I made it into the first team. Any fears that I might not be big or strong enough, at 5ft 9in and under twelve stone, were calmed by taking a look at him and realising he was ever so slightly smaller and lighter than me.

He was one of the easiest men to play with. He nearly always wanted the ball; he was easy to find and could control it in an instant. A player who got too close soon found himself a beaten man. Indeed, with regards to Len I can think of only one person who could tie him down – the late great, incomparable Duncan Edwards of Manchester United.

It was my job to get the ball and give it to Len. I was the fetcher and carrier, as they say.

I don't share the opinion of some of his critics that Shack would spend too much time trying to impress the Roker Park crowd by 'clowning around'. Yes, he did like to delight spectators, but never at the expense of allowing a game to slip away. Shack would only lay on the entertainment and laughs when things were going right or we'd already sewn up the match. Otherwise he'd be as committed to victory as anyone else in a red and white shirt, as long as it was at Roker Park.

Len was also a good trainer, and at the pre-season training he was always near the front on the long runs which stretched from the ground up to Whitburn and to South Shields and back, around seven to eight miles at a decent pace. Like many others at the time he smoked cigarettes but he wasn't a heavy drinker.

One of his party pieces was to toss a coin, catch it on his instep and flick it into his top pocket. It particularly engaged Ray Daniel, who tried in vain for ages to master the trick. He didn't have Len's technique and we used to laugh as the coin flew everywhere but into his top pocket. Shack could also cut across the ball so it went five yards and then had so much backspin on it that it came back to him.

In April 1954 I managed to grab my second league goal but it was in a 4-2 home defeat by Sheffield Wednesday and that left us facing the possibility of relegation. No other Sunderland side had ever gone down so it was a nerve-wracking experience when in the next match on Easter Friday at home to Sheffield United a nineteen-year-old lad from Horden Colliery Welfare strode up to the penalty spot with Sunderland 2-1 down with just ten minutes left. I still can't recall how I came to find myself in such a situation. I had taken penalties in the reserves but this was a bit different.

Now Roker Park could be a noisy place but it was deadly silent when I put the ball down on the spot. Fortunately I rammed home a right-foot drive that gave 'keeper Ted Burgin no chance. It was probably one of the most important goals I ever scored for the club, especially as Middlesbrough, with whom we were competing to avoid the drop, alongside Liverpool, had lost at home.

A goalless draw in a scruffy match with Middlesbrough at Ayresome Park meant we were safe. But it had been touch and go for our expensively assembled team for much of the season.

One of the keys to Sunderland staying up had been the decision to replace Cowan in goal towards the end of the season with Bill Fraser, another Scot who had been signed from Airdrie in March 1954. The new man was a fit lad who played brilliantly on his debut at White Hart Lane to help us to a 3-0 victory. His confidence in coming out and collecting high balls inspired the rest of us and was just what we needed. It meant defenders didn't have to back into the six-yard box to try and get the ball clear.

Sunderland won three of the seven games he played that season and lost just the once.

So it had not been the easiest of seasons. The players and fans had believed when it started it would be a success, which made the failure to challenge for the league or

FA Cup difficult to understand. But I was pleased with my efforts. I had played in thirty-four of the forty-two matches, scoring three times. I knew I still had a lot to learn but was confident that I could do so while playing first-team football in a side I was certain would improve the following season. It wasn't a bad time to be around.

Chapter 5

So near but so far...

I was fourteen years with Sunderland and the only medal I won was with the reserve side at the end of the 1951–52 season. I should have got at least one more, as in 1954–55 we had, I am still convinced, the best team in the country. So to finish fourth in the league and to lose out in the semi-finals of the FA Cup rankles even now, though more than half a century has passed.

Unlike previous summers the club was content to leave the transfer market alone and the squad that re-assembled for pre-season training was familiar.

We were looking in good shape and we started at home to West Bromwich Albion, who had come close to the double the previous season, having won the FA Cup and been runners-up to bitter rivals and neighbours Wolves in the league.

Up front West Brom had Ronnie Allen, who'd scored twice in the FA Cup final. He was only 5ft 8in but centre-halves had to work hard to get the ball off him and he had a good eye for goal. He didn't manage to score this particular day at Roker Park but he was to end up as the league's top scorer with twenty-seven goals.

There were more than 56,000 at the match and I scored Sunderland's opening goal of the forty-two-match campaign. On twenty-eight minutes Billy Elliott was brought down in the box and I slotted the resultant penalty past Jim Sanders. We eventually won a cracking game 4-2. Les Dodds made his goalkeeping debut after the Army refused to allow weekend leave to Bill Fraser, who was doing his national service.

The win was part of a great start; after five games we'd taken eight points from a possible ten. I was now twenty and enjoying every moment of being a professional footballer, playing in front of tens of thousands of people every weekend.

I did, however, lose my self-control during the first half of the home game against Sheffield Wednesday. It was a robust match. Tackles were flying in and in truth the fury got to me. It was probably lack of experience, but when Jackie Shaw and I clashed for the ball and his legs finished over mine I reacted by pushing him off me as hard as I could. There was a bit more pushing and shoving before the referee dashed over and told us: 'You two off'. We trooped dejectedly down the tunnel.

My mam and dad were sitting in the main stand but I didn't dare look up as I was terribly embarrassed. I had left the shower when the team came in at half-time and Bill Murray told me rightly I was a 'stupid bugger', although I disagreed with him when he later said I was 'too hot-headed'. Generally I didn't let incidents on the field affect me. This proved to be the only time I was dismissed in England during my long career. It meant a trip to Sheffield to appear before an FA Enquiry, where Jackie and I escaped a ban but were warned as to our future conduct.

I thought that if we finished in front of Wolves and West Brom we would win the league. It was therefore disappointing to return from Molineux after the sixth game of the season beaten 2-0. Nevertheless, we were starting to play as a unit. Joe McDonald had been signed from Falkirk to play left full-back with only four games left of the previous season and he remained in the team as we moved towards the top. Also Ray Daniel, who'd had a bit of an up and down time the previous season, was starting to show why he had cost such a huge fee.

On his day there were not many better centre-backs than Ray. Often he seemed to reserve his best matches for when he was facing the top centre-forwards. Against, for example, Trevor Ford or Nat Lofthouse, of Bolton Wanderers, Ray would play brilliantly. He seemed conscious of the need to prove that the large fee was money well spent. But against lesser lights he'd often appear uninterested.

You had to goad Ray into playing well by whispering casually in his ear, 'This fellow you've got today has been banging them in regularly, Ray.' That would intrigue him enough to go out and prove he could tame his opponent.

At the Portsmouth away game I scored my second goal of the season, a repeat of the first. Billy Elliott was fouled and I stroked home the penalty, which was the final goal of a 2-2 draw.

The Newcastle game at home that season was a real thriller, played before more than 66,000, including many youngsters who had been passed down over people's heads to sit close to the touchline. We ended up winning 4-2. Shack, playing against his old club, mesmerised the Newcastle defence to set up a goal for Ken Chisholm and generally had a great game, while Billy Bingham scored twice, including a beautiful lob from twenty-five yards. To round off the victory we were now top of the league, and I, for one, felt that we now had the players to stay there.

A couple of weeks after the derby we won for the third consecutive season at Highbury, where Shack was again in his element. He laid on the first two goals before I knocked home my third penalty of the season with eleven minutes remaining to make it 3-1. The crowd on the day was 65,424.

This meant that in October 1954 Sunderland played five league games attended by 283,000 spectators, an average of nearly 57,000 a game – great days indeed.

After the Arsenal match the team suffered a very frustrating few weeks, drawing seven out of ten league games, including 1-1 on Christmas Day against Huddersfield Town. Thankfully, unlike the previous season, we didn't have to jump straight on the coach. This time the game at Leeds Road took place two days later. We again drew 1-1 in a thrilling match.

I was respsonsible for Huddersfield opening the scoring on twenty minutes. Ray Daniel had deflected the ball past Bill Fraser and as Tommy Cavanagh moved to put the ball into an empty net I brought him down. It was a cynical foul and today I would have been rightly sent off. However, referees were a lot more lenient back in the '50s and I wasn't even booked. Little good it did, though, as Vic Metcalf hammered home the penalty.

Despite our run of drawn matches we were just off the pace at the top. Wolves were only a couple of points ahead and it was proving a tight contest. I was confident that if we could pick our form up just a little we could be the first Sunderland since 1936 to be First Division champions.

We drew Burnley at home in the third round of the FA Cup, which gave me the chance of revenge. With five minutes of the match remaining most spectators appeared to be resigned to a replay, but I was able to force my way beyond my marker to cross to the far post. Billy Elliott had time to direct a header well out of the goalkeeper's reach and into the net. Billy was especially pleased because the goal came against his old club, although it has to be said that Ray Daniel was the man of the match.

But I wish he hadn't been so strong defensively because in hindsight I really wished we had lost. That might seem a strange thing to write, but the further we went in the FA Cup the more convinced I became that it caused our league form to suffer; the players' minds had wandered off in the direction of a little part of north-west London. But as a relative youngster I didn't really have the confidence to speak out. Even if I had I am not so sure my teammates would have listened.

This is because in those days the FA Cup was *the* tournament, bigger than the league and the World Cup.

There was a special excitement as players crowded round a transistor radio to hear the Monday lunchtime draw, and as you progressed the thrill intensified up to the semi-final, when you could hardly bring yourself to listen. You didn't really want to know who might bar your way to Mecca – or Wembley, to give it its proper name.

Playing well in the final could bring footballing immortality. Every professional footballer dreamed of playing at Wembley, and every fan hoped some day to see their side lift the famous trophy. Sunderland's players and fans were no different, and although there wasn't the hatred that exists today, the fact that Newcastle had lifted the trophy in 1951 and 1952 was never far from the minds of Sunderland fans.

In the fourth round we drew Preston North End at Deepdale. While most of football wanted the great Tom Finney to finally get a cup winner's medal it didn't include us at Roker Park. The first match was thrilling, with both Shack and Tom Finney absolutely outstanding; they had the large crowd cheering their every move in a game that finished 3-3. Sadly Tom was injured and missed the replay. His deputy Bobby Foster was never going to prove as effective and was blotted out of the match by Joe McDonald. The ninety minutes was poor, but two second-half Ken Chisholm goals were enough to ensure we progressed to meet Swansea Town in the next round.

Ken was a real character – one of the funniest men I've ever met. And how he could talk. I reckon he could have been in politics. He wasn't a great footballer, and he'd be the first to admit it. But he was no fool; he was a quick learner and a keen listener. He was the sort of bloke who would have been a success no matter what business or trade he chose.

He was breezy and full of life. No one could deflate him. This meant that no matter how many mistakes he made on the field he still continued to want the ball. If he missed a sitter he'd be back in the box the next instant looking for a shot at goal. He could be very frustrating one minute and a hero the next. While skill on a football field is important, attitude doesn't come far behind and Ken Chisholm had that in abundance.

The week before the fifth round at Vetch Field we played Charlton Athletic at home. We had beaten them easily away, 3-1, in September although they were now in third, one place below us. But we were unbeaten in fourteen home league games. We attacked most of the match, but in truth rarely threatened Charlton's famous 'keeper Sam Bartram; the match finished 2-1 to Charlton and I missed a penalty at 1-0.

These days reporters would say the performance lacked enthusiasm; my view is that some of the players were already thinking of Wembley.

This feeling intensified when we beat Swansea, again needing a replay, courtesy of a Charlie Fleming header, to set us up with a quarter-final home tie against Wolves. With Newcastle also making it through to the last eight the whole region was thinking this could be the year when we would get to play each other in the final.

Newcastle, though, had the advantage of not needing to worry about winning the league, whereas we were still very much in the hunt and we had what was always a special satisfaction of recording the double over them, winning at St James' Park 2-1, Ken Chisholm grabbed both, with the winner arriving just a minute before time, when he headed home a well placed Jack Hedley free kick. But then we lost 3-0 at Bolton where the side simply didn't play.

I still have a newspaper cutting from the *Journal* for that match.

It reads:

Sunderland, moving only at half speed, ran into all sorts of trouble in this match, and the result was they never

54

had the slightest chance of winning and displacing Wolves at the top of the table. The responsibility for this lapse has to be on the shoulders of the forward line that seldom revealed scoring potential. Neither did the line show any semblance of teamwork or understanding.
Shackleton must shoulder a lot of the blame. He was slow, played far too much behind his colleagues and rarely went into the tackle.

And the players certainly wouldn't have listened to me after we beat Wolverhampton 2-0 at home in the quarter-finals with Ted Purdon scoring both on his twenty-fourth birthday. The Wolves left-back Bill Shorthouse being carried off after only four minutes helped us and although we continually pressed after that against the remaining ten it wasn't until the hour that we took the lead. When we scored the second the crowd went absolutely wild.

After the game I went to the cinema with Marjorie, my childhood sweetheart. I have no idea what the film was that night after the Wolves game, but I remember vividly that at the interval there was a short Pathé news piece and it included some action from the game earlier that day at Roker Park. I was thrilled; it was the first time I'd seen myself on the big screen, even if only for a second. New technology was revolutionising the world and football was to be dramatically changed by television.

Only a few short weeks earlier a growing TV audience had watched the second half of Wolves v Honved, the Hungarian club who included a number of players from the national team which had hammered England 6-3 and 7-1 the previous season.

Marjorie and I had met at the church social club in Horden. It would seem odd to today's youngsters, but in those days we boys would all troop to the church hall to meet girls. The social was run by Miss Stoute – she was, very – and you would have your ears checked to see if they were dirty, your hair in case you had nits, and you had to be smartly dressed or you wouldn't be let in. We would be taught to dance. And that's how I got to know Marjorie. We were about fourteen. She also came to play netball at our school because hers didn't have a court. I watched her play and then she would come and watch me play football.

As you might expect after we had beaten Wolves, whose manager Stan Cullis had declared them the 'Champions of the World' following the Honved victory, our supporters were eagerly remembering that the only time the club had won the FA Cup, in 1937, they had also overcome Wolves in their quarter-final.

We listened to the draw on the following Monday before our game at Sheffield United, which had been re-arranged because of the cup tie. That was a decision by the League that caused me a small problem!

I had expected to be taking part in a rather different, but certainly just as important, match that particular day – I was supposed to be getting married.

When I heard about the Sheffield United date I approached Bill Murray to tell him of my plans, hoping that as friends and relations had already arranged to travel he would give me permission to miss the match. Not a chance. As I said, he was a man of few words and all I got was 'You'll have to re-arrange it.' So I had the awkward job of telling Marjorie's family that the wedding had to be held a week later.

It was just as well that I always got on with her parents and we got married the following Monday – March 21 1955 – at St Mary's Church, Horden. The best man was my cousin Alan Mason and the bridesmaids were Dorothy Wright and Elizabeth Harrison, who like the bride had to hold their dresses up high to avoid the slushy snow. The Reverend W.H. Walton, the vicar of Horden, performed the ceremony. The rest of the team was in preparation for the forthcoming semi-final so none of them could attend. We had a big do afterwards at the Co-operative Hall and it was a great day. Marjorie and I were to be together for more than forty-five years before she died in Doncaster Royal Infirmary in 2001.

As Newcastle had drawn 1-1 at Huddersfield we had faced the possibility of a Tyne–Wear semi-final. In fact, we drew Manchester City, winners by a single goal away to Birmingham City. Newcastle drew Third Division York City. Our semi-final was scheduled for Villa Park two weeks later, theirs for Hillsborough.

There wasn't much of a crowd at Bramall Lane that Monday night. If we'd won we'd have gone level with Wolves at the top, but the *Journal* got it just about right the following morning when it stated: 'Perhaps it was the reaction following the previous cup tie but the weakened Sunderland side rarely seemed to show any urgency. The finishing of the forwards was woefully weak and it was a dreary game with few incidents to rouse the interest of the small crowd.'

Without Len Shackleton we lost 1-0 in a scrappy game and although I was pleased with my own performance I felt that as a team we never looked like winning. But we were still very much in the title hunt. We had lost fewer games than any of the other clubs in the top nine and we were separated by only six points.

Chelsea, who had never won the league, were making a real effort to knock Wolves off the top and we knew we had to play them the week after the semi-final. Squeezed in between was what on paper seemed a pretty easy game against a struggling Arsenal, whom we had already beaten 3-1 at Highbury. We did hit the bar twice, and had another effort cleared off the line, but we weren't good enough and we lost 1-0. It was one of the most disappointing results I experienced but there was little time to dwell on it; there was the little matter of my wedding forty-eight hours later.

I knew, though, that a victory in our next game at Stamford Bridge would be vital if we were to have any chance. We had to win, it was as simple as that.

First came the semi-final. We had beaten Manchester City 3-2 at home in December so were confident. In goal City had Bert Trautmann, a real character who, following his time as a prisoner of war, stayed in Britain rather than return to Germany. He was a goalkeeper I always rated. At number nine there was Don Revie, who had followed the Hungarian tactics of the time by playing a deep-lying role rather than staying up front facing the centre-half as was the tradition. I was to get to know Don pretty well when he signed for Sunderland before falling out with him after I moved to Tyneside and one of his Leeds players broke the leg of a Newcastle lad.

Shack was fully fit and the team stayed at Buxton in the week leading up to the match. One good performance and we'd be running out in front of 100,000 in May. It was a great thought – and then there was the prospect of playing Newcastle in the final. They were favourites to reach Wembley. Manchester City, Sunderland, Newcastle and York in the semi-finals of the FA Cup – it might be some time before that happens again!

What happened next was a farce. When Saturday arrived the heavens opened and from Buxton to Birmingham there were floods everywhere. Villa Park was in a dreadful state and try as they might the groundsmen were making no impression on the pitch.

Bill Murray called us together to say that it looked like the game would be off but that the referee was prepared to inspect the pitch half an hour later. As it just kept pouring down no one seriously expected him to do anything other than postpone the match. It was a shock therefore to be told that he intended starting the game but that if it got worse he would abandon it. Obviously this was not the right sort of atmosphere to be playing a semi-final.

It seemed the only reason for starting the game was that spectators had travelled long distances. It stills seems a daft decision to play the game.

It was farcical. George Aitken, a big strong left half, tried to hit a ball upfield and managed to shift it only five yards. Despite the conditions I felt we were the better side and only a fluke prevented us taking the lead. Shack wriggled his way past the City defence to the byline and squared the ball across to Charlie Fleming, who hit it powerfully enough. Trautmann, in a desperate attempt to block the shot, actually slipped and his momentum helped stop the ball and it dropped just over the bar for a corner.

This was a time when you didn't argue with referees but at half-time, as we walked down the tunnel, players from both sides asked him to call it off. Ironically, as neither team looked as if they would score the tie seemed certain to be settled another day anyway.

However, early in the second half City's left winger Roy Clarke beat Bill Fraser with a header to give his team the lead. There was no way the referee was going to call the game off now and try as we might – Len especially worked tirelessly to fashion an equaliser – we couldn't recover. We just didn't have enough up front to punish Manchester City.

It was a very quiet dressing room afterwards and I have often wondered if the rest of the players were thinking the same as I was, namely that you should never rely on one single match to make or break a full season.

Despite my pleasure as a newlywed, my misery was made almost complete the following weekend when we lost a tight match at Stamford Bridge. We conceded two goals in the first quarter of an hour, Roy Bentley and Stan Willemse the scorers, although we played much better in the second half and were back in the game on fifty-two minutes when Charlie Fleming, taking the ball in his stride, flashed past two defenders before beating Chick Thomson in the Chelsea goal. In the last quarter of an hour we penned Chelsea into their own box but the ball just wouldn't drop kindly and we lost 2-1.

The result meant we were now outsiders to win the league. We drew at home with relegation-bound Leicester City in the next match on Easter Friday, and I then missed another penalty at Roker Park to leave Manchester United 2-1 in the lead. However, Ken Chisholm scored a hat-trick to make it 3-3 and with just four minutes left I managed to score the winner. I lofted the ball into the box and with Chis challenging Ray Wood, the United 'keeper totally misjudged its flight and it ended up in the net. We were still, just, in the race for the title.

Manchester City, again, put paid to our hopes, with Don Revie scoring in the first minute of the following day's game as we went down by a single goal. Although we won our final three games we were well out of contention, as shown by the fact that little more than 20,000 were at the final home game at Roker Park.

Chelsea proved to be the most resilient side that season, finishing with fifty-two points, four more than Wolverhampton, Portsmouth and us in fourth. It still rates as Sunderland's second highest finish – after third in 1949–50 – since the last league success in 1936 but that was, and still is, little consolation. Fourth might mean something these days with qualification for the Champions League as a reward but it counted for little in 1955. Certainly no one was celebrating, least of all me although at the time I was consoled by the thought that we might be in a position to challenge again over the next few seasons.

I still believe we threw it away. Chelsea had more than their fair share of good players, including Roy Bentley, a very strong inside forward who I played against many times. He had two good feet and was very good in the air, getting on the end of many a cross from Peter Brabrook. But we lost our concentration because of the FA Cup. To make matters worse – and how could it be? – Newcastle had to replay with York, which they did at Roker Park. And then they won the cup for the third time in five seasons, beating Manchester City 3-1.

Chapter 6

The start of the long decline

As an established first-team footballer and newlywed man the last thing I needed was a spell in National Service. But that was just what happened. Starting in the summer of 1955 I was helping defend Queen and country – well, at least looking after a petrol station!

The country, of course, had a regular army but it was not up to strength for the Second World War, which was why National Service was introduced in 1939. After the war a new act of Parliament decreed that all men aged between eighteen and twenty-five, barring coal miners, had to do eighteen months' National Service in one of the three services.

This went up to two years at the outbreak of the Korean War in 1950. While many National Servicemen served alongside Army regulars in military operations in places such as Malaya, Korea and Kenya the furthest I went was Catterick in north Yorkshire.

My call-up also cost me a pretty packet. National Service pay was the princely sum of 13s and 6d (68p) per week. Sunderland weren't too generous either. In fact they never were during my time with them. They agreed to pay me just a £1 a week to retain my services. It's true that I received a £6 match fee every time I turned out for the first team, which made a grand total of £7 13s and 6d. But this was still only about half what the other first-teamers at the club were getting.

The start of the long decline

There were rumours that under-the-counter payments were being made to attract star players and I wouldn't have minded getting some! Especially as in order to ensure I spent Sunday nights at home I was paying colleagues in the service £2 to do my job while I was absent. Shack was right: it was ridiculous. We were playing in front of many thousands of people every week and getting a minuscule percentage of the gate receipts.

Feeling hard done by, I spoke to Bill Murray about it. He assured me that if I kept quiet he would make it his business to ensure that when I came out of the Army I would get back all the money I would have earned had I not been drafted. Foolishly as it turned out, I trusted his word, consoling myself with the knowledge that there would be a good nest egg for Marjorie and me in the summer of 1957.

Catterick, for those unfamiliar with the geography of northern England, is about sixty miles south of Sunderland and for the next two seasons I would be away during the week and, all being well, return at weekends to play First Division football for Sunderland and to see Marjorie.

After basic training I was put into the Royal Tank Regiment alongside Middlesbrough players Derek McLean, Doug Cooper and the eighteen-year-old Geoff Smedley.

I didn't hate being in the army. It was fun learning how to strip down a machine gun and to shoot, and I had no problems with the discipline side of things. But once the initial training had ended it became pretty boring, especially as I spent most of my time in the stores dishing out tank parts and occasionally working on the fuel pumps filling up tanks.

As if being away from home wasn't bad enough, Marjorie got pregnant and when our daughter Sherley was born in 1956 I missed her first few months. I deeply regret that. You can never make up that time.

Consolation came in the form of football. The regimental team was under the control of Captain Rice and I was duly selected to play. Then Colonel Mitchell, knowing I played First Division football, chose me for the full Army team. Over the next two seasons I played more football than at any other time in my career. Combined with my Sunderland appearances, I notched up more than eighty-five games a season.

The Army side was packed with First Division Footballers – Bobby Charlton, Bill Foulkes and Eddie Colman from Manchester United, Dave Dunmore of Tottenham Hotspur, and Alan Hodgkinson and Graham Shaw from Sheffield United made it a very strong side. Dave Mackay, then of Heart of Midlothian, also played although there was no place for Maurice Setters, even though he was a regular in a very fine West Bromwich side.

One of the Army games was against the Football League, who included Jackie Milburn, and 30,000 turned out at St James' Park. The inter-services cup matches were often fierce encounters, but with so many good players to choose the Army side was virtually unbeatable.

As usual with football teams there was dressing room banter and Phil Woosnam, who played fifteen times for Wales, was often the butt of the jokes. As an educated man, with a degree in physics, he had been made a second lieutenant and was the only officer in the team. At the time Phil was playing for Leyton Orient as an amateur, although he turned professional when he moved to West Ham United in November 1958, quitting his job as a physics teacher. We'd do mock salutes when he entered the dressing room and shout out 'Good morning, sir!' He took it in good humour. He had to, otherwise he would have just got more of the same. Phil later went on to be one of the most important people in the development of football in the United States.

At one point with the Army we toured West Germany,

playing against top sides and losing only one of the six matches we played.

One of them was played in the 1936 Berlin Olympic stadium, the place where in 1938, under instruction from the FA, England players had raised their arms in Nazi salutes. The stadium facilities were still remarkable more than twenty years later, and we won the game 2-0.

The trip also meant a chance to see the differences between the west and the east of Germany following the enforced partition after the war. The differences were remarkable; American money had restored, and in many cases improved, conditions on the western side but in the east it was as if the war had only just ended – shrapnel, bullet holes and buildings half blown to bits were everywhere.

In the east we found people staring at us. I was more than happy not to take too careful a look – in fact during my playing career I was, stupidly, never too bothered about examining the places I visited. I heard years later that when West Bromwich Albion became the first western club to tour China in the late '70s the vast majority of the players preferred to stay on their coach playing cards rather than get off to see the Great Wall of China.

That would have been me as a player. I visited a number of places I have never had the chance to go back to and did nothing to try and see the sights. Of course, the clubs should have done more by laying on trips. But most of the time players simply hang around their hotel; any moments of relaxation usually involved going for a beer in a nearby bar.

National Service did little for me and although I must admit I enjoyed playing in the Army team I was glad when I finished the two years at the end of the 1956–57 season.

When we won three of our first four games of the 1955–56 season, scoring fourteen goals, my hopes that this would be our season rose sky high.

Len Shackleton scored a superb goal when we won 4-1 at Villa Park. With Billy Elliott injured, Shack was playing outside left and in the final minute he picked up the ball on the halfway line and dribbled past three Villa defenders before clipping it over the 'keeper, Ken Jones. Shack had turned around with his hands in the air before the ball dipped into the net.

Then came Blackpool away, and although we took the lead through Shack, Joe McDonald was so badly injured he was forced to limp out the remaining seventy minutes. It was a nightmare for us and particularly for me.

I was asked to fill in at left back for Joe and was torn apart by Stanley Matthews. Imagine playing in a position for the first time in an emergency and facing the most famous footballer in the world. He went one way and I went the other. At half-time we were 2-1 down and there were eighteen minutes left when Stan Mortensen made it 7-1. As it was early in the season there were a number of fans down from the north-east for a holiday weekend but I am not sure how many were still in the ground when we grabbed a couple of consolation goals to finish with the very flattering scoreline of three goals for and seven against. Bill Perry, the man who scored the winner in the 1953 FA Cup final, managed a hat-trick. I don't think I ever played left back again!

Despite this experience I am of the opinion that Matthews was not as good a player as Tom Finney. Tom had the ability to play in a number of forward positions and he also scored a lot more goals than Sir Stanley. I am a big admirer of Tom Finney; he had pace, could dribble past players, centred superbly, rarely misplaced a pass and in front of goal was so deadly that he scored 210 times in 473 first-team appearances for North End, his only club. I was very pleased when Tom was made a knight. It was deserved recognition for such a superb player.

The start of the long decline

The result at Bloomfield Road hardly seemed to matter as the club began the best run I experienced as a First Division footballer with Sunderland between 1952 and 1958. We won six and lost just the one. I was lucky in that I played in the six we won, missing the seventh after being called into the England squad for the friendly against Denmark in Copenhagen. It was my first call-up for the senior team and came after I'd made my under-23 debut in a 5-1 thrashing of Denmark at Fratton Park.

We really did play some cracking football as Chelsea, Bolton, Arsenal, Birmingham, West Brom and Tottenham Hotspur were all beaten.

The Chelsea match at Roker Park was one of the best I ever played in, although I didn't feel like that when just before half-time we were three down to the champions and looking at a thrashing of Blackpoolesque proportions. Our confidence soared, however, when Shack made an opening for Charlie Fleming to reduce the arrears and then shortly after the restart Ray Daniel, showing good close control, presented Fleming with his second. Ken Chisholm hit the equaliser and with four minutes left we took the lead with his second. We finished 4-3 in front, although it was just as well Peter Sillett's last-minute shot hit the post.

At The Hawthorns we scored a last-minute winner to move within a point of Blackpool at the top of the league, a position we occupied the following weekend after beating Spurs 3-2 at White Hart Lane, where Ted Purdon had one of his best matches in a red and white shirt. We had played twelve matches, winning nine and losing three.

We drew the next three but were still top when we had the privilege of playing Russian giants Moscow Dynamo in a high-profile friendly under floodlights. More and more clubs were installing floodlights, and although the Football League initially refused to sanction games under them they finally buckled with the first fixture under lights coming later that season when Portsmouth took on Newcastle United at Fratton Park.

Although we lost by a single goal to the Russians I was confident that we now had a side capable of finishing top. Sadly I couldn't have been more wrong: from November 19 the team and club went gradually downwards for the next four and a half seasons, halfway through which came relegation to the Second Division for the first time in Sunderland's long history.

It started with an 8-2 defeat at Luton Town's compact Kenilworth Road ground and although we had a chance to return to the top two weeks later when we were at Old Trafford we blew it. I have often wondered what might have happened had we taken a number of chances in the first half hour. But it took us until the thirty-fifth minute before Ted Purdon struck the opening goal. The match was played at a cracking pace and there was an abundance of skill on display, even though Len Shackleton was missing through injury. The Manchester United side, who had already earned the title of 'The Busby Babes' by then, were not short of confidence but had we managed to hold on for more than the five minutes before they equalised perhaps we might have dented their self-belief.

The sides that day are worth recording:

Manchester United: Wood, Foulkes, Byrne, Colman, Jones, Edwards, Berry, Doherty, Taylor, Viollet, Pegg.
Sunderland: Dodds, Hedley, McDonald (J), Anderson, Daniel, Aitken, Bingham, Fleming, Purdon, Chisholm, Elliott.

My schoolboy friend Dennis Viollet scored the winner with just five minutes left. As might be expected I got some gentle ribbing about the result when I next played in the Army side with Bill Foulkes and Eddie Colman. United ran away with the title that season, finishing eleven points in front of second-placed Blackpool.

After that defeat we were never seriously in with a chance of winning the league and our supporters were starting to feel frustrated that the considerable sums invested in expensive players were failing to find success. Some pointed in the direction of Old Trafford, noting that Matt Busby had largely relied on developing young players through the youth and reserve teams to produce a team that threatened to sweep all before them over the next few seasons.

It was Ted Purdon who suffered the most at the hands of the crowd. He'd only scored once at Roker Park in the first part of the 1955–56 season and the crowd weren't shy in letting him know what they thought.

Fans in those days were less vitriolic in their attitudes towards opposing teams but much more critical of their own players than today. Sometimes when I watch games at the Stadium of Light I am amazed that spectators will even clap if a player simply passes the ball in the direction of another player, never mind to him – that would never have happened back in the 1950s.

Ted, in my view, suffered through his association with Ken Chisholm; let's rephrase that – through going drinking with Ken and Bill Fraser most nights. Ken could handle alcohol better than most, but I don't believe players could run it off in training as they used to say. Certainly Ted couldn't, and his fitness levels went down compared with what they were when he signed. I think training became an effort and his form suffered. He was very popular at the start of his career at Sunderland but not at the end.

Bill Fraser also didn't work as hard as he should have in training. Bill had it in him to be one of the top goalkeepers and he should have been able to play for much longer. But he retired when he was just turned thirty. So perhaps the drink also got to him; as it certainly did later to another

Sunderland player, Jim Baxter, who signed for the club from Glasgow Rangers before the start of the 1965–66 season when I was at Newcastle United.

Early that season I arranged to meet up with Jim in the La Strada nightclub following Newcastle's game with Manchester United earlier in the evening. Jim had been at the game, in which his great friend Paddy Crerand was playing. I was writing a weekly column for a Sunday newspaper and it was thought it would make a good piece for us to chat about the progress of Newcastle and Sunderland after half a dozen games.

I'd played against Jim as part of the defeated England side at Hampden Park in 1962 and those who saw him in his prime have little doubt he was a brilliant footballer. He particularly liked playing for Scotland against England and twice inspired his country to victory at Wembley in 1963 and 1967. After the latter the Scots claimed they were the world champions!

When I walked into La Strada I was greeted by Jim asking me what I wanted to drink. After ordering a lager and lime we sat down. Jim's drink was Bacardi and Coke and almost before we'd started chatting he'd finished it and shouted for the waitress to bring him another while enquiring if I fancied the same. I was fine with what I'd ordered.

When the waitress arrived Jim was very polite but told her that rather than waste time coming over to take an order every few minutes she should just bring a fresh drink for him every ten minutes. This meant that after an hour or so there were a good number of glasses on the table. Today someone would have snapped our picture on a mobile phone and it would have been in the papers the following day, but we were never disturbed. It might have been better had we been, however. Although I was not drinking anything like as much as Jim I did consume more than was good for me and began to feel slightly unwell. As a consequence I was in no fit state to drive, so ordered a taxi home. Although I wasn't really able to say for certain, in comparison with me Jim didn't look too bad. In the circumstances I think we did pretty well to get together a decent article.

I had to ring Joe Harvey to tell him I couldn't train the next day.

'What've you been doing?' asked Joe.

'I had a night out with Jim Baxter for an article,' I replied.

'Silly bugger,' Joe said.

I met Jim years later after he'd retired and I was manager at Bolton. It was at a golf tournament in Lancashire and I spotted the Liverpool and Scotland international Ian St John. After greeting him, I was walking away when I realised that Jim Baxter was sitting next to him. I returned and apologised for not having recognised him. 'Don't worry, Stan, lots of people say that,' was Jim's response.

The man I spoke to that day was not the man I admired so much as a player. Nicknamed 'Slim Jim' during his days at Glasgow Rangers, he had now become bloated, putting on so much weight that his face had changed; he died aged only sixty-one in 2001.

Bill Fraser was between the sticks when I was part of the side that suffered the club's record home league defeat, losing 6-1 on Boxing Day. To make matters worse it was to Newcastle United. Six-one! I thought it was a fluke; I still maintain that there wasn't that much between the sides apart from the finishing of Jackie Milburn, who was at his magnificent best. The statistics show we had nine corners and Newcastle five, and that Ronnie Simpson, who was in goal for Celtic when they became the first British club to capture the European Cup in 1967, took thirteen goal kicks compared with Bill's nine.

I was a great admirer of Jackie Milburn, as I was of Bobby Mitchell, the Newcastle outside left, who always seemed to be available and who created many of the chances finished off by Jackie.

Ted Purdon was left out for the following day's return, replaced by a new signing, Bill Holden from Burnley. Bill gave us the lead after only five minutes and we should have been two up shortly afterwards when the new boy set up a simple chance that Charlie Fleming should have put away. At half-time we were still ahead and I felt we would have our revenge. But not long after half-time Newcastle equalised and then Milburn put them in front, and at the end it was 3-1. Two games: Newcastle 9 Sunderland 2. Still, we didn't have to play them again that season and perhaps with little to worry about in the league we could concentrate on the FA Cup – Len would be pleased!

The highlight of our route to the quarter-finals was a goal from Ray Daniel. He strode up the field from centre-half before striking the rock-hard ball, as it was then, from forty-five yards. It flew past Ted Burgin in the Sheffield United goal and into the top corner of the net. Ray was the joker in our team and he lived on that goal for months afterwards.

We were to face Newcastle in the quarter-finals, and early on, during a delay when a player was getting treatment, Billy Elliott pointed out that Jimmy Scoular had on a knee bandage.

'Yes, I see,' I said, not thinking anything of it until a grinning Billy said, 'Well, somebody ought to test his knee out for him.'

Jimmy, a sailor during the war on HMS *Dolphin*, was a real hard man but Bradford-born Billy was anyone's equal. During the war he served on a frigate hunting U-boats. I don't know if he captured any Germans, but I wouldn't have wanted to be in their shoes if he had.

In 1955 I had roomed with him on an end-of-season tour of the United States and Canada – Bill Murray had managed to get permission from the Army for me to go with the squad – and we were away for over a month.

As well as playing local clubs we lined up against Huddersfield Town on four occasions. In the first game, played in baking hot conditions in New York, there was a tussle on the far side and by the time I got over there Billy was having a right wrestle with about half the Huddersfield team. The air was blue and George Aitken, a big strong lad, had his arms in a bear hug around Billy, restraining him.

Bill Murray came on the pitch to get Billy to calm down and I could hear Billy telling George to let him go as he was all right now; he promised not to continue the argument. When George let go Billy whacked one of their players. I can't remember who it was but he went straight down. Bill Murray ordered Billy down the tunnel before the referee did.

Somehow we managed to pacify the Huddersfield players and by the end of the game everything seemed to have been resolved. We went back to the hotel to get ready before having something to eat and a drink. I was ready before Billy and told him I'd see him in the bar. When I came out of the lift on the ground floor I was met by four Huddersfield players asking where Billy was. They were staying in the same hotel, and one of the quartet, Bill McGarry, said they wanted to talk to him as 'He was out of order.' I was able to persuade them that wouldn't be a good idea. When I told Billy about it later on he just shrugged his shoulders and said 'Well, they know where I am' and carried on drinking.

So Billy Elliott could be a nasty, hard lad and in the quarter-final it wasn't long before he conducted his own first aid test on Jimmy's left knee, which left our opponents with only ten fit men for most of the match. It was just before half-time when we took the lead, Bill Holden throwing off his marker to head home. In the second half, despite Newcastle pushing up the field, I never felt they were going to equalise. When Holden hit the second with just seven minutes left I knew we were going to get our chance to reverse the previous season's semi-final defeat. This time it would be different.

We were up against Birmingham City with Manchester City, our nemesis the previous season, facing Tottenham in the other semi. We'd beaten Birmingham earlier in the season at St Andrew's and with the bulk of the 65,000 Hillsborough crowd behind us I was confident we'd win again. In fact we were collectively very disappointing. We fell behind after just nine minutes when Joe McDonald scored an own goal. And although we were only a goal down at half-time and still in with a chance, this disappeared when their right winger, England international Gordon Astall, grabbed the second with twenty-five minutes to go. Eddy Brown scored their third with only seven minutes left. Our hopes were dashed and although I couldn't know it now, so were mine. The furthest I was to go in the FA Cup after that was a quarter-final place in 1960–61.

Birmingham went on to lose in the final 3-1. The match is best remembered because Bert Trautmann played the last seventeen minutes with a broken neck. They were hard times back then!

Having managed to capture eighteen points from the first twenty-four it was a sign of how far we fell when, by the end of the season, we managed only another twenty-five from the last thirty games. Spread over the whole season that would have been relegation form. We'd done all right in front of goal, scoring eighty league goals, but we really struggled defensively, conceding the most of any club – ninety-five, the highest number by any Sunderland team. We had, of course, let in eight at Luton, seven at Blackpool, not to mention six at home to Newcastle.

It was hardly surprising that crowds plummeted – there were only 19,865 for the visit of League champions

Manchester United at the end of the season. In a side that was just starting to blossom, England captain and left back Roger Byrne was a magic player; Bill Foulkes was solid and would still be around twelve years later to play in the European Cup Final at Wembley when Matt Busby's refashioned side won the European Cup by beating Benfica 4-1. Eddie Colman at right half was one of my favourite players of all time; they said he had swivel hips and he always played with a big smile on his face. Playing in the same Army side was a pleasure and a privilege.

Then there was Duncan Edwards, a colossus of a man, arrogant, not unlike Wayne Rooney today, and a brilliant footballer. There was also Tommy Taylor, a great goalscorer, and my good friend Dennis Viollet, who was an excellent player. Had the tragedy of Munich not intervened and the team managed to stay together I think that they would have dominated English football for the next eight to ten years. I am not certain Spurs would have been the first twentieth-century club to do the double of League and Cup.

I got to know Matt Busby pretty well when I moved into management. What a manager. He survived Munich by the skin of his teeth and recovered to fashion a truly great club. He also had the courage at the end of the 1955–56 season to ignore the Football Association, who had called for the Old Trafford club to follow Chelsea's lead of the previous season and refuse to participate in the fledgling European Cup.

Matt Busby was having none of that. He wanted to compete with and prove himself against the very best. I would have liked that to have included Sunderland, but sadly the side was now in freefall and we were plunged straight into a fight for survival at the start of the 1956–57 season, losing the first game 6-2 at Luton Town. Bill Fraser was dropped and John Bollands, signed from Oldham Athletic in April, was given the 'keeper's spot for the rest of the season. He was top class, very quick off his line, great at diving at the attacker's feet to smother the ball and a very good handler of the ball. He proved a great asset to the side.

It was not just our form that was making me unhappy. I didn't like being asked to move from the number four spot to inside right. It was a position I never enjoyed playing and I made this clear to Bill Murray, but he wasn't prepared even to listen to my complaints. It was true that playing number eight gave me a greater opportunity to go forward but I always much preferred playing right half, where I felt my ability to pass the ball gave me a greater influence on the game.

After we beat Blackpool 5-2 in mid-September the side suffered a terrible run, losing nine and drawing just one, with only eight points from eighteen games. I feared I was about to become part of the first Sunderland side to get relegated. So in November I was delighted when the club bought Don Revie from Manchester City. Ultimately he was to have little success at Sunderland, but I felt his experience would help us and in the wake of his arrival I was moved back to my favoured position. Later another England international, winger Colin Grainger, joined us from Sheffield United.

In December 1956 we managed to scramble our way to three victories, one of which was in my final Christmas Day match, a 1-0 win over Aston Villa at Roker Park watched by just 18,000.

At Tottenham in February 1957 we came up against Ted Ditchburn, then the England 'keeper, and he had an inspired game. We lost 5-2 but might have won. One of our best results came the following weekend when, in the best game played by Don Revie in a Sunderland shirt, we beat Sheffield Wednesday 5-2 at Roker Park – we had played better at White Hart Lane. Football can be an odd game at times.

Our struggle on the pitch was being complicated by events off it. In January 1957 a letter from an unidentified 'insider' at the club had suggested Sunderland were breaking the rules by making illegal under-the-counter payments as a way of subverting the rules on the maximum wage.

Trevor Ford's autobiography the previous year had lifted the lid on under-the-counter payments thought to be operating at a number of clubs to attract and then keep their best players. In his book Ford had named Sunderland as one of the guilty parties and Bill Murray subsequently admitted to having handed over £250 in a parcel to the Welshman in the summer of 1951.

Football League Secretary Alan Hardaker examined the club's books and found they had been making illegal payments. They totalled just over £5,000 – not a great deal when divided among the players, but the rules had been broken. In April, four of the club's directors, including Stanley Ritson, a magistrate, were banned for life.

I wasn't one of the players who received the illicit money but I was dragged into the affair when I was informed I was to have six months' benefit money taken from the £750 I was owed from the club after five years as a professional. I have no idea why that happened. I can only assume that when the directors were asked who had received payments they wrongly mentioned my name. Later I got the benefit money back.

There were rumours that we were going to be dropped into Division Two or docked points, which considering our perilous position was as good as relegation. All we could do was to put the issue to one side while we fought to finish out of the bottom two. Perhaps it was because they didn't want to see their side relegated for the first time ever but as we moved into March 1957 the crowd at Roker proved a great inspiration.

Although I didn't like it one bit I was switched back to inside right and grabbed the winner with only twelve minutes left at St Andrew's as we beat Birmingham 2-1. Joe McDonald, however, was the man of the match.

I was determined we wouldn't go down, and the following weekend I did it again, scoring the only goal at home to Arsenal after half an hour. Billy Bingham and I linked up well down the right and with a little more luck we would have won a lot more comfortably. We were slowly dragging ourselves to safety. I then scored my third in four matches as we beat Leeds United to almost guarantee survival.

The game attracted the largest home crowd of the season – more than 56,000. A lot came to see the Leeds centre-forward John Charles, who it was known was off to play for Juventus in Turin when the season ended. John ended up as the First Division's top scorer that season with thirty-eight goals.

John went on to be a big success in Italy, which wasn't the case with other players such as the great Jimmy Greaves. John had immense strength, and he was very talented whether playing centre-forward or centre-half. You'd look at him and think 'I bet he can play' and he could. On the field he had this air of superiority, but off it he was a very unassuming man. I met him many times and always enjoyed his company.

Manchester United won the league but lost 2-1 to Aston Villa in the FA Cup final. The Villa forward Peter McParland flattened United 'keeper Ray Wood early in the game and Jackie Blanchflower had to go in goal. McParland's barge would have earned him a straight red today, but in the 1950s 'keepers were expected to withstand some fearsome challenges. Shack didn't waste any time in repeating his well-known belief that no side could win the First Division title and FA Cup in one season.

In the final week of the season Ray Daniel, Billy Elliott, Willie Fraser, Johnny Hannigan and Ken Chisholm, all big-money signings, were forced to appear before a joint FA–Football League commission into illegal payments. After they refused to incriminate themselves, remaining silent on advice from the Players' Union, they were each given a lifetime ban. Only later did it transpire that those involved in the enquiry did not possess the powers to suspend the players.

I was glad to see the end of 1956–57, in which the shocking form of the latter half of the previous campaign had continued for much of the season.

There was also another personal reason to look forward. In the summer of 1957 I was finally finished with National Service and could now spend more time with Marjorie and Sherley. The three of us were able to live together for the first time. We rented a house from the club not too far from Roker Park. It used to be Billy Elliott's but he had a shop which had a house attached so he moved out. We were there for the next eight years, and had fantastic neighbours in Ritchie and Joyce Wilkinson. With it being no distance at all from Seaburn there were plenty of opportunities to get down to the sandy beach. It was close enough to Roker Park for me to walk to work. Billy Elliott was the only player who lived near us until Bill Fraser moved in nearby.

Sunderland was a much bigger place than Horden. It had a large, busy shopping centre and the people were friendly, especially if the team was doing well. Later in my career nightclubs arrived in the town, and it was great to visit them during the close season and on special occasions. Sunderland had at one time been the biggest shipbuilding town in the world, and while the numbers of ships being built had declined by the late '50s the industry still dominated the River Wear.

Marjorie and I would often walk along the banks of the Wear, pushing Sherley in her pram and looking down on the ships being built. Their launches were always special occasions; thousands would turn out and I'd often be among them. The waves would hit the other side of the river seconds after the boat hit the water. As a family we'd also walk down to Marsden Grotto near South Shields, and all in all Sunderland was a great place to live.

Chapter 7

Playing for England

When you start playing football one ambition is bound to be to play for your country. I was lucky, I managed to achieve the thrill of pulling on the full England jersey, but not before I suffered more than my fair share of setbacks. Finally I played two games in April 1962 to earn a place in the World Cup squad which travelled to Chile.

By the end of 1954 I felt comfortable playing regularly at right half for one of the best-supported clubs in the country. I had previously played for England Schoolboys and I was keen to get a chance to play for England at a higher level.

So it was exciting to be selected as part of the England Under-23 squad for a match at Stamford Bridge against Italy on January 19 1955. There was to be a training session the week before at Highbury.

Now over the years there has been considerable speculation about whether Walter Winterbottom, the England manager from 1947 to 1962, picked the England team or whether he made do with players chosen by the FA. Arguments have been made for both but I think my experience in January 1955 can end these.

At the training session I felt things went really well. I was lifted when Winterbottom started telling me about the player I would be up against, saying he was very good and the Italian team's playmaker but that his weakness was he was all left foot. We even shared the train back up to the north-east – he got off at Darlington – and the discussion about my opponent and the Italian side in general lasted all the way home. I felt certain I was going to play. If I wasn't then it was a very strange conversation, that was for sure.

After I played for Sunderland at Sheffield Wednesday on the Saturday the lads wished me all the best. There was absolutely no doubt in my mind I was playing.

I trained with the rest of the players with the manager not saying too much to any of us. Then on the Tuesday morning I received a letter that started 'Dear Anderson' and when I looked a line had been drawn through 'selected' and above it the word 'reserve' had been written in.

I know Manchester United's boy wonder Duncan Edwards was picked instead of me, and he had an outstanding game as England won 5-1, but the right and proper thing for Walter Winterbottom would have been for him to explain why he had changed his decision. Problem was, I am sure it wasn't his decision. He'd wrongly assumed I was in the team and when that turned out not to be true he simply didn't know how to tell me. I was naturally very disappointed and when I got back home to see my Sunderland teammates I felt a little awkward in describing what had happened. Some assumed I must have fallen out with the manager.

Thankfully I didn't have to wait too long to make my debut at Under-23 level. It came in disappointing circumstances for another player, Robert Ayre, the Charlton Athletic centre-forward who broke his collarbone early in the game against Scotland at Shawfield Park on February 8 1955. Unusually for those days it had been agreed that substitutes would be allowed, so I made my debut aged twenty as a substitute. Forced to reshuffle, the man in charge for the night, Bill Nicholson, then a Spurs coach, pushed Duncan Edwards up front. We finished 6-0 winners with Duncan scoring a hat-trick. He was by a mile (and more) the best player on the field, using to the full his strength, pace and deadly shooting ability. Duncan could have played any position on a football field and been outstanding.

Although I had played nowhere near as well as him I was still pretty pleased with my performance. I felt I'd been able to control the ball well and use my passing ability to bring others into the game. And 6-0 against Scotland; it's the sort of thing about which Englishmen dream.

The full international between the countries that season was set for Wembley in early April. With Sunderland in the thick of a challenge for the league title and FA Cup, and with a wedding to arrange, I never gave the game a second's thought. Len Phillips, of Portsmouth, the man who taught me a few things on my league debut, was regular choice at right half. However, he suffered an injury and about ten days beforehand Sunderland manager Bill Murray pulled me to one side and said that he thought I was going to be selected. He didn't say much more, but from experience I suspect a selector had rung him to enquire about my form and availability. There was also an article in the *Daily Mirror* saying that I was being considered. So you can imagine my disappointment when Chelsea's Ken Armstrong got the nod. It marked the end of a disastrous couple of weeks in which Sunderland lost out to Chelsea in the fight for the title and to Manchester City in the FA Cup semi-final. England, incidentally, won 7-2 with Dennis Wilshaw, of Wolves, scoring four times. I could hardly claim I was missed!

I started for England Under-23s for the first time the following season when on September 28 1955 I was part of a team that beat Denmark 5-1 at Fratton Park, Portsmouth. Alf Stokes and Johnny Haynes each scored twice and Bobby Robson got the other.

It was after this game that I received the news that I was wanted for the senior squad. As it was a friendly, league games were still to be played that weekend so the FA had agreed to limit selection to one player per club –

in the previous match there had been seven players from Wolves, Chelsea and Manchester United. I was selected as the travelling reserve. Despite knowing I would not have been picked had it been a full international I still regarded it as an honour. Newcastle's Jackie Milburn went out of his way to make me feel at home, helping me considerably. England won the game comfortably with Don Revie and Nat Lofthouse each scoring twice in the 5-1 victory.

England: Ron Baynham (Luton Town), Jeff Hall (Birmingham City), Roger Byrne (Man Utd), Bill McGarry (Huddersfield), Billy Wright (Wolves), Jimmy Dickinson (Portsmouth), Jackie Milburn (Newcastle United), Don Revie (Manchester City), Nat Lofthouse (Bolton Wanderers), Geoff Bradford (Bristol Rovers), Tom Finney (Preston North End)

Denmark: Per Henriksen, Poul Andersen, Verner Nielsen, Erik Pondal Jensen, Christen Brogger, Jorgen Olesen, Jorgen Hansen, Jorgen Jacobsen, Ove Andersen, Knud Lundberg, Poul Pedersen. Sub: John Jorgensen for Christen Brogger (28 mins)

As expected I was not selected for the next match, a Home International against Wales three weeks later, and little did I realise it would be almost six years before I got back into the senior squad and seven before I finally got to put on the full England jersey.

My third appearance for England Under-23 came against France on October 17 1956 at Ashton Gate. It was a very proud moment as I was made captain but it was a disappointing goalless draw, a match marred by a terrible injury to a wonderful prospect, Doncaster's Alick Jeffrey. The broken leg practically ended his top-class career. The whole atmosphere was soured, and I was glad – as I suspect was also the case for most spectators – when the referee blew the final whistle. There is no doubt in my mind that

Alick would have enjoyed a highly successful career had he not been injured that Bristol night.

When I was chosen as captain I got a message from Walter Winterbottom to look out for a youngster at Doncaster Station. As the train drew in I opened the window to see this big, strapping lad. Once on the train he introduced himself as Alick Jeffrey. He was built like Duncan Edwards and he seemed to have the same confidence.

He didn't say a lot but he was asking all the right questions and I thought that if he played as well as he talked then the crowd were going to be in for a treat. Doncaster were in the Second Division and Alick had made his debut aged just fifteen. He was now seventeen and before the game many newspapers reported that because of his pace, punch and determination he was already being considered for a full England debut.

There could be no blame attached for the tackle that broke his leg. The French player made a a genuine attempt to win the ball but Alick got there first and unfortunately his opponent couldn't stop his follow-through. I was only about ten yards behind the incident and it was the first time I'd heard the sound of someone breaking a leg; it was like the snapping of a twig.

The game petered out after Alick was taken off. In those days it would take a player much longer to recover from such an injury, and the other players' minds were diverted from the match as a result of what we'd experienced.

There were fears that Alick would never play again. Thankfully he did but it took him a long time to recover. I understand he was helped by George Raynor, the manager who took Sweden to the 1958 World Cup final, but even he could not restore the electrifying pace and power that would have taken Alick to the very top. Instead, the peak of his career came in 1964–65 when he top-scored in Division Four with Doncaster Rovers with thirty-six league goals – not bad for a crock!

Apparently before his injury Matt Busby had given Alick £200, the equivalent of around three months' wages, with the promise that he would buy him in due course at a fee that would probably have smashed the British record. Staggeringly, after the injury Alick even offered to pay it back!

When I was manager at Doncaster Rovers in the 1970s an ex-player, Laurie Sheffield, asked if I'd be willing to play in a fund-raising match at Pontefract and when I expressed the opinion that I was a little too old he attempted to persuade me by saying Alick Jeffrey had agreed to turn out.

I was amazed; I'd seen him a few weeks previously and he was a big, round barrel of a man who looked like he couldn't even jog never mind play football. He was the landlord of the Black Bull in Doncaster marketplace and clearly enjoyed a pint. Come the match and Alick could hardly get his jersey over his gut. There were a few murmurings among the crowd of close to 2,000 about his appearance, with some younger spectators giving him stick about his weight. He'd hardly had a kick when a cross from the left was headed back out by a defender, and I can see it now, the ball soaring into the air with Alick just moving backwards ever so slightly. My reaction was 'no way can he hit that', but he leaned back and struck a volley that rocketed twenty yards into the top corner of the net. It was some goal and nobody laughed at his appearance after that. He never made it back on to the field for the second half, but that goal was worthy of any match so no one was complaining.

I thought afterwards how 'form is temporary, class is permanent'. That was Alick. It was a great shame what happened to him.

Six months later, on February 6 1957, I was chosen to play at St Andrew's against Scotland in a B international.

At centre-forward for us was a twenty-one-year-old from Middlesbrough, one Brian Howard Clough. It was the first time I'd met him. I'd heard of him of course, because while football didn't receive the blanket coverage it does today, which meant you wouldn't get a report of Manchester United v Arsenal in our north-east papers, the local matches were covered so I knew about 'Boro's goalscoring sensation. He lived up to his reputation by hitting our second in a 4-1 win.

At the season's end I was off on the England Under-23 European tour. As it coincided with the termination of my National Service, my difficult time for Sunderland in the league and the run-in with the Football League when I was wrongly docked ten per cent of my five year's service money I felt this was the time to show what I could really do.

Three matches were planned, against Bulgaria, Romania and Czechoslovakia. Although eighteen players in total were selected only twelve were available for the first game – the other five, plus Bolton's Dennis Stevens as the reserve, were on duty in a World Cup qualifier in Dublin the evening of our first match in Sofia. They were later to link up with us in Romania.

The match has to go down as the most disappointing in my career. With Clough at centre-forward, we didn't play well. Brian scored an equaliser but the match was a niggly affair. Many of us had our shirts pulled, which didn't happen much in England then, and with fifteen minutes remaining we were still 2-1 down. That was bad enough but it was to get a lot worse for me.

The ball had gone out of play and as I was running to take the throw a Bulgarian player deliberately stepped in front of me and spat at me. Nobody had ever done that to me before and I saw red and punched him. It was a good enough blow and the player went down. I knew I was in trouble even before the Hungarian referee, Steven

Jolt shouted 'Get off!' He pointed towards the tunnel and I followed his finger.

I later heard that a spectator had tried to attack me and had to be manhandled away by the police, but I was oblivious to everything as with my head bowed I marched off the pitch into the dressing room. I was the first player to be sent off playing for England.

Although what I'd done was wrong I had no regrets and I still haven't. I'd been spat at, which is reprehensible. But I knew the Football Association would view the dismissal very seriously. True, this wasn't a full international but that didn't mean it would be ignored and the 'hard lines' of my teammates when they appeared a few minutes later, while appreciated, were of little consolation. Neither was the knowledge I learned the following day that the player I'd thumped, the outside left Doicho Batchev, had the previous season received a year's suspension for rough play.

'England player is sent off in disgrace' screamed the headline in the following day's *Daily Mirror*. Frank McGee reported that there had been a scuffle and I had tried to kick the Bulgarian. The chairman of the selectors, Frank Adams, was reported as being grave-faced and upset when he said: 'I do not disagree with the referee.' Bill Nicholson, in charge while we awaited Walter Winterbottom's arrival from Ireland, was good enough to point out I had 'been provoked immediately before the incident', but that was of little consolation.

I knew I was going to be suspended and the chances of playing again were diminished because two right halves, Ronnie Clayton, of Blackburn, and Duncan Edwards had joined us from Ireland. They were buoyant because England had scored a last-minute equaliser to deny the Republic a famous victory. This was a game in which my soon-to-be Sunderland colleague, centre-half Charlie Hurley, had made an outstanding debut. The draw meant

England rather than Ireland qualified for the 1958 World Cup finals in Sweden.

I couldn't wait to get home but I knew there would be awkward questions when I did – being sent off in 1957 was a big thing, and being sent off playing for your country was seen as shameful. I even thought about packing in football but fortunately my wife Marjorie and friends persuaded me not to be so daft and while it's true that I was a qualified plumber I much preferred playing football.

I knew my actions were likely to have ended any chances of earning a full cap for some time. What made it so annoying was that I had wanted the chance to explain myself – I hoped that as we made our way through Romania and Czechoslovakia one of the many FA officials would have taken the trouble to speak to me – but not a chance. In fact they hardly glanced in my direction.

Charlie Hurley has spoken about how the Irish players sometimes turned up at the airport to discover there were so many officials that there wasn't room for all the players on the plane. England wasn't as bad as that but there was still a big class divide. We were expected to address the officials as 'sir' but such courtesies were never extended to the players. FA officials used only our surnames.

It was said that FA secretary, and later FIFA president, Sir Stanley Rous was a great administrator who did a lot for English football. Yet he was one of the most aloof, unapproachable people you could ever hope – or not – to meet.

It was therefore difficult for the players to suppress their laughter when following the second tour game we approached the Romanian border with Czechoslovakia to be stopped by armed guards. After the driver had returned from speaking with them he said we would have to get off and carry our cases and equipment across before getting back on board.

Sir Stanley was not impressed. Announcing to all and sundry 'We shall see about that' he stormed off the coach and straight into the faces of the border guards – we couldn't hear what he was saying but it was clear that they couldn't understand his English. Mind you, neither could most of the players so the guards had no chance. He continued to argue with himself until he was reduced to silence when suddenly one of the guards raised a rifle and pointed it at him. Sir Stanley took the hint and marched back to the bus, to announce, 'We will have to disembark and carry our luggage across.' How people kept a straight face was a miracle.

If Sir Stanley Rous didn't speak to me about the dismissal, there was no chance anyone else would. I wasn't told I wouldn't be playing again; I heard rumours I wouldn't be considered for another four years or so but no one told me officially, or even unofficially. My side of the story was never listened to.

It was to be four years before I got anywhere near playing for England again. It's true that during that time Sunderland struggled badly. However, my form couldn't have been that bad because Manchester United's Matt Busby wanted to buy me so I am convinced it was the events in Bulgaria which prevented me getting selected.

In 1961, having largely given up on the idea of being selected for England again, I was surprised and delighted to be chosen for the England squad for a World Cup qualifier in Portugal followed by friendlies in Italy and Austria at the end of the 1960–61 season. There was little doubt that Sunderland's FA Cup run had raised my profile in the national media, especially as two of the ties were against top London sides in Arsenal and, more importantly, Tottenham Hotspur. Yet I remained convinced that despite the positive rumours my sending off would bar me from selection.

At the same time I was aware that the Sunderland chairman, Syd Collings, was now on the selectors' panel and he wasn't shy in letting me know he was putting in a good word for me. In truth this was a ridiculous situation. The manager should have picked the squad and then the team but after my experience with Walter Winterbottom I knew exactly how it worked. Would I have got in if Collings hadn't been on the selectors panel? Who knows. I'd like to think so but I doubt it.

Having been selected to travel I really hoped my long wait might come to an end. I reckoned it was unlikely to happen in the first game against Portugal – especially because in their previous three games England had beaten Mexico, Scotland and Wales 8-0, 9-3 and 5-1 respectively. Nevertheless I was a proud man when we arrived in Portugal, where we were met by a group of Portuguese officials at the airport. They had arranged for us to bypass the large queue without showing our passports before getting on the bus to take us to our hotel.

I was towards the back of the group, which contained great players such as Jimmy Greaves and Bobby Charlton, already household names. So I had to laugh when an obviously well-to-do English 'gentleman' wearing a trilby looked us up and down and said in a loud voice to his wife and anyone else within earshot, 'I told you the peasants were taking over the world.'

West Brom's Bobby Robson kept his place at right half and England grabbed a deserved draw thanks to a late Ron Flowers goal. After that the squad moved on to Italy, where I roomed with Jimmy Greaves.

This was just after Chelsea had accepted an offer of £100,000 from Italian giants AC Milan. Jimmy had scored forty-one league goals that season, finishing top scorer for the second time in Division One even though he'd only just turned twenty-one.

It was obvious that he wasn't that happy about moving to Milan and when we reached Italy the best-known agent from the time, Gigi Peronace, rang our room. In fact Gigi was probably the only agent anybody knew then. Jimmy refused to answer the phone, saying very quietly, 'Tell him I've gone out, Stan.'

Gigi wouldn't have that, though, and he kept ringing. I kept lying for Jimmy, and when Gigi said he was coming to the hotel I was even persuaded by Jimmy to say that wasn't allowed under FA rules. Gigi duly turned up and I deliberately kept a low profile out of embarrassment. Of course Jimmy did go to Italy, but although he scored nine times in just twelve games, an unbelievable record in a country that prided itself first and foremost on defence, he was back in London before Christmas to play for double winners Tottenham Hotspur.

He had a great ability to find space in the penalty area. I played against him a few times and he had to be marked very tightly in the box; he had quick, nimble feet, and could shoot and also dribble. He wasn't at his best outside the area but he scored two magnificent goals that I remember because they came against Sunderland and Newcastle. As these matches were televised they were repeated dozens of times; Jimmy ran from the halfway line before beating a number of players and rounding the 'keeper. Charlie Hurley was one of the players chasing him in the Sunderland game and Bobby Moncur and Ollie Burton were among the Newcastle players involved.

I know that Jim was naturally very upset when Alf Ramsey left him out of the 1966 World Cup final and his replacement Geoff Hurst, of course, did a magnificent job as striker. There are still a lot of different opinions about whether England would have won had Jimmy played instead of Geoff. I don't have any doubt that we would have won for the simple reason that ours was the best team that year.

Despite missing out on England's finest day, Jimmy still had a fantastic career. Whatever era he'd played in

I think he'd have finished as top scorer in the league. Jimmy Greaves was a great footballer and I was delighted for him, and the other England lads, when he was finally presented with a World Cup winner's medal in June 2009. He did, after all, play in the first three England games in 1966 before injury forced him to miss the quarter-final with Argentina.

In all he scored 357 goals in the First Division and thirty-five in the FA Cup for Chelsea, Spurs and West Ham and also rattled home forty-four goals in just fifty-seven England appearances.

Back on the England tour it was a pity from my viewpoint that England's only change for the match in Rome's Stadio Olimpico was at centre-forward, Aston Villa's Gerry Hitchens replacing Bobby Smith. Gerry scored twice before Jimmy Greaves popped up with the winner with just four minutes remaining. The 90,000 crowd were not happy at seeing their side beaten and gave their players some stick.

I honestly thought the next match at the Praterstadion in Vienna was a case of now or never for me. Changes were made to the team to face Austria – the forwards were the same in Bryan Douglas, Jimmy Greaves, Gerry Hitchens, Johnny Haynes and Bobby Charlton but at the back Middlesbrough's Mick McNeil was replaced at left back by Burnley's John Angus.

Another Burnley man was brought in to replace Bobby Robson – Brian Miller being naturally elated to be making his debut, in what proved his only England appearance. Yet Brian's true position was left half and this meant Ron Flowers, who'd always played left half when he turned out for England, being moved to right half. I could see the logic of Brian being given his debut because of his club partnership with John Angus. England's selectors clearly favoured keeping club pairings, as shown by the example of Ron Springett in goal with Peter Swan, his Sheffield Wednesday teammate, at centre-half. But to swap one of your most consistent performers and play him in an unusual position was something I could not fathom. I wasn't the only one to think like this. Frank McGee, in the *Daily Mirror*, quoted an unnamed player as saying, 'I feel sorrier for Stan Anderson than anyone. We all thought he was supposed to be the reserve right half, the man who would fit in naturally in the same style and plan.'

It meant I would just have to wait, perhaps for ever, to play for England. I was absolutely gutted and my mood was not raised by watching an out of sorts England lose 3-1.

Bobby Robson was back at right half for England's next four matches that season, helping us qualify for the World Cup finals in Chile that summer. Having failed to make the squad for any of those games I felt my chance had passed. So I concentrated on helping SunderFland make their first serious attempt on promotion since being relegated at the end of the 1957–58 season. If I never played in a full England international it would be disappointing but not the end of the world.

However, in March 1962 I finally got my chance. I was picked to play against Austria in a friendly at Wembley. I was to be the first Sunderland player to play for England since Len Shackleton had scored when England beat the then World Champions West Germany in 1955.

I found out I was in the team when I received an early morning call from the *Daily Mirror*'s Charlie Summerbell, asking for a comment on my selection. As I hadn't received official confirmation I told him he must be joking. Thankfully, I got a letter from the FA the next day confirming I'd been picked. I was delighted: I'd played for my country as a schoolboy, at Under-23 and B level but to be chosen for a full international was extra special. It marked a great period in my career; after a poor start Sunderland were in with a real chance of promotion, I was playing well and now I was due to play in the white of England and for the first time at Wembley. The teams were:

England: Ron Springett (Sheffield Wednesday), Jimmy Armfield (Blackpool), Ray Wilson (Huddersfield), Stan Anderson (Sunderland), Peter Swan (Sheffield Wednesday), Ron Flowers (Wolves), John Connelly (Burnley), Roger Hunt (Liverpool), Ray Crawford (Ipswich), Johnny Haynes (Fulham), Bobby Charlton (Man Utd).

Austria: Gernot Fraydl, Heribert Trubrig, Karl Stotz, Erich Hasenkopf, Rudolf Oslansky, Karl Koller, Adolf Knoll, Erich Hof, Hans Buzek, Ernst Fiala, Friedrich Rafreider. Sub: Rudolf Flogel for Fiala (40 mins).

I knew most of the players but there was no team meeting and Walter Winterbottom did not say anything. There were no dossiers on Austria or on my direct opponent, the number ten Ernst Fiala.

Once you know you're playing you have to try and treat the occasion as if it's just an ordinary game, but that's difficult. Even though Wembley wasn't full it was still a fantastic experience to play there.

I was given an almost immediate touch of the ball. We kicked off and it was played back to me by Johnny Haynes. I pushed if out to John Connelly just outside at right wing.

We scored after just seven minutes through Ray Crawford, in only his second, and last, match for England. Ray, equal top scorer with West Brom's Derek Kevan in Division One that season as Ipswich under Alf Ramsey finished as champions, hadn't been selected to play originally. But Middlesbrough's Alan Peacock had suffered a broken cheekbone on the Saturday during the Tees–Wear derby at Ayresome Park in a clash with Charlie Hurley. It would have been Alan's first cap.

Ron Flowers made it two and in the second half Roger Hunt scored a third before Hans Buzek reduced the arrears.

During the game I managed to hit a couple of 'trademark' right-footed long balls across to Bobby Charlton on the left wing and this drew a polite round of applause from some fans, which boosted my confidence. I was aware that many fans probably knew little about me and some had possibly never seen me play.

I helped play a part in the third goal by linking up with Connelly. Afterwards Walter Winterbottom said 'Well done' and I was delighted to have played in a winning side.

After the game my dad said to me: 'Well done, son, but you played a couple of bad passes.'

He couldn't tell from the stands, nobody could, that the pitch was terrible. It looked immaculate but they'd filled in the divots and even painted them green. So the ball often bobbled. No wonder Bobby Charlton said as we came off, 'What a bloody mess.'

I was aware that England's next game was just ten days away and what a game – Scotland at Hampden in the Home International Championship, the oldest international rivalry in football. I was hoping to play, but had to wait for three days to receive official confirmation, even though the newspapers reported I had been picked. This meant I was missing when Sunderland played at Kenilworth Road, my replacement Martin Harvey scoring one of the goals in a vital 2-1 win.

Two changes were made to the team from the game against Austria: Bryan Douglas replaced John Connelly at outside right and Bobby Smith took over from Crawford. Bryan was a very easy lad to get on with. I knew that he could play both on the wing and at inside forward but I felt he was slightly more effective as a winger. He was very clever with the ball, could dribble past the full-back and could centre or cross extremely accurately.

The teams were:

Scotland: Bill Brown (Spurs), Alex Hamilton (Dundee), Eric Caldow (Rangers), Paddy Crerand (Celtic), Billy McNeill (Celtic), Jim Baxter (Rangers), Alex Scott (Rangers), John White (Spurs), Ian St John (Liverpool), Denis Law (Torino), David Wilson (Rangers).

England: Ron Springett (Sheffield Wednesday), Jimmy Armfield (Blackpool), Ray Wilson (Huddersfield), Stan Anderson (Sunderland), Peter Swan (Sheffield Wednesday), Ron Flowers (Wolves), Bryan Douglas (Blackburn), Jimmy Greaves (Spurs), Bobby Smith (Spurs), Johnny Haynes (Fulham), Bobby Charlton (Man Utd).

I was always interested in what programme notes said about me and in this case it was: 'Gave an impressive exhibition against Austria at Wembley last week and it was not surprising that the England selectors "capped" him again for today's match. A far-seeing, industrious middleman, assertive and with a telling shot. Such is his stamina that he seems able to keep going in attack and defence without halting in his stride. His colleagues will find his power having an impact on how the game will veer this afternoon, while we may have cause to fear his judgement as he dashes through seeking a chance to have a shot at goal.'

The Scotland match was the biggest of my long career. England were up against a side packed with talent. I felt they should have done better in the '60s than they did. Sadly John White was killed by lightning in 1964, but he and Caldow, McNeill, Crerand, Baxter, St John and Law were very good players. Yet they failed to qualify for the 1962 World Cup (although perhaps in view of how their group opponents Czechoslovakia went on to do in Chile that was no disgrace) and I feel the pressure applied on them by their fanatical support might have hampered their performances.

I had been slightly injured during the home league game with Southampton in between the England matches. It was my thigh and I needed a couple of days of treatment using a heat lamp and massages to bring out the bruising. I was able to train by the Wednesday but missed the round of golf with other players at Troon the following day. I was fit enough on match day but would not have liked to have been hit on my thigh, that's for sure.

There were more than 130,000 in Hampden Park. Unlike many players I can think of, crowds, big or small, never got to me, and I was lucky in that I didn't get too nervous before even the biggest of matches. I think this is why I was often chosen as captain. I was so laid back that Peter Swan, of Sheffield Wednesday and England, the man who was imprisoned for betting on matches, gave me the ironic nickname of 'Jet' because I walked around as if I'd got all day.

But I was affected by tension this day. We went out first and the booing and hissing was deafening; it shook the living daylights out of you. And what a noise when Scotland came out; the sky seemed to move, never mind the stadium. It was terrifying and to make matters worse there didn't seem to be a single person in the crowd supporting England. Mind you, even if there had been it would have been best to have kept quiet.

Backed by such support, and determined to reverse the previous season's 9-3 Wembley hammering, Scotland pushed forward and when they scored after thirteen minutes Hampden Park went absolutely berserk. David Wilson was the scorer and from our point of view it was a poor goal. We failed to clear a corner and when it came back into the box the Rangers outside left was unmarked and he struck the ball past Ron Springett, me, Jimmy Armfield and Peter Swan all close to the goal line. The roar was terrifying; I could see players on our side shouting at each other out of disappointment but you could not hear what they were yelling.

There was little doubt that at half-time the Scots were full value for their lead but in the second half we were much more in the game. Bobby Smith was able to unsettle their defence, Johnny Haynes, making his fiftieth international appearance, saw much more of the ball and Jimmy Greaves's runs were promising to pay off.

Although we didn't exactly silence the crowd we could at least communicate with each other. With our confidence increasing I felt we might get an equaliser and I am convinced we did when with fifteen minutes left Johnny Haynes unleashed a powerful drive that beat Bill Brown in the Scots goal. The ball rebounded from the crossbar and, standing on the edge of the penalty area, I could see it had clearly crossed the goal line before bouncing out. One-one, great. Yet the referee, Holland's Leo Horn, did not give it. We were going mental. Haynes, the captain, ran over to argue on our behalf but Horn was not going to change his mind and we were left bitterly disappointed.

It knocked the stuffing out of us and it was no great surprise when Scotland got a second with just two minutes left. Peter Swan made a late challenge on Denis Law and the resulting penalty was stroked home by the Scots captain and left back Eric Caldow.

At the end the crowd was even crazier and the Scottish lads did a lap of honour. Most of the England players couldn't wait to get off but I watched the Scotland side enjoy the applause as I couldn't help but be fixated by such enthusiasm from the crowd.

But I was bitterly disappointed by the result, especially as I knew, and as photographs in the following day's papers confirmed, we had scored a goal. I felt I hadn't played too badly. One of my roles had been to try and keep Denis Law quiet and I felt reasonably pleased that in many respects I had achieved that. I was also heartened by reports which said I had been one of the better England players. I had not disgraced myself, that's for sure.

But the fact was that Scotland had beaten us and the selectors were bound to be both upset and not a little angry. It was England's biggest game of the season, and no Englishman likes losing to Scotland.

So I wasn't too surprised to find that I was left out for the next international, at home to Switzerland. Bobby Robson was again selected at number four, while up front Smith was dropped and England experimented by moving Bobby Charlton from left wing to play alongside Gerry Hitchens. We won 3-1.

Bobby Robson was one of my main rivals for an England place. He'd made his debut against France in November 1957 and became a regular after the 1958 Sweden World Cup following his move from Fulham to West Bromwich Albion.

He tended to play a little bit further forward than me and was a good passer of the ball, rarely wasting it. He was also very fit and could be relied on to last the full ninety minutes. He had developed a playing relationship with the England captain Johnny Haynes at Fulham and the selectors were obviously keen to see that maintained in the national team.

As he was born not far from me in Sacriston, County Durham, we always got on very well. He was a Newcastle fan but didn't go on too much about it.

I was not surprised he went on to become a top-class manager. In 1959 Walter Winterbottom had persuaded him to take an FA coaching course at Lilleshall and when you were in Bobby's company he would talk football, football and football. He was keenly aware of the tactical changes in the world game that were taking far too long to come to Britain, and he would engage the other players in conversations about them. He and Don Howe, who went on to coach England and manage West Brom and Arsenal, were always chatting away. Bobby knew the strengths and weaknesses of every player at each club in England and Scotland.

Because Walter Winterbottom tended to say little before a match, Bobby would talk to the other players about how best to tackle the opponents. He was an organiser was Bobby. Only Alf Ramsey has got the national team to the last four of the World Cup. We were unlucky to lose on penalties to West Germany in 1990 in Italy. It was a very sad day when Bobby died.

I was really hopeful that I would be selected alongside him for the squad to go to the 1964 World Cup finals and so was overjoyed when the twenty-man squad was announced. It was:

Ron Springett (Sheffield Wednesday), Alan Hodgkinson (Sheffield United), Jimmy Armfield (Blackpool), Ray Wilson (Huddersfield), Don Howe (West Brom), Stan Anderson (Sunderland), Ron Flowers (Wolves), Bobby Moore (West Ham), Maurice Norman (Tottenham), Bobby Robson (West Brom), Peter Swan (Sheffield Wednesday), Bobby Charlton (Man Utd), John Connelly (Burnley), Bryan Douglas (Blackburn Rovers), George Eastham (Arsenal), Jimmy Greaves (Spurs), Johnny Haynes (Fulham), Gerry Hitchens (Inter Milan), Roger Hunt (Liverpool), Alan Peacock (Middlesbrough).
Team Manager: Walter Winterbottom. Trainer: Harold Shepherdson. Coach: Jimmy Adamson.
Officials: J. Richards, JP (chairman of selection committee), Lt. Col. C.F. Linnitt (chairman, international committee), H. Shentall, S.S. Collings, Sir Stanley Rous, Denis Follows (secretary).

There were only sixteen teams in the finals in those days and England were drawn in Group Four with Hungary, Argentina and Bulgaria. It was hoped we would do better than the three previous times we'd qualified for the finals: 1950, which saw an embarrassing defeat to the USA in the first round group stages; 1954, when England were defeated by Uruguay in the quarter-finals; before failing to get through the group stages four years later.

Brazil, having won the 1958 tournament with arguably the greatest side ever, were naturally favourites to retain the trophy, especially as the tournament was taking place in South America. Brazil were also looking for revenge, having lost out to Uruguay when the tournament was staged in Brazil in 1950.

One member of the squad was a good friend of mine, Middlesbrough's Alan Peacock. I was delighted at his inclusion. He was a good player whose company I always enjoyed and the two of us roomed together in Chile with Gerry Hitchens. On the back of his successful end-of-season tour with England the previous summer, Gerry had left Aston Villa for Inter Milan and done well in Italy. He was to stay there until 1969, also playing for Torino, Atalanta and Cagliari. Although he enjoyed success at all four clubs he missed out on being selected for England when Alf Ramsey took over as manager, because he preferred home-based players.

It was Gerry who introduced me to a new range of football boots. In comparison with my big awkward boots with hard toecaps I couldn't help noticing he had brought with him boots that were much more supple. They could be bent in half. I was fascinated and when I got the chance to try them I was impressed. When we returned home I asked Gerry to send me a pair. Alan Brown at Sunderland didn't approve of my new boots and told me to change them. I would slip them on just before we left the dressing room. I kept those boots for years, getting them mended and patched. People of my era will remember them as 'continental' boots.

I was fully aware that I was unlikely to be an automatic choice; two caps, including the defeat at Hampden Park, meant I was an outsider. It's an odd situation: you want the team to do well, but if they do then you've got no chance to get on the field and show what you can do. I made up my mind I would train as hard as I could, be enthusiastic, encourage those lucky enough to start and if I didn't get a game then so be it. It would also be a chance to watch some of the finest players in the world at first hand. All things considered I felt privileged to be picked and all the players at Sunderland were delighted and wished me well.

I was really looking forward to Chile. Yet even before we set off I should have seen the warning signs. When we turned up at Heathrow to fly to Peru for a warm-up friendly, eight of the players, me included, were informed we were to follow the main party of twelve players – and the selectors – the following day. So we arrived, after flying to the United States first, only three hours before kick-off. It was clear many of us were just making up the numbers and morale, ever so important in any squad, especially when you're a long way away from loved ones, plummeted.

One of the interesting aspects of the Peru game was the international debut of West Ham United's Bobby Moore, playing at right midfield that day. Despite press reports I felt Bobby had a very ordinary game. I felt he did not have the pace to play in midfield and I very much doubt whether he would have played every game in Chile had Peter Swan not fallen ill with tonsillitis, and then contracted dysentery when he arrived in Chile. It left the way clear for Bobby to partner Maurice Norman at centre-back. As teams began to drop a fourth defender back to support the centre-half and the two full backs Bobby blossomed and, of course, he went on to become a world star in this 'new' position.

Together with Ray Wilson, Jackie Charlton and George Cohen he helped forge a formidable back four for England at the 1966 World Cup finals, at which he was one of the tournament's stars.

Peter Swan might also have gone on to win many more England caps but he was later found to have been part of a betting ring with two other Sheffield Wednesday players, Tony Kay and David Layne. They had bet on their team to lose a match at Ipswich Town in December 1962. The amount of money they gained was peanuts but Peter was sent to prison and banned from playing until 1972. I wasn't totally shocked when I heard what they'd been up to – when I was in their company all they talked about was betting, not on games but on almost anything. I think they were hooked on gambling and might well have not even considered the consequences of their actions.

The match against Peru was a good workout but nothing like what would be faced in the qualifying group. When we eventually got to Chile the organisation was just as poor – Roy Keane would have gone mad but this was 1962, not 2002.

We were billeted – I use the word deliberately – in the Braden Copper Company's huts. It wasn't quite a prison camp but it certainly wasn't the Ritz. There were no telephones which would have let us ring home, and with little to do it wasn't long before boredom kicked in. Incredibly, I read later that newspapers back home had reported we were living a life of luxury – I wish.

It would have been good to have seen something of the country, but we rarely ventured far. Even the established players were not happy and it wasn't long before opinions were voiced, mainly to Harold Shepherdson, the Middlesbrough and England trainer. It was probably a good thing that the first match was just a couple of days away as it meant we just got on with training and passed the rest of the time as best we could.

The ground at Rancagua was only about twenty minutes' drive from our base and it was the venue for England's three group matches. The first, against a more than useful Hungarian side, turned out to be the most difficult.

The atmosphere wasn't what we had expected for a World Cup. There were only 8,000 fans in the small, run-down stadium. Local people couldn't afford the admission prices, and as a result there were usually more people outside the stadiums than inside. The World Cup was happening in their country but the vast majority of the Chilean people were not invited to the party. As such there was very little of what could be called 'World Cup euphoria' on display – especially as the location meant very few of our own supporters could afford the trip. At most 200 or so were at each game.

The little we did manage to see of Chile revealed gross disparities in wealth. When all the players went to a sumptuous dinner at a big mansion we passed shoeless people in the streets, cooking food on top of an oil drum. Others were clearly sleeping rough and you could see people working in terrible conditions on farms with wooden huts for accommodation.

Chile had suffered a massive earthquake in 1960, but there was little to indicate it was on the way to recovery. I was not too surprised when a decade or so later the people revolted.

Hungary started the first match better than us and led as early as the sixteenth minute through Lajos Tichy but England got back in the game and deservedly equalised with a Ron Flowers penalty. A point against decent opponents wouldn't have been a bad result. But with twenty minutes left Florian Albert, a two-footed player with a blistering shot, who five years later was voted European Footballer of the Year, grabbed the winner. Everyone was disappointed but most players accepted that the better team had won.

We returned to the training camp and I am sure at least some were expecting to see changes for the next match. George Eastham, Alan Peacock and Roger Hunt seemed to be the strongest candidates for places but I'd be lying if I denied we were all secretly hoping to be picked. In fact the inclusion of Alan, making his debut, for Gerry Hitchens, turned out to be the only alteration. This simply confirmed to many of the squad that we were really there just to make up the numbers. I felt that at the very least George Eastham and Bobby Robson, with their vast experience, should have been used in some way.

England, unlike other top international sides who were now playing 4-2-4, were still committed to the old system of 2-3-5 and at the 1962 World Cup it was clear it wasn't working. We had strength in the team but we were still playing too many long balls and failing to hold possession for long enough spells.

Argentina, our next opponents, had suffered a number of injuries in their 1-0 win against Bulgaria, and the side they turned out against England was weak. England played well in spells to emerge as worthy winners with goals from Bobby Charlton and Jimmy Greaves and another Ron Flowers penalty against just one from José Sanfilippo. Alan Peacock had a fine debut and he and Bryan Douglas had been the best England players.

Everyone was delighted. Because Hungary had hammered Bulgaria 6-1 England had only to draw with the group's poorest team in the final match to go through. Everyone was very confident that we would win comfortably to set up a quarter-final against either Brazil or Czechoslovakia, who both had three points from their opening two matches in Group Three.

I'm sure that everyone who was at the 1962 World Cup would say that England–Bulgaria was the worst match of the tournament. It even beat the Chile–Italy game, which was dubbed 'the Battle of Santiago' and famously introduced by commentator David Coleman on BBC television as 'the most stupid, appalling, disgusting and disgraceful exhibition of football, possibly in the history of the game.' At least in that game a couple of goals were scored.

It was clear from the start that Bulgaria were happy just to avoid a hammering. They sat back, inviting England to attack. Yet with plenty of possession England rarely looked like scoring and might have even suffered a surprising defeat had Kostov shown more confidence in front of goal, rolling a chance past the post with four minutes remaining. Had that gone in, Argentina, who drew 0-0 with Hungary in the other match, would have replaced England in the last eight.

I'm sure most of the players who played were as embarrassed as those of us watching. Even the small crowd jeered every bad pass and both teams were laughed off at the end. England might have gone through but no one watching the debacle could have been confident we'd get past our next opponents, Brazil, who by beating Spain 2-1 had finished top of Group Three.

I felt that if I was going to get a chance to play in the World Cup this was it. Surely whoever was picking the team would make changes now.

My hopes were lifted when Harold Shepherdson told me that Walter Winterbottom wanted to speak to Bobby Robson and me the following morning. I felt this must be my chance. Speaking to Bobby I know he felt the same, and I suffered one of the worst nights' sleep of my life, so anxious was I to know if I'd be playing for England against Brazil in the World Cup quarter-finals at Vina del Mar. It would undoubtedly have been the highlight of my career.

It was not to be. When we went to see Walter all he wanted us to do was set up a practice for the forwards. I spent most of my time collecting balls that had gone astray. By now I was simply looking forward to getting home and I was pretty certain that it wouldn't be too long before I was back in Sunderland. I had little doubt that Brazil would knock England out. I could envisage no other result and before kick-off, looking at those lucky enough to be picked, I was sure they felt the same.

Brazil were a brilliant side, even without Pele, the world's best player. Their passing and movement was as good as anyone's, even in present day football. Garrincha, nicknamed 'Little Bird' because his name means 'wren' in Portuguese, was only 5ft 6ins tall, but he outjumped Maurice Norman, at 6ft 2ins, to head home after half an hour.

England equalised when Jimmy Greaves rose above the Brazilian defenders to head a corner from Johnny Haynes against the bar and the ball bounced down for Gerry Hitchens to force it into the net. Gerry was playing only because Alan Peacock had food poisoning, a direct result I believe of the conditions we endured. Alan had sought something to supplement the inadequate food we were given and suffered the consequences.

Not that England learned of course, losing goalkeeper Gordon Banks to similar problems in Mexico eight years later just before another quarter-final. In his absence Chelsea's Peter Bonetti played badly against West Germany and a team arguably better than the one which won the 1966 World Cup had to go home.

At 1-1 there was real hope for England, especially as Didi and Amarildo, Pele's replacement, were limping. Didi had gone off after just four minutes, returning fifteen minutes later. But Brazil re-took the lead on fifty-three minutes when from twenty-five yards Garrincha hit such a powerful free kick that Ron Springett couldn't hold on to the ball. When it bounced off his chest Vava nodded it home.

Six minutes later the amazing Garrincha beat the England 'keeper with a wicked dipping shot. I was amazed afterwards to read that some reporters felt Springett should have saved it. Ron was a good goalkeeper but he couldn't perform miracles.

After that Brazil simply wouldn't let us have the ball, passing it from player to player, backwards and forwards and making England chase shadows. When their 'keeper got the ball he threw it to the full back and they played the ball to each other's feet. It was embarrassing, not quite England 3 Hungary 6 as in 1953 at Wembley, or 1-7 in Budapest shortly afterwards, but bad enough. For the last quarter of an hour England hardly had a touch such, was the supreme skill of the Brazilians.

For me England's impotence was summed up by our failure to utilise the one player who really could pass the ball around and bring others into the game. Bobby Charlton was playing, of course, but he was stuck out on the left wing, forced to wait for the ball when he should have been in the middle of the park and involved in everything.

England, under Walter Winterbottom, had failed to move with the times and in some respects almost fifty years later that's still true of our national team and its football, when passion is often elevated above the crucial aspects of the game – namely ball control, passing and movement. Forty years after our defeat against Brazil in 1962 the same sides met in a World Cup quarter-final, this time in Shizuoka during the 2002 World Cup.

England had taken the lead through Michael Owen only for Brazil to score twice through Rivaldo and Ronaldinho. However, when the latter was sent off with more than thirty minutes left the difference in class was shown once again, with Brazil using their abilities on the ball to lead England a merry dance. No matter how hard England worked to get the ball, they couldn't get close enough to the ten men to take it back. And when they did have it England just didn't have the skills to exploit their one-man advantage.

For me the match was confirmation that we still have a long way to go before we can compete at the highest level internationally. We must raise our players' ability to control and pass the ball if we hope to again win the World Cup. In 2009 I found myself agreeing with the criticism of the FA's head of development, Trevor Brooking, by former England youth team coach John Cartwright. He argued that it had taken the former West Ham and England midfielder much too long to back his belief that coaching for youngsters needs to concentrate on developing individual skill.

John made his points after Brooking picked out Brazilian Lucio as a defender who was relaxed on the ball and able to pass it accurately. Cartwright was correct in attacking FA coaching schemes that have for too long concentrated on the long-ball coaching beliefs promoted by Charlie Hughes.

Speed, strength and a willingness to work hard are vital, but so too is ability on the ball, moving into space and the awareness of it, being able to control the ball instantly and to look up and pass it accurately. Give me someone who can pass it over a runner any day.

Improving a youngster's ball skills needs to start in the schools, of course. But it will also require brave managers to defy the crowd's expectations, built on more than a hundred years of tradition, that the aim is to get the ball forward as quickly as possible.

Following their victory over England in Chile, Brazil went on to beat the hosts in a cracking semi-final in which Garrincha again grabbed two as they won 4-2. In the final they met Czechoslovakia, who took the lead through their impressive left half Josef Masopust but ended up losing 3-1. Brazil thus captured the trophy for the second time. Chile finished third by beating Yugoslavia in the play-off match. By this time I was back home in England watching on television.

It was a great disappointment not to have played in the World Cup and I don't think I would have let my country down had I taken part. However, it was still a great experience to have been part of the squad. What I couldn't know, of course, was that it was the end of internationals for me. Yet playing twice for England provided two of the highlights of my career. It meant I had achieved one of my boyhood ambitions.

Chapter 8

That sinking feeling

Bill Murray quit as Sunderland's manager in the summer of 1957. I'm not sure if he could be accused of abandoning a sinking ship, but as he had been heavily criticised for failing to win either the League title or the FA Cup I feel that the fear he might go down in history as the manager who took Sunderland down for the first time, plus the FA enquiry, was a bit too much.

Although I hardly knew him I was sorry to see him go. It meant he was not there to explain to the club secretary George Crow that he had indeed promised me compensation for getting only around half what the other first-team players earned during my National Service. George told me he knew nothing about any such arrangement and that was the end of the matter. It meant that, with the vast majority of my five years' service money spent on furniture for our new home and on repaying the £200 I had borrowed from my gran to buy a car, five years as a First Division footballer had left me with only a couple of hundred pounds in the bank. That would be worth about £10,000 these days.

The players had no idea who would replace Bill Murray, and we were back in pre-season training when it was announced that Alan Brown of Burnley would be taking over. They had finished seventh in Division One at the end of 1956–57 season and he arrived with a good reputation. It was said that he was among a new breed of managers with fresh ideas. We certainly saw more of him at training than Murray, but that wasn't difficult.

Brown was the first Sunderland manager to be born in County Durham and part of his attraction for the directors must have been that he had based his Burnley team on young players, many stolen from the north-east right under the noses of Sunderland, Newcastle and Middlesbrough. The Sunderland board was looking to end their big-spending days and concentrate on developing home-grown talent.

From the start Brownie made it clear he was in charge and that if we were to play in the first team we were to do exactly as we were told. Players were given specific roles. He made it clear that he wanted me to play more defensively. This disappointed me – I thoroughly enjoyed playing football at any level but especially when I was able to go out and play by getting on the ball and linking up with the forwards. What thrilled me was to play a defence-splitting pass to set up a forward for a shot at goal. My new role made this much more difficult.

Brown also treated all the players completely the same, which on the face of it might seem a good thing. But players are not all the same – some respond to words of encouragement and an arm round their shoulders to reassure them. Others do better if you tell them straight that they're playing poorly as they like to prove the manager wrong. Brown did much of the latter but very little of the former. Within a few weeks players were beginning to have doubts about the new man.

We started the season by losing 1-0 at home to Arsenal. We hadn't played too badly so there was no need to panic, although the announcement over that weekend by Len Shackleton that he was to retire immediately was a big blow, even though everyone realised he was in the latter stages of his playing career.

That's the one thing about Len that is still a mystery to me – the circumstances surrounding his retirement. We were in the dressing room before training on a Monday when Billy Elliott asked us if we'd heard that Shack had retired because of an ankle injury. Then the coaching staff confirmed it. I was astonished. He never mentioned an ankle injury to me and none of the other players could remember him ever talking about it. We would have asked him but Shack never came back to say his goodbyes – he simply disappeared. It was months before I next saw him.

He had trained as hard as the rest of us in pre-season and then all of the sudden he plays one game and he can't play again? He could have insisted the club sent him to a specialist and even if it had taken him half a season to get fit no one would have complained. The previous season he played in more than half the games. I am convinced he had another couple of years left in him. His retirement deprived the side of its most experienced and creative player and, I am convinced, ultimately played a significant part in our relegation.

When I finally got the chance to ask him what had happened he wouldn't answer me when I wanted to know if he'd gone because he didn't want to play for Alan Brown. All he did was smile. I knew Len very well, and I know that had I said something wrong he would have said, 'Wrong question – you're bloody crackers.' So the fact that he just smiled confirmed my belief that he'd made up his mind about Alan Brown, that he didn't rate him and was looking for a way out.

I believe, although I have no proof, that Len and the directors came to a financial arrangement. The club would claim compensation on insurance for the loss of his services – he was, after all, coming towards the end of his career – and he might have got a year's salary.

Len became a football reporter after he retired. He was a good one. He would come and see me once a month and only twice did he write anything that caused me real problems. He would work with you on a piece and you could trust that he wouldn't misrepresent what had been said or look to sensationalise it. I always got on well with him and when I became a manager at Middlesbrough I gave him loads of stories and he was very grateful.

Len also knew managerial talent when he saw it. It is well known that when Derby County were looking for a new manager in the late '60s he recommended the then Hartlepools United manager Brian Clough. The rest is history.

I remained friends with Len right up until the day he died and often think of him. I suspect Sunderland fans of that period do the same. He was a cracking player was Len Shackleton.

After Len left, the manager gathered us together and said he intended sticking with thirteen or fourteen experienced players for the first seven or eight games of the season. It must have been his way of boosting our morale, but when we slumped 4-1 at Leicester in the second match Jack Hedley and Charlie Fleming were dropped for the game at Wolves to be replaced by two youngsters, Alan O'Neill and Allan Graham. They lined up alongside another young lad, John Maltby, who'd replaced Shack at Leicester and stayed in the team. Not surprisingly we were hammered 5-0 and we were lucky to get nil. Having quickly discarded his declared policy in light of one poor result, Brown then added to the players' confusion by quickly bringing back Fleming and Hedley. It made for a poor atmosphere among the players, but fortunately three home wins, including one against Newcastle, lifted us out of the relegation zone.

The manager had decided to replace George Aitken at centre-half with a new man, twenty-one-year-old Charlie Hurley from Millwall. I'd not seen him play but I knew that he'd made his international debut for the Republic of Ireland against England during the summer and had marked Manchester United's Tommy Taylor out of the game. That meant he couldn't be too bad. He had also played more than a hundred league games for Millwall in Division Three South.

With hindsight it is amazing that Alan Brown even considered signing him – Charlie was a ball-playing centre-half, quite prepared to take chances in defence to beat players. True, he was also extremely good in the air, essential at a time when teams played with two wingers to supply crosses to big, battering-ram centre-forwards. But Brown had hardly shown during his first few weeks a desire to play open football – and certainly not at the back.

Charlie was, of course, to go on to become a Sunderland legend but his debut at Blackpool wasn't one of his better games as we lost 7-0. Charlie had a nightmare, being responsible for at least a couple of the goals. He did play better the following week at Burnley. Nevertheless, he put his foot on the ball and tried to beat someone only to lose it. It was quickly in the back of the net. We lost 6-0. Charlie must have wondered what on earth he'd got himself into.

On my part I feel that my own performance at Turf Moor was one of my worst for Sunderland. Brown had moved me to inside right at Blackpool but at Turf Moor I couldn't complain about playing out of my natural position. Alan Brown had put Don Revie at inside right and restored me to right half. It was just that nothing I tried came off. I honestly felt I might be dropped for the first time in more than five years. Fortunately I kept my place.

When you're fighting relegation every point is precious, and we threw one away at Hillsborough when, with only seconds remaining, Redfern Froggatt, the Sheffield Wednesday centre-forward, managed to get free of Charlie Hurley for the first time and head home a cross from the right to make it 3-3. Thankfully, when we were next on our travels Don Revie scored twice against relegation rivals Birmingham City. They helped us to our first win away from home that season.

My only league goal in the 1957–58 season was against Manchester City, Don's old side, in a 2-1 win. This was at Roker Park and I was a little unlucky not to get a first hat-trick as I twice hit the post with crashing shots that beat Bert Trautmann. The goal I did score wasn't too bad; I went past a couple of players and ignored cries from two teammates before driving the ball from twenty yards into the top corner. To beat a 'keeper as good as Trautmann was especially satisfying and that goal was one of the best I ever scored at any level of football.

February 8 1958 was one of the most depressing days for any footballer. It was bad enough that we were absolutely hammered at Kenilworth Road, again, losing 7-1 to a Luton side we had beaten 3-0 earlier in the season. But no games should have been played in England that weekend. For two days earlier had come the news from Munich that the plane carrying Manchester United home from their European Cup tie against Red Star Belgrade had crashed attempting to take off after refuelling.

Twenty-one people – players, reporters and staff – were killed instantly. They included friends of mine – Eddie Colman in particular I knew well, but also Roger Byrne and David Pegg. Duncan Edwards had survived but was in intensive care. I was certain from having played with and against Duncan that he would survive. He was a colossus. I felt that if any man could pull through it would be him. Tragically he was to die fifteen days after the crash; the world lost a great footballer and a decent man.

While I am not blaming our defeat at Luton on the disaster I know I was not in a fit state to play a game that weekend.

When we crashed at home 4-1 to Blackpool it meant we had conceded seventy-five goals in thirty league games. If you added the previous season's total it meant 170 goals in seventy-two matches. No team could hope to stay up with such a record.

With my partner, Sue and our dog, Oscar.

East Durham Schools. (Players back row – left to right) Hinds (Shotton), Hawkes (Shotton), Alderson (Shotton), Holmes (Horden RC), Baker (Horden M), Me. (front row) Smith (Horden RC), Forrest (Horden M), Shutt (Wheatley Hill), Willis (Easington), Wetherall (Blackhall). My teacher, Joe Herron, is third from the right on the back row.

England Schools v Scotland at St James' Park. (Players [in white] back row – left to right) Whitefoot (Stockport), Me, Matthews (Aldershot), Bassham (Ealing). (front row) Birkett (Newton le Willows), Vickers (Rotherham), Ames (Wareham), Jackson (East Northumberland), Viollet (Manchester), Chamberlain (Islington), Young (Derby).

Aged 20 and a first team regular at Roker Park.

Wearing the type of kit that was supposed to stand out under the new-fangled floodlights. This was probably taken before the match with Moscow Dynamo in November 1955. It was obviously a cold night because I'm wearing a T-shirt.

Relaxing before playing Portsmouth. Standing – Ted McNeil, Billy Elliott and Arthur Hudgell. Sitting – Ray Daniel, Dicky Davis, Tommy Wright, Billy Bingham, George Aitken and me.

My one and only outing at left back. I was given the runaround by Stanley Matthews.

Against Spurs in 1960 FA Cup quarter-final at Roker Park. I'm making sure goalkeeper Peter Wakeham has protection.

Not the best weather but still a great day to marry Marjorie.

Marjorie and three-year-old Sherley.

Winning promotion with Newcastle and sharing champagne with Dave Hilley. Jim Iley is behind us.

Less muted celebrations in the dressing room. (left to right) Jim Iley, Bob Cummings, Gordon Marhsall, Tommy Knox, Frank Clark, David Craig, Bryan Robson, Dave Hilley, Me, John McGrath, Willie Penman, Bill Thompson, Joe Harvey, Jeff Allen.

Shaking hands with Sunderland captain Charlie Hurley before my Roker Park testimonial.

Scoring for Newcastle against Bury.

With the Second Division trophy. Presented to me on Newcastle station!

The Andersons. Jim, Dad Tom, me, Mam, Frank and Bob.

Manager of Middlesbrough.

Joining Doncaster as manager. Ben Raynor, the chairman, watches carefully.

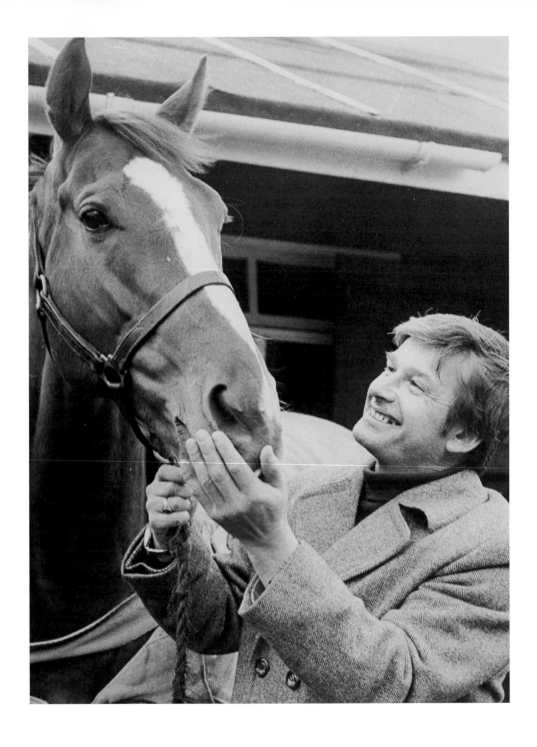

Me and Badsworth Boy, one of the greatest ever steeplechasers.

Signing Brian Kidd when I was manager at Bolton. I didn't have a lot to smile about there.

Playing golf. I preferred it to cricket.

We needed to sign at least a couple of players with First Division experience to try to steady the side but Alan Brown clearly didn't feel the same. Teenagers Graham Reed, Harry Godbold and Alan Spence were given tough, and I thought premature, introductions to first-team football.

Some of the experienced players we did have were unable to play their natural game for fear of upsetting the manager. For instance, Colin Grainger had played for England; he could beat players and cross the ball. But Alan Brown made clear that he wanted Colin to track back all the time. Colin hated him for it.

We were tumbling towards the Second Division and preying at the back of everyone's mind was the club's proud boast of never having been relegated since entering the Football League in 1890. No other club could lay claim to such a feat and the players were reminded of it constantly by supporters. Only natural really, as the fans were desperate for Sunderland to stay up.

We beat Tottenham at White Hart Lane when Don Revie scored the only goal of a match in which George Aitken, standing in for Charlie, was outstanding in blocking their battering-ram centre-forward Bobby Smith. Alan Brown had bought a similarly built player in Don Kichenbrand from Glasgow Rangers to play up front for us and he and Don Revie scored the following weekend when we recorded our first back-to-back victories that season, beating West Brom 2-0 at Roker Park before a crowd of more than 38,000.

Earlier in the season Alan Brown had signed Ambrose Fogarty from Irish side Glentoran. Ambrose and Don were tireless workers but with due respect to both we needed a bit more than that. After first playing Ambrose mostly at inside left, Alan Brown moved him to the right wing for the last eleven matches of the season. This meant he left out Billy Bingham. I loved playing with Billy; he had exceptional control, and you knew when you gave it to him he would not lose it lightly. He was also quick and could cross with deadly accuracy.

I was very disappointed when he was allowed to leave for Luton in July 1958, especially after he had played really well in Northern Ireland's five matches at the summer's World Cup finals in Sweden.

After more than 200 Sunderland appearances and forty-seven goals Billy was allowed to leave, as was Joe McDonald at the same time. He signed for Nottingham Forest for £5,000. Joe played his last Sunderland game on the day we got walloped 7-1 at Luton Town with the manager preferring Billy Elliott for the last thirteen matches of the season.

Both Billy Bingham and Joe McDonald prospered after leaving Roker Park. They ended up facing each other in the 1959 FA Cup final, which Forest won. Bill was still going strong in the top flight four seasons later, playing a big part as Everton won the First Division title in 1962–63. So he was certainly good enough to have continued playing for Sunderland. I am still good friends with Bill and I know he would have been happy to have stayed at Roker Park.

Only Charlie Hurley won more caps while playing for Sunderland than Billy, thirty-eight for the Republic of Ireland compared with thirty-three for Northern Ireland. Billy, though, won more overall with fifty-six to Charlie's forty.

Billy started as a coach with Southport in April 1965 and quickly assumed the position of manager. After spells in charge of the national team and Linfield he became one of the first British managers to work in Greece when he took over the national team. When I was offered a post at AEK Athens I rang Billy to gather some idea of the task I faced. After managing Everton, Billy took over again as manager of Northern Ireland between 1980 and 1993. In 1982 and 1986 he somehow got them to the World Cup finals. In 1982 Northern Ireland shocked the world by beating the hosts Spain 1-0.

Bill was so softly spoken I hadn't thought of him as manager material. Yet he shared my passion for the game, always looked disappointed when we lost and was more than happy to discuss the strengths and weaknesses of opposing players and teams. He was also a proud Ulsterman, and having played so well for his country at the 1958 World Cup finals, his experience must have been invaluable in 1982 and 1986.

Don Kichenbrand, nicknamed Rhino for obvious reasons, was never my cup of tea as a player. He scored a few goals but there was no chance that he would bring other people into the game by holding up the ball till midfield players could get forward in support. Don would either score or, much more often, lose the ball. As it was hard work getting it back I could never feel kindly disposed to someone like Don who gave it away so easily. I hate seeing players give the ball away cheaply.

The crucial game in 1958 was our defeat at home to Birmingham City on Easter Saturday. We were four goals down in less than twenty minutes and by losing 6-1 equalled the club's record home defeat against Newcastle at Christmas 1955.

To have any hope of avoiding relegation we really needed to beat Manchester United at Roker Park. Their makeshift team had thrilled the country by winning its way through to the FA Cup final to face Bolton Wanderers, but they hadn't won a league game since the Munich disaster. So when we took the lead through Ambrose Fogarty I thought we were certain to record a morale-boosting victory; United's players were strolling.

Sometimes, though, the slightest thing can change the course of a game and this happened that day. Billy Elliott kicked one of their players – I can't remember who – but that annoyed little Ernie Taylor. Ernie was a wonderful player who had won an FA Cup winner's medal with

Newcastle as well as Blackpool. He could beat opponents, see little openings and make space for himself. Ernie was also a Sunderland lad, so I guess given the chance he wouldn't have minded seeing us stay up. But he wasn't having any of Billy's nonsense and he inspired Manchester United, playing a part in both of their goals, and we finished a sorry lot, losing 2-1. Like Billy, Ernie had served in the Navy during the war, only he was in the Submarine Service. He certainly sank us that day.

Ironically, Alan Brown had tried to buy Ernie Taylor but withdrew after Manchester United, desperately seeking new players following the Munich disaster, also made a bid for him. He did join us in December 1958 but that was too late. If we'd been able to get someone like him the previous season I felt we might just have stayed up.

We did beat Nottingham Forest in our penultimate match, which meant that if we won our last game at Portsmouth and Leicester City failed to beat Birmingham City we would stay up. But I was never confident that Birmingham would beat Leicester. And although we beat Portsmouth 2-0 we got back to the dressing room to find out we had been relegated. In those days it took some time to find out the other results and eventually we heard that Leicester had won 1-0.

So we went down with Sheffield Wednesday. I might have been anticipating relegation but when it happened I was devastated. I was a Sunderland supporter as well as a Sunderland player. They were my team. We'd never been relegated; we'd won the First Division six times; only Arsenal had won it more. And there was I, a part of the first ever Roker Park team to go down. It was bloody terrible. To make matters worse we made an overnight stop in London on the way down to Plymouth for a testimonial match and we bumped into the celebrating West Ham United side returning from Middlesbrough after winning 3-1 to gain promotion as our replacements in League One.

I do think that following the events of the previous season Sunderland would have struggled whoever the manager was. The club was in turmoil, but Alan Brown was wrong to introduce youngsters during such a difficult time. He would have been better buying a couple of experienced players, or keeping those already on the books in the team. That might have kept us up.

It wasn't until the fixtures for the new season were announced that it really hit home that Sunderland would no longer be playing in the First Division.

The first game we played in Division Two was at Sincil Bank, home of Lincoln City. It was packed; Lincoln's fans couldn't believe they were playing the 'famous Sunderland'. Don Revie had been left out after asking for a transfer and with Charlie Hurley injured I was asked to be captain. This was a great honour and maintained my record of having been skipper of every club team I played for. That was about as good as it got, however, as we were well beaten 3-1. We had the double done over us by Fulham, losing 2-1 at Roker Park and 6-2 at Fulham, where we actually led at half-time before Johnny Haynes inspired the Cottagers with a hat-trick.

Haynes was a good player but he would come back to collect the ball. I thought he dropped too deep at times and when I had played for England B against Scotland at Birmingham in 1957 I ended up having an argument with Bill Nicholson, the assistant manager. Haynes kept drifting deeper to take the ball from me. I said he should get forward and I would supply him with it; certainly I had the ability to do so. I have occasionally heard people suggest Haynes was as good as Sir Bobby Charlton but I just laugh. I would take Bobby 100 times out of 100 in a choice between the two.

When Charlie returned I expected to be replaced as captain but he offered me the chance to continue and

I was more than happy to accept. It was a job I was to perform for the next five years.

At Swansea we lost 5-0, with Ivor Allchurch grabbing four, but if that was bad our trip to Hillsborough was even worse and we lost 6-0. Two games, eleven goals against and none scored. Three days later we ran out before a crowd of just 27,000 at home to Ipswich Town. The manager had made up his mind to give youth its chance. Out went Jack Hedley and Billy Elliott at full back to be replaced by Cecil Irwin and Len Ashurst, while Jimmy McNab came in at left half. The Wednesday game also marked the end of Bill Fraser's time in goal at Sunderland. After Peter Wakeham was signed from Torquay United Bill was sold to Nottingham Forest. With the kids in we didn't play too badly, but we were still defeated 2-0.

One of the goals was as a result of a mistake by Alan O'Neill and this led to him getting abuse from the crowd. It meant he was dropped for the game with Derby County. I was moved, once again, to inside right, with Jimmy McNab switching to right half. The crowd was even smaller at just over 23,000. They saw me score twice as we won 3-0. Two weeks later, however, we suffered a humiliating 3-0 defeat against Charlton Athletic before losing 4-1 at Bristol City, where England international John Atyeo scored. I played with John in the England Under-23 side. He was a very strong and powerful centre-forward with the fantastic scoring record of 314 goals in 598 matches.

Cecil Irwin's shaky start, meanwhile, saw him replaced by Colin Nelson at right back and Colin and Len Ashurst retained their places as full backs throughout the rest of the season.

Don Revie had never been happy playing under Alan Brown's direction and when Sunderland agreed to accept Leeds United's £14,000 offer he was only too glad to move south and start what proved to be a fifteen-year association in which he managed the Yorkshire club to success at home and abroad.

In truth, his time at Roker Park was not a success. The deep-lying centre-forward plan never worked at Sunderland. At Manchester City Don had been the star of the show; the side was built around him and he was its focal point. Although Sunderland were struggling when he arrived in 1956 we had a good number of expensively purchased 'star' players who were not prepared to have him as the centre of things.

I thought highly of his ability. I felt the loss of another experienced, skilful player was bound to leave the side struggling. Ironically, Don's move benefited me as I was given the chance to drop back to play at right half for the rest of the season. I'd been filling in at inside right but Brown decided I was needed at right half and he brought in Ernie Taylor to play at number 8.

Our trips around the smaller grounds took us to the Old Showground, Scunthorpe on Boxing Day 1958. We lost 3-2, with the game throwing up the odd statistic that Colin Nelson's goal was the first by a Sunderland right back since Jackie Stelling had scored against Burnley in October 1950, nine years earlier. These days full backs are expected to be able to support the front men and where possible overlap. That wasn't the case in the 1950s. Their job was to stop the opposing winger. This restricted their opportunities to get up the field and they rarely scored a goal. Len Ashurst, who went on to make more than 400 appearances for Sunderland, scored only three times. He did score at Scunthorpe that day as well – sadly it gave Scunthorpe the lead. Sorry about that, Len.

Len was one of football's strong players and I doubt many wingers enjoyed facing him. His tackling wouldn't be allowed today, but I've no doubt he would have adapted his game to enjoy a professional career in any era. He was solid and reliable. I wasn't surprised that he did well when he entered management as he was always his own man, unafraid to take decisions. Len's book *Left Back in Time*, published in 2009, sold well and was a credit to him, especially considering he wrote it without much professional help. I have to say, however, that I have no knowledge of the events he refers to at Swansea in 1962 and at home to Norwich in 1963 when players from these clubs were apparently willing to be paid to throw matches.

Three victories pulled us away from the ignominy of suffering relegation in successive years but it was hardly surprising to see little more than 12,000 at the final home game against Brighton. Don Kichenbrand scored three times to end up as our top scorer with twenty-one league goals. We finished with a record of sixteen wins, eight draws and eighteen defeats, which meant fifteenth with forty points. Sheffield Wednesday recovered much more quickly than us and went up as champions. Joining them were Haynes's Fulham.

There wasn't much to laugh about between August 1957 and May 1959 but a couple of incidents do stand out – the first was when Cecil Irwin made his debut. I got the ball, turned and played it back to him. I wanted him to get a first touch to boost his confidence.

As I played it I turned to move forward and all I heard was whack and the ball smashed into the back of my head. Balls then were pretty hard and after getting up I gave him a right mouthful. A few weeks later when Colin Nelson made his debut at Bristol City I thought I'd give him an early touch. I pushed the ball back and moved forward. Whack and the ball smashed into the back of my head again and over I rolled. I didn't know whether to laugh or cry.

Of course, in time Colin and Cec, in particular, did pretty well for Sunderland. Colin Nelson was a steady player who could move across the pitch pretty quickly to cover the opposing attacking players and he was a more than able tackler. He played a smashing game in the sixth round of the FA Cup against Spurs in 1961 to keep Terry Dyson at left wing quiet for much of the time.

Colin was the regular right back for three seasons from 1958 before Cec took over and more or less made the position his own for a long time. Cec is a lovely man who was a very good player with a whole-hearted attitude. During my time playing in front of him he rarely got a chasing – he also became, after that first kick, someone I could rely on to get the ball over me and away!

Chapter 9

On the up

I hadn't been long as assistant manager at Bolton Wanderers in the late '70s when Willie Morgan, their Scottish international winger, wondered if I fancied a game of golf at Lytham St Annes, the British Open course near Blackpool.

Willie had played in the World Cup finals in West Germany in 1974 when he was at Manchester United. Bolton had signed him in 1976 after he had returned to Burnley, and as a fast-raiding winger with a trick or two he was always popular with the Burnden Park fans.

This particular day he was looking for a partner in a foursomes. Our opponents, he informed me, included his manager at Old Trafford, Sir Matt Busby. I was naturally thrilled. Although we'd spoken, and Matt had been gracious in praising my Middlesbrough side in the early '70s when we played Manchester United in the FA Cup, this would be a good chance to get to know him better.

A game of golf with Matt Busby – brilliant! It was a competitive event; you'd expect it to be if Sir Matt Busby was involved, of course. Word had got round he was playing because when we arrived the whole of the club committee had their jackets on and were shaking his hand and saying 'Lovely to see you.'

I found Matt to be softly spoken but he obviously knew his football. I was aware that all the Manchester United players loved him to bits but he also had a reputation of being a bit tight with the wages – there is a story about Denis Law finding out, not long after the maximum wage was lifted, that Matt and Bill Shankly, his counterpart at Liverpool, had agreed between them not to pay players more than a certain sum. Players such as Law, Charlton and Best were, however, prepared to forego a little bit of extra cash in order to win things.

This culminated, of course, in the famous 1968 European Cup final victory after extra time against Benfica, reward for being forced, with Jimmy Murphy's help, to refashion the team after the Munich air disaster. At Munich Busby suffered multiple injuries and wasn't expected to survive. Indeed, he twice received the last rites but was back at his desk for the start of the following season. Busby was a hard man, but he was the sort anybody would want to play for, including me.

We sat having a cup of tea after the round and he said, 'I remember making an enquiry about signing you. They wouldn't let you go. I signed Maurice Setters from West Bromwich Albion instead.'

I was staggered. I could not remember when Matt Busby had signed Maurice Setters but that didn't matter. I replied, 'I would have walked down to Old Trafford from the north-east to have played for you,' while continuing to shake my head in astonishment and frustration.

'They wouldn't entertain me even making a bid, so I let it be. They didn't tell you, then?' asked Sir Matt.

I think my silence told him they hadn't. Nobody at Sunderland ever mentioned that Manchester United were interested in what must have been late 1959 or early 1960. Setters for £30,000 in January 1960.

Setters had been part of the England 1958 World Cup squad and was to help United win the 1963 FA Cup before leaving for Stoke City the following season. I played against him a few times, and he'd scored at The Hawthorns when Sunderland lost 3-0 during our relegation season. He was a good player and I ended up replacing him as manager at Doncaster Rovers in the mid 1970s.

I was sickened by Matt's news. When I checked the chronology I was even more upset. In general I am not the sort of person who gets angry easily, but in 1959 playing at Sunderland was not a pleasure. Indeed at Christmas that year there was even a chance the club would slide into Division Three just two seasons after being relegated from Division One. To have swapped that for a place at Old Trafford would have been an easy choice – especially as I had had even found myself being asked to play centre-half on a couple of occasions!

We began the 1959–60 season in reasonable form. Ian Lawther, signed from Belfast Crusaders, had replaced Kichenbrand up front and went on to do well. At one time Ian had been on Manchester United's books but homesickness took him back over the Irish Sea to Belfast – we might have been Old Trafford teammates, therefore. Thankfully, he returned to English football with Sunderland and made his debut against Aston Villa. He didn't score but did in his second match and by the time he left Sunderland for Blackburn in the summer of 1961 he had scored forty-four times in just eighty-three matches, an impressive strike rate at any level. Unlike Don, Ian, despite not being a big lad, could hold up the ball and pass it accurately.

We hammered Sheffield United 5-1 in mid-September, with Ian scoring once, and there were signs of a revival in the club's fortunes. Charlie Hurley, however, got injured in that game and was missing when we played Ipswich Town at Portman Road. We were routed 6-1.

Alf Ramsey, who'd played with distinction in the Spurs 'push and run' Championship-winning team of 1950–51, was starting to build a team that would surprise the football world before he moved on to manage England. One of Charlie's international colleagues, Dermot Curtis, scored a hat-trick, as did Ted Phillips. Dermot was to find his chances limited over the next few seasons by Phillips' partnership with Ray Crawford, topped off when Ipswich won the First Division title at the end of 1961–62, their first season in the top flight. Crawford ended up as joint top scorer in the League with Derek Kevan of West Brom, both with thirty-three. Phillips and Crawford were good players, but it was Ramsey's genius which really made them. He got the midfield players to exploit the space between the full backs and centre-half at a time when teams mostly played with a back three. Ramsey's tactics were helped by the pitch at Portman Road, which was spacious and well maintained.

His value was shown when he left to manage England as Ipswich went back down to Division Two within two years.

A few weeks after the thrashing at Ipswich, with Charlie again missing, Alan Brown decided to give Martin Harvey, a youngster from Northern Ireland, his debut. He picked him at right half and pushed me to centre-half. I had never played at number five before and although we scrambled a 0-0 draw at Plymouth Argyle I came off the field hoping I would never do so again.

My Christmas was ruined when, to my great surprise, Alan Brown dropped Charlie Hurley, among others. It was true we were in the middle of a terrible run of five straight defeats, but shifting me to centre-half left me totally dumbfounded. Little good it did. We lost 4-2 at home to Lincoln City on Boxing Day. I spent so much time trying to keep Imps centre-forward Fred Graver quiet – he didn't score, which was pleasing – that I was unable to offer any help to my teammates. Charlie came back the following day and we fought like tigers to bring home a valuable point from the return fixture.

Our form improved in 1960, not by much but enough to keep the side away from the bottom of the league. Ian Lawther's goals were crucial and he ended up with seventeen by the season's end – a very good total for his first season. Colin Grainger, however, had struggled, and I wasn't surprised when he moved to Leeds United in the close season, leaving a manager he hated. Their left winger Jackie Overfield moved in the opposite direction a few weeks later.

Colin was more than just a footballer. He could sing like an angel. When we had him and his wife around I'd persuade him to sing and I'd try and accompany him on the piano. He sang on the same bill as the Beatles and at the London Palladium.

With the manager deciding at the start of the next season to keep a regular goalkeeper and back five – Wakeham in goal, Nelson and Ashurst at full back and me, Charlie and the increasingly important Jimmy McNab at half back, the team began to have a familiar feel. And the more we began to play together the better we became. We weren't making much of an impression on the top clubs, but our form was such that we had no worries about relegation.

In November 1960 we beat Leyton Orient 4-1 at Roker Park, a match I thoroughly enjoyed, not least because I scored what I reckon was my best goal for Sunderland. It was described in the *Journal* – and the cutting is one of my many treasured football possessions – as: 'Credit Stan Anderson for giving the Roker players their bonus. He was the star of these "Phantom Frolics". For sixty-six minutes it looked as if Sunderland had lost their way to goal in the fog. Then Stan called for the ball from a hesitant Lawther. He ambled wingwards then suddenly cut back in and from thirty yards out unleashed a rocket shot that flashed into the net. It was a goal worth all the bonuses put together. For it sparked off the Roker goal machine.'

Goals, of course, win matches and finding new ways to get them was always on my mind, especially as during my career I was always regarded as the more attacking of the two wing-halves that featured in teams at that time.

Stuck between the two wing-halves was the centre-half. Before they changed the offside rule in 1925, when it required three rather than two players to be beyond an attacker, the centre-half had been the attacking fulcrum and the man who made teams tick. However, that changed and by 1960 centre-halves rarely advanced beyond the halfway line. They were expected to concentrate on blotting out their direct opponent – the centre-forward. Once they got the ball they were expected to get rid of it – end of story. This emphasis on negativity was why I hated being asked to play there.

Charlie Hurley was different from other centre-halves. True, he was a good defender but he was also very good, especially for such a big man, with the ball at his feet. My feeling was that if he'd played up the field Charlie would have been fine. He certainly wouldn't have given the ball away as easily as some Sunderland centre-forwards I had previously had the 'pleasure' of playing with.

Charlie was almost unbeatable in the air and I thought we should use his undoubted talents at free kicks and corners. I didn't bother asking Alan Brown, as I considered he'd not be too happy, especially if he felt the idea had originated from me. So I simply suggested to Charlie that he go forward.

We did it first against Ipswich Town in December and Charlie should have scored with a header but the linesman missed Roy Bailey, father of Gary, Manchester United's goalkeeper in the 1980s, scooping the ball out after it had crossed the line.

Charlie did get his name on the scoresheet in the Boxing Day match with Sheffield United, blocking an attempted clearance in the six-yard box. He followed this with another in a 7-1 rout of Luton Town on New Year's Eve when he headed home my indirect free kick. It was this performance that earned him the title of 'King Charlie', courtesy of Vince Wilson in the Sunday Mirror.

Charlie went on to score more than twenty more goals for Sunderland. He was helped over the next few seasons by some tremendous crossers of the ball in Harry Hooper, Jackie Overfield, John Dillon and George Mulhall. The crowd would go wild when he went forward. They'd chant 'Charlie, Charlie, Charlie' and if it looked as if he was hanging back they'd urge him forward. He'd be knackered some matches if we had a lot of corners. Alan Brown never mentioned the fact that Charlie was going forward, but after seeing it work he wasn't daft enough to stop it.

Charlie had almost quit the club during the previous summer after an incident at the end of the season when the club went on a short tour of Switzerland. We played Winterthur and when we lost after missing two penalties Alan Brown was furious. The following morning he walked us down to the big lake and had us rowing up and down in two big boats. Everyone thought this was ridiculous, and this soon turned to anger when he then told us we all had to be back in the hotel at 10.30pm.

Many players were already upset by accommodation that wasn't exactly salubrious and there was a lot of grumbling as we set off for a pint or two. As we started drinking, like a lot of young lads, we started to talk more bravely than we were really feeling. At first we weren't going back; then as it got closer to 10.30pm the daring started to dissipate.

Charlie was more sensible than most and felt we should go back, and the vast majority of the squad went with him. Ernie Taylor and I didn't join them, but not long afterwards Ernie thought better of it and decided to head to the hotel. I felt that I might as well be 'hung for a sheep as a lamb' and anyway I was having a good night talking to one or two English people. It was probably about 1.00am when I crept round the back of the hotel and managed to make it into the lift and up into my room, where Reg Pearce was fast asleep.

Next morning I was down for breakfast very early and sitting there when Alan Brown walked in. 'Oh no,' I thought, but he was full of life, asking how was I and had I slept well. He was being very friendly, I thought, and I couldn't work out what was happening. When the players started coming in and sitting at the other end of the room I started to get more than concerned.

Afterwards I found out that there had been a big row. Some players had gone back to Charlie's room and were complaining about the accommodation and what had happened earlier in the day, and specifically about Alan Brown. What they'd failed to realise was that the walls were paper thin; Brownie had heard everything. Next thing he'd crashed through the door, picked up Ernie Taylor and literally hauled him one-handed out of the room and back into the bedroom he was sharing with Len Ashurst, chucking him on the bed. Now Len's nickname was 'Lennie the Lion', but he swears he was asleep through all this. Alan Brown then marched back to Charlie's room and shouted at him: '… and you, you're nothing but a playboy' – a charge so utterly ridiculous it was laughable. A family man who hardly drank or smoked, never in a million years was Charlie ever a playboy. Charlie was furious and told me he was leaving the club. He was already set to leave the tour as Ireland were playing West Germany. I gather he had a great game in a famous 1-0 victory.

When I saw him go I wasn't too certain I'd see him playing for Sunderland again – thankfully, I understand Alan Brown apologised and smoothed things over and he was back for pre-season training. Alan loved Charlie, not surprisingly as he was his best player and signing.

Charlie played a key part in one of my favourite matches, one that a lot of fans from my generation raise when I meet them. It was the third-round FA Cup tie with Arsenal at Roker Park. Charlie didn't score. But he was instrumental in ensuring I did: the Arsenal defence were so distracted by his presence in their box during the second half that they left me with a simple header from a corner kick. I nodded it past Jack Kelsey, to make it 1-1.

We'd gone twelve games unbeaten in the league and the goal further boosted our confidence, so it was no surprise when we took the lead. I made a twenty-five-yard run into space and Harry Hooper found me with a superb defence-splitting pass. Kelsey, who played forty-one times for Wales, including at the 1958 World Cup finals, rushed out to narrow the angle and attempted to spring down at my feet to snatch the ball. I decided not to try and beat him at the near post and although for half a second I felt my shot was going wide of the far side of the goal it crept just inside the post to bring the loudest cheer heard at Roker Park for many a year.

When the final whistle sounded the 59,000 crowd was ecstatic. So, too, were the players. While we knew it was only one match, the fact we'd deservedly beaten a First Division side showed us we could compete with the best. The feeling was that Sunderland were at last on the road back.

We extended our unbeaten league run to fourteen by beating Lincoln, where I scored again, and Portsmouth to set us up for a fourth-round FA Cup tie at Liverpool. Bill Shankly hadn't been there too long and the Merseysiders were in the Second Division, but we knew it was certain to be a difficult game.

A large and noisy following backed us and they would have left very pleased after we won 2-0. Harry Hooper, a scorer along with Ian Lawther, was outstanding. It was a hard match and the applause we got from the Kop at the end was both pleasing and merited.

Our reward for beating Liverpool was a tricky tie at Norwich City. They were in the same division as us but had thrilled the football world in 1959 when as a Third Division team they had reached the semi-final, ultimately falling to Billy Bingham's Luton Town in a replay.

On the up

Even though we were in fine form we knew we were in for an exacting time. That's the way it turned out, although it was also one of the most satisfying games I ever played in. Charlie Hurley was magnificent. I still rate it as his finest game during my time at Sunderland. And Jimmy McNab at left half was as solid as a rock.

Although it was not the sort of football I usually enjoyed, I was being made to play more defensively. We were not making much progress up front and our backs were against the wall for most of the match as we were forced on to the back foot. We were helped by a massive following that turned Carrow Road almost into Roker Park. Norwich were relentless in pushing forward and it looked only a question of time before they scored. But credit to our backs, who stuck to their task.

I'd have been delighted with a draw, but with about ten minutes to go we managed to break forward and force a corner on the right. As he'd had such a hard, exhausting game I was surprised when I saw Charlie Hurley coming forward. True, the supporters loved seeing him do that but in the circumstances I wondered what might happen if the ball was cleared – how would he get back in time? I needn't have worried as what happened next still gives me a special thrill.

As I ran towards the near post Harry Hooper floated over the corner and with absolutely no chance of getting it I turned to see Charlie roar in and power the sort of header I had never seen before, or since. The ball flashed past the 'keeper and stuck in the stanchion. It is a shame that TV in those days wasn't as good as it is now because if the experts had looked at it from every angle then all fans, not just those at Carrow Road, would have been talking about that goal for a very long time. The players mobbed Charlie; there must have been about half a dozen on his back. The Sunderland fans were going crazy and one or two ran on to the pitch in celebration.

After we scored we came under even more pressure. Norwich couldn't believe they were losing. Somehow we managed to hold on for a great victory and it still remains the match I remember with most pride. Not because of how I played but because of what the rest of the players did, particularly Charlie Hurley, who more than anyone was responsible for the win.

His defensive play was without blemish and yet he still had enough in him to score the vital winning goal. I was really proud to have captained the side and as we came off Norwich's Bill Punton said, 'How the hell have we lost that game?'

When the draw for the quarter-finals was made we found ourselves pitted against Tottenham Hotspur, who were being openly touted as a team who would become the first double winners since Aston Villa in 1896–97.

Few people outside the club and its supporters gave us any chance of beating Bill Nicholson's side. But I felt that we might have a shout; we were in good form, having lost only one of twenty-one league and cup games, and our confidence was high. The noise of the Roker Park crowd that day was also extra special. Danny Blanchflower, the Spurs captain, said it was the loudest he'd ever played before. I'm not sure about that. As I've said, Hampden Park for Scotland and England in 1962 was more deafening, but it was still a great thrill to be involved against Spurs in 1961, I can assure you.

At half-time we were a goal down. We'd started nervously, and went behind on only nine minutes when Cliff Jones scored. We battled hard but might have gone in further behind; Bobby Smith rounded Peter Wakeham but with Charlie getting back to put the Tottenham man under pressure the ball hit the post. At half-time the feeling in the dressing room was that we could play a lot better and that at only 1-0 down we weren't out of the match by any means.

On the up

Harry Hooper hit a shot wide as we pressed and Spurs seemed unsure whether to hold on to what they had or try to kill the tie with a second. One or two of their passes were going astray and the crowd, particularly the Roker End towards which we were now kicking, were providing magnificent backing. We got a corner on the right and when Harry Hooper floated it over Charlie rose magnificently to power a header that Bill Brown stopped only because it was straight at him. He couldn't hold it, though, and Willie McPheat followed up to push the loose ball into the net.

Some of the crowd invaded the pitch; nothing malicious and many of them were youngsters. But it meant it took the referee some time to get the game restarted and I read later that Blanchflower said this helped them to regroup and that they were able to play out the rest of the match fairly comfortably. I have to say that this is nonsense; the faces of the Spurs players showed how shocked they were. Danny's face was almost white; the goal and the roar of the spectators had knocked them for six. They kicked the ball anywhere. Dave Mackay tried to rough up Charlie, and might have paid the consequences had I not persuaded the big Irishman to concentrate on the game rather than revenge. We forced three corners and there was pandemonium in the Spurs defence; Bill Nicholson was out of his dugout urging his players to keep tight to Charlie.

With ten minutes left we should have taken the lead, and had we done so we would have won. John Dillon was put clean through but he couldn't make up his mind which foot to use to knock the ball past Brown. Sadly he ended up doing neither and the Spurs 'keeper dropped on it gratefully. Poor John; even now when the players get together he takes some stick about this and shakes his head with disappointment. The match thus ended in a draw at 1-1.

In the replay, with Jimmy McNab injured, the manager replaced him with Martin Harvey, switching me to left half. I thought it strange. It meant two changes rather than one because Martin was left-footed and I was right. There were 65,000 at the match. Tottenham's record gate is 75,038 for the 1938 sixth-round tie, also against Sunderland, and if the ground had been large enough that would have been broken in 1961. An estimated 30,000 were locked out.

I felt that we had missed our chance at Roker Park as a team as good as Spurs were unlikely to give us a second chance. So it proved. We were heavily beaten, 5-0, with two goals from Les Dyson and others from Dave Mackay, Bobby Smith and Les Allen.

Nevertheless I have often wondered what might have happened that night had Ian Lawther managed to take one of his two very good scoring opportunities in the first ten minutes – especially as they were the sorts of chances Ian normally gobbled up.

Spurs went on to do the double. They finished eight points clear of Sheffield Wednesday at the top of the First Division and they won at the first attempt in every other round of the FA Cup. The final was no classic. Leicester City had full back Len Chalmers injured in the first half and Spurs were never fluent. But they won 2-0 – and to think we nearly denied them the double.

Spurs had some exceptionally talented players such as Dave Mackay and John White in midfield, barnstorming centre-forward Bobby Smith and the wingers Cliff Jones and Terry Dyson. To cap it off they had Danny Blanchflower. True, he was close to the end of his career but he still had a real touch of class. They were ten per cent above any other team in the country and deserved to win the two trophies. I would compare them with the Manchester United side of recent years and the great Arsenal sides of the past.

Sadly we can only speculate whether they would have been better than Manchester United had the tragedy at Munich not occurred. But we can be sure that, had that United team matured together, their 1961 games with Spurs really would have been special. Mackay against Duncan Edwards in midfield would have been worth watching, that's for sure.

Of course we were disappointed at being beaten at White Hart Lane, but we reckoned we had shown we were good enough to play in the First Division. It was now our job to prove it by getting there. Our fine run had pushed us up the table and after we beat Brighton at home we were just five points behind second-placed Sheffield United. And we had a game in hand. It was a long shot, but with nine matches left the opportunity was there. Sadly, in our next game at Eastville, Charlie Hurley was injured very early and although he stayed on it might have been better for him to have gone off. He aggravated his injury and consequently missed most of the rest of the season. Bristol Rovers' 1-0 victory made it a long journey home, especially when we heard that Sheffield United had won.

With Charlie missing for the home game with Norwich, Alan Brown chose not to call in our reserve centre-half Dickie Rooks, deciding instead that I should deputise at centre-half with Martin Harvey taking over at right half. The match was a nightmare, and although I was at least able to help out my colleagues with some passes we got walloped 3-0. Terry Alcock, the man I was marking, hit the second. For the return at Carrow Road three days later I was back at number four and Rooks came in for his debut. We still lost 3-0.

We finished sixth, good enough these days to qualify for a play-off spot and a shot at the Premier League. But in those days only the top two went up and we were far behind surprise champions Ipswich and Sheffield United.

Still, we had played well in the second half of the season and after going on tour with England I was looking forward to boosting my pay as the maximum wage rules, imposed before the First World War, and under which payment was restricted to £20 a week, had been abandoned. Now we had to negotiate our own contracts with the club. Everyone who liked football in those days knows that Johnny Haynes was to become the first £100-a-week player; the rest of us had to get what we could. So Charlie Hurley, George Mulhall, Johnny Crossan and I got together and agreed none of us would sign a deal before we'd all been to see the manager.

After the tour and a holiday in Scotland I returned to Roker Park to find that this agreement was no more. The others had met Alan Brown and agreed new deals. None of them was willing to tell me how much they had negotiated.

Brown offered £32 a week, which he assured me was what the other 'top players' were getting. I wasn't sure he was telling the truth and resisted signing. I didn't want a transfer, but that's how it was spun, especially in the press, when it became known I was the only player who hadn't signed a new, improved contract. It led some fans to question my commitment to the club.

I was later offered a further £6 a week, but only for being captain. That happened because chairman Syd Collings said I should be earning more. Of course £20 to £38 a week was a big leap. But many years later I found out that others had been given more than me. Len Ashurst was on £40 a week and Charlie double that amount. In that respect I was clearly underpaid and Collings, of course, knew it. George Mulhall told me many years later that I was a 'mug' for signing. And I was – but Alan Brown was adamant that I wouldn't get any more.

With this newfound wealth some players bought their rented houses from the club. I decided against this, regretting it later when I moved to Newcastle. It had been agreed, by two directors – Laurie Evans, the man who owned the firm I'd worked for on leaving school, and Syd Collings – that as part of the transfer dealings I could stay living there as long as I wanted. But at the start of the 1965–66 season I received a letter asking me to vacate the house. Thinking there had been a mistake, I went to Roker Park and spoke to Laurie and Syd to remind them of their commitment, which had been made in front of Alan Brown.

They denied making such a promise, saying they couldn't remember speaking to me about it. I left the ground fuming, but realised I was in a difficult position, not least because Alan Brown had since moved to Sheffield Wednesday and our relationship could never have been described as good. I had no reason to believe he would verify my side of the story.

Which just shows how wrong you can be sometimes! At the beginning of the 1965–66 season, following promotion, Newcastle played at Hillsborough. I had told Joe Harvey, the manager, about the letter I had received and he said he would sort it out by speaking to Alan Brown. I wasn't too confident Brown would offer his support but I was wrong. After the game I went to Alan Brown's office and he threw his arms around me like I was a long-lost friend. He said he would be prepared to go on record that he was present when the two Sunderland directors had made their promise and even go to Roker Park if necessary.

As he embraced me I wondered what was going on and it wasn't difficult to work out why he was so willing to help. I reckoned he was still very angry about the events which led to him quitting Sunderland. The board had been unwilling to reward him for gaining promotion in 1963–64. Most of the players had got around £1,000 each, but he received nothing, even after approaching the board. When they refused he left, but not before the players, desperate for him to stay, had a whip round, paying in £50 each. I have no idea who approached him with the money but I am glad it wasn't me. If Alan Brown had made his mind up on something nothing, not even money, would change it. He would have felt insulted.

When I let it be known that Brown was willing to testify on my behalf Sunderland dropped their demands, even though they sent new signing Neil Martin to view the house. I was very polite with Neil but made clear he wasn't moving in just yet. When I signed for Middlesbrough in November 1965, and bought a house in Billingham early the following year, I returned the keys to Roker Park.

Chapter 10

Last day double disasters

I think everyone believed that because we'd played so well in the 1961 FA Cup we would win promotion the following season. This feeling intensified when Alan Brown travelled just down the coast to sign the Middlesbrough centre-forward Brian Clough, who had scored 204 goals in 222 matches for his hometown club.

The club had also bought George Herd, a slightly built inside right from Clyde, towards the end of the previous season and together the pair had set them back close to £90,000. This was a considerable sum at the time and showed that the directors were intent on the club recovering their place in the First Division, even if they weren't too generous with my contract.

My relations with Brian didn't start well. After we lost our opening game 4-3 at Walsall he had a go at the defence. As captain it was my job to sort that out. 'Don't you start that here,' I told him. 'We play as a team.'

His approach – and you couldn't argue with him – was 'give me the ball as I'm the bloke who will score the goals to take the side to success'. He felt he was the best centre-forward in the country and when the England teams were announced and he wasn't in them he'd be very angry. He wasn't that great outside the box, he couldn't beat defenders, but inside it he had this uncanny knack of being in the right place.

The ball might ricochet off a couple of players and Brian would be there to push it into an empty net. I don't know how he did it as I certainly never had such ability around the goal, but it wasn't luck. He scored too many goals for that.

Players at Sunderland would say 'Who does he think he is? He only came from Middlesbrough,' and yet when I asked my good friend Alan Peacock he told me Brian had been exactly the same when he was at 'Boro. An example he told me was that Brian was furious after he'd scored four at Charlton in a match that 'Boro lost 6-5.

I think coming to Sunderland was a bit of a culture shock for Brian. He was very opinionated and would say what he thought. But at one training session Alan Brown was talking to us when a young lad on a bike rode along and shouted, 'Hey, Brian.'

After he'd done it two or three times it was obvious that Brian was not listening to Alan Brown. 'Get over there and tell your mate', said Brown menacingly, 'that if he doesn't go away I'll throw him, his bloody bike and you as well over that fence.'

The rest of us were laughing but Brian realised Brown was not joking. He'd never been spoken to like that before. He had a lot of time for Alan Brown after that.

We also lost twice to Liverpool in our first four games but despite the setbacks, with Cloughie in the side things were bound to get better. He scored hat-tricks against Bury in September, Plymouth Argyle in October and Swansea, when we won 7-2, in December. He didn't score, though, when his old club came north for the first Wear–Tees derby. Nevertheless we won 2-1, with 'Boro finishing with ten men after Arthur Kaye had been sent off. I'd handled his header on the line in the fifty-seventh minute and he'd cut our lead to a single goal with the penalty. Ten minutes later the referee awarded us a free kick for an innocuous challenge and Arthur moaned about the decision and was sent off.

England winger Eddie Holliday, up against Cecil Irwin and having a difficult time, was generally very quiet but was ranting in my ear about the referee so I suggested he go and have a word with him. The 'Boro man stormed over to do just that and after giving the official a tongue-lashing was booked for what I believe was the only time in his career! I hadn't honestly set out to get him booked, but I must have added to his anger by laughing loudly.

What was less funny was an incident in the Walsall game just before Christmas, which led to my own exit from the field. I think it must go down as the quickest ever injury in football. We kicked off and Jackie Overfield passed the ball from the centre circle. As I looked down to see who to move it on to the next thing I knew was that full back Bill Guttridge had clattered into me. His head shattered my cheekbone and left me sprawling on the floor. It was an accident, but after less than ten seconds I was out of the game. To my amazement Alan Brown ran on to the pitch, picked me up and carried me off in his arms.

Still in my strip, I was taken directly to hospital, where a doctor inserted his hands into my mouth and pushed the bones back into place. I was actually back home the following day.

In my absence we still managed to win 3-0, which left us level on points with second-placed Orient, but eight points behind runaway leaders Liverpool.

Despite our surge up the table I felt that we should have been doing even better. Jimmy Montgomery, a young 'keeper, had made his debut in the league cup against Walsall in October and I had also watched him in training and for the reserves. I was convinced he was ready to make the number one spot his own. I felt the current incumbent, Peter Wakeham, had made one or two mistakes that had cost us valuable points.

As the captain I would meet with the manager every Monday to discuss the weekend's performance. I often found this to be frustrating because I'd want to talk about how we could improve while Alan Brown would spend more time talking about how he wanted me to play; and this usually involved him suggesting I played a bit deeper. I put my case for Jim Montgomery to be given a chance, but if the manager was listening it certainly didn't have any effect because it wasn't until late February, at home to Derby County, that 'Monty' made his league debut.

As everyone knows, once he got into the side he was hardly ever out of it for the next fifteen years. Indeed, during my final eighteen months Jimmy played every game bar one. He was a magnificent goalkeeper; from the start he made it absolutely clear that he didn't want defenders dropping deep into the penalty area. He wanted them out beyond the eighteen-yard line and so if a ball came into the box it was his. He was also a magnificent shot stopper, and at Huddersfield in December 1962 he virtually played the home side on his own, making one save that even surpassed his efforts in denying Leeds a goal at Wembley in 1973 when Sunderland won the FA Cup. Even the Huddersfield players applauded him off at the end of a game from which we stole both points.

Cec Irwin also came back at the same time as Jimmy, who in his first twelve matches suffered only one defeat – and even then he was unlucky. It was away at Plymouth Argyle. Alan O'Neill, deputising for the injured Clough, had put us into a two-goal lead within the first quarter of an hour and I was not too concerned when George Kirby reduced the arrears soon after. We were well in control.

I was shaken, though, by Kirby after half an hour, when he barged me to the floor. We were both booked after I got back up to argue vociferously with him. But I was lucky compared with Dickie Rooks. Two minutes later Kirby committed one of the worst challenges I witnessed during my years as a professional footballer. Dickie, then only twenty-one, was playing centre-half as Charlie was injured. He went to head clear only to be flattened by

146

Kirby's outstretched elbow smashing into his cheek. Dickie, a hard lad it has to be said, was poleaxed with a broken left cheekbone and had to be carried off the field. In fact, he had to be left behind in hospital when we travelled back home later that evening.

Amazingly Kirby was not sent off. In fact I don't think the referee even spoke to him. We were outraged and as captain I had to prevent one or two, including me, from seeking revenge. It was going to be hard enough with ten men, never mind nine or even eight.

Wilf Carter equalised with twenty minutes left and it looked like we would grab a deserved point until we were left heartbroken by a second from Carter late on. The loss was to prove crucial at the season's end. There are some days in football when justice simply isn't done and Jimmy Montgomery's first defeat was one of them. I left the field really hoping someone would get Kirby – and do you know somebody did, although I have to say the way it happened wasn't exactly planned!

It occurred at Southampton in mid-September the following season. Coincidentally Dickie Rooks had again taken Charlie's place, one of only four games he played that season.

George Kirby had moved to The Dell during the summer and was again making a nuisance of himself. Cloughie scored another hat-trick and we were winning comfortably when, with around twenty minutes left, they were awarded a free kick just outside the penalty area.

We lined up our defensive wall under Monty's instructions, but Kirby started to try to break it by muscling in. His elbows were everywhere and I was looking to see if the referee was going to do anything about it. He wasn't taking a blind bit of notice, so when the ex-Plymouth striker pushed me and then flicked back his boots to put his studs into me I thought 'To hell with this' and thumped him in the lumbar region with my stronger left hand. He collapsed and certainly wasn't acting, although he did get up fairly quickly. This annoyed one of the Southampton stars, winger Terry Paine, who shouted to him to stay down, no doubt to get me into trouble.

The referee and the linesman hadn't seen anything and, doing my best to appear as inconspicuous as possible, I suffered no punishment. For the rest of the game I stayed away from Kirby. When we were going off he said he would get me in the future. It was a threat I took seriously enough to make sure that when we played Southampton at home I held on to the ball for as short a time as possible. All I could hear every time I got it was these great big lumbering strides coming towards me. It reminded me of my time in the Houghton and District League as I got rid of the ball as quickly as I could to avoid being clattered.

George and I have spoken about it since we retired. We don't especially get on, but as far as I am concerned he couldn't complain too much at what I'd done to him.

The defeat at Home Park meant we really needed to win our next away game at Ayresome Park. Brian Clough was returning to his old ground for the first time since moving to Sunderland but it was his one-time colleague up front who was the centre of attention as, after just ninety seconds, a clash with Charlie Hurley left Alan Peacock clutching his broken jaw. As Alan was set, like me, to make his debut for England against Austria only a few days later he was naturally extremely upset and angry – he still is fifty years later!

Even with ten men, Middlesbrough proved to be a difficult side to break down. It was Brian Clough, some might say inevitably, who scored the winner. Somehow he managed to wrestle himself free of Bill Gates to dive and head home my lob, leaving Bob Appleby with no chance. Brian was a good header of the ball; he was also very brave, being prepared to dive in when boots were flying.

I had to miss our next game – at Luton Town – because I was playing for England at Hampden Park and I was delighted to hear the news that we had won 2-1. It was Sunderland's fourth win in a row and it became five when we beat Newcastle 3-0 at Roker Park. George Herd scored twice and the result in a rough encounter might have been more convincing. Newcastle might have had no chance of going up, but they weren't going to make it easy for us.

Two games followed against Rotherham United and, looking back at the scores, victories by 4-0 and 3-0, they fail to give a true impression. In both matches the Millers pushed us all the way. It was Charlie Hurley's heading ability that was key. After fifty-eight minutes in the first game, when we were 1-0 up, he headed a beauty from Jack Overfield's cross. In the second, on seventy-one minutes he headed home a cross of mine to make it 2-0. Only then did ten-man Rotherham, Ray Lancaster having been forced off the pitch with a fractured cheekbone, give up the struggle. Charlie scored six goals that season, not a bad return for a centre-half.

It left us needing to win at Swansea Town in our final game. Vetch Field, of course, was the scene of my first really big game, when England Schoolboys lost to Wales in the late '40s. Would I be lucky this time? We had won our last seven games; could we make it eight?

Before the match Leyton Orient were level with us but with a slightly inferior goal difference. They, however, had a home game while we faced a tougher encounter. Swansea were threatened with relegation, being level on points with Bristol Rovers. In fact Bristol lost their final game 2-0 so Swansea needn't have battled so hard! We had a good number of our supporters in the crowd and took the lead on twenty minutes when Brian Clough scored his twenty-ninth league goal of the season. After beating two defenders, he left Johnny King in the Swansea goal with no chance. But we couldn't get the crucial second, which I am convinced would have seen us clinch promotion. So at half-time it was 1-0.

On the restart I managed to find enough space to hammer a left-foot shot that hit the Swansea 'keeper rather than him making a save. We then had a strong appeal for a penalty turned down for what I was sure was a foul on George Herd. Swansea, though, were not out of the game. They'd hit the woodwork twice in the first half and although we had pinned them back for much of the second period they forced a corner on sixty-six minutes. Up came Mel Nurse, and when he and Charlie went for the ball it dropped among a crowd of players. Brayley Reynolds hooked it back over his head and with Len Ashurst, Jimmy Montgomery and Cec Irwin trying desperately to prevent a goal the ball seemed to take an eternity as it floated past them and into the net. One-one and twenty-four minutes to get the winner and clinch promotion.

I honestly thought I'd scored it when I met Harry Hooper's cross from the right. But as the ball flashed towards the net, Johnny King in goal came from nowhere to push it round the post. Thanks, John! It was a great save. We fought right to the end. Jimmy McNab made a desperate effort to head home a loose ball and had to be carried behind the goal to receive attention. But we couldn't make the breakthrough and the match ended in a draw.

We had no way of knowing if we had gained promotion or not – it all depended on Orient's result – and with our heads bowed we all trooped from the field at the end. It was a very quiet dressing room. I don't think anyone really believed Orient hadn't won, but it was still disappointing to have it confirmed that they had beaten Bury 2-0; at the start of the season no one could have predicted Orient would do so well.

I was gutted, although this personal disappointment was tempered shortly afterwards by my selection for the

England squad for Peru and then Chile for the World Cup.

We kicked off the next season by winning four of the first six matches, losing only at Elland Road, where Willie McPheat suffered a broken leg in a challenge from Bobby Collins that still annoys some of my teammates to this day. It was an injury that ended Willie's top-flight career, although he went on to play for Hartlepools and Airdrie. I'm still not sure whether it was an accident or not.

Don Revie was fashioning a team to be reckoned with, but they had a vicious streak. This was somewhat surprising; Don had been a delicate player and I'd guess he'd never had his name taken during his career and rarely, if ever, made rash, nasty tackles.

Leeds were also the first side to really pressurise referees over decisions, with Billy Bremner and Jack Charlton, in particular, being prepared to run to the official and argue. In some games the entire Leeds team might crowd round the referee, a habit bitterly resented by other clubs' players and supporters, not to mention the press. Many reporters hated Leeds' attitude towards the game.

Leeds won more competitions with Don in charge than at any other time in their history. They also finished second a lot, though, and had one or two decisions that went controversially against them. For example, in 1971 West Brom's Tony Brown scored a goal, which ultimately cost Leeds the title, which was obviously offside. I think referees got sick of Leeds. Of course they didn't sit down and discuss it – they just got to the point where they said: 'I'm not having that.' Leeds' reputation went before them and they suffered from it.

But you have to say that Don did a magnificent job as manager after taking over at Elland Road from Jack Taylor in the summer of 1961. He turned them into a formidable outfit with players such as Billy Bremner, John Giles, Peter Lorimer, Alan Clarke and Terry Cooper.

I wasn't surprised he made a first-rate manager. From his short period at Sunderland, and having played against him, it was obvious he didn't lack confidence. He was very quiet but he would get very passionate on issues that concerned him.

As the captain he would be prepared to say what he thought to Alan Brown. But he was wasted at Sunderland because all Brown wanted was to get the ball up quickly to the centre-forward – either big Don Kichenbrand or George Whitelaw – and they didn't have the skill to keep hold of it until Don got up with them. So it would come back and Don found himself constantly running backwards and forwards. He was being cut out of the game. His ability wasn't utilised and it frustrated him, as it would any player.

I was very disappointed when he left because he was my type of player and it was another sign that the team was disintegrating.

Don, of course, became one of the national team's most controversial managers when he replaced Sir Alf Ramsey following England's failure to qualify for the 1974 World Cup finals in West Germany. I felt the FA's dismissal of Alf was a mistake; he had won the trophy in 1966 and been unlucky in 1970 when the side lost to West Germany in the quarter-finals.

Don's record as England manager never came anywhere near Sir Alf's. At the time I thought he was an odd choice. He had built a Leeds side that would run through brick walls for him, but doing that takes day-to-day involvement and working closely together. That was never going to be the case with England, where the manager has the players together only a few times a year. Don's reign in charge came to an inglorious end when he agreed a deal to coach in the Middle East after failing to get England to the World Cup finals in Argentina in 1978.

Cloughie scored his first hat-trick of the season as we beat Southampton 4-2 away in the match during which I tangled with George Kirby, and he scored another in November when we beat Grimsby Town 6-2 at home. Making his debut that day was Northern Ireland international Johnny Crossan, who joined us from Standard Liege in Belgium. He was a player who scored goals, was never intimidated even by the roughest of opponents and was clever on the ball. I felt he was going to be an important addition to the side and he quickly linked up with George Mulhall on the left, the Scotsman having travelled south from Aberdeen to sign in September 1962. That result left us in third, only a point below table-topping Chelsea. When we beat Leeds United at home on the Saturday before Christmas we moved into second.

However, disaster was just around the corner. I was unable to play in the Boxing Day fixture against Bury. The conditions were poor, with a rock hard surface and a chilling wind. Sitting in the Main Stand alongside my dad, I watched as Brian Clough ran on to a ball over the top of the Bury defence and hurtled into and over the Bury 'keeper Chris Harker. When he didn't get up immediately I feared the worst; Brian wasn't one to stay down. My dad said, 'It's a bad one, that.'

Sadly it was and Brian, despite Herculean efforts, never made a full recovery – the fact that he made any recovery at all from what was a cruciate ligament injury was a miracle in those days, and to have played three times and scored a goal in the First Division at the start of the 1964–65 season says a lot about Brian and his absolute love of the game of football and his desire to do well at it.

Bob Stokoe, then Bury player-manager, suggested to the referee that Brian wasn't badly injured. Brian never spoke to him again unless he had to.

I visited him several times but Alan Brown felt he should be allowed to rest and recuperate. I didn't get the opinion that he felt he wouldn't play again, but he knew it was bad. I had no idea if he would come back, but our physiotherapist Johnny Watters told me it was 'a very serious injury', which I took to mean that his career might be over.

Of course everyone was devastated – for Brian and, although this might sound slightly selfish, ourselves. With him we looked certainties for promotion. He'd already scored twenty-four league goals before Christmas and was on for at least forty or more by the season's end.

I was not the least surprised that he became one of the great managers as he was always very sure of himself. Having failed to sustain his recovery, Brian did exceptionally well coaching the Sunderland youth team to the FA Youth Cup semi-final. And if George Hardwick is to be believed, the board failed to extend his manager's contract at the end of the 1964–65 season because he told them that Brian would be his right-hand man within two years. There was no way those in charge at Sunderland were having that, and after the club received the insurance money paid for the loss of a key player, Clough and Hardwick were gone within months. It was Sunderland's loss.

Apart from those at Leeds, none of the many players he managed have a bad word for him. He was strict but always honest and players appreciate that. Frank Clark is one of the most placid players you could hope to meet and he never had a bad word to say about Brian. Brian also managed Dave Mackay, known for his volatility, yet he handled him pretty well. And Roy Keane seemed to do as he was told under Brian at Nottingham Forest.

If Brian was a friend he always stood by you. When I quit my job at 'Boro he was one of the first on the telephone, asking me to come and watch a match with him.

Mind you, that never stopped him getting annoyed if his team lost. He was bitterly upset when I took Middlesbrough to the Baseball Ground one year and we won. Afterwards he went on about how lucky we were. That was nonsense: we'd deserved to win – but he hated losing.

His most controversial appointment was as manager of Leeds United at the start of the 1974–75 season when he took over from Don Revie. Leeds had won the First Division the previous season, although after a fabulous unbeaten start to the season they'd stuttered a little towards the very end.

When the fixtures for the new season came out, Leeds' opponents in their first home game of the season were Queens Park Rangers, where I was then assistant manager. What happened has stayed with me.

We won 1-0 and there were murmurings both in the crowd and in the corridors downstairs that Brian wasn't the man for Leeds.

Afterwards we went for a meal, and by chance the Leeds team were booked into the same hotel. Brian was with them and the atmosphere wasn't great. I asked if he fancied a drink, and how was it going?

'Not great,' he replied. 'I've had a few problems.'

I said I was sure that things would work out fine.

'You were lucky today. Wish I could get a bit of that luck,' he said.

I repeated that he'd be all right.

'I'm not sure about that. I don't think I will be here too long,' he said. It was a statement that shook me. I smiled but he was gone.

I got the impression his heart wasn't in it. He didn't have Peter Taylor, his assistant manager at Hartlepools, Derby and Brighton, alongside him although his chief coach Jimmy Gordon had joined him at Elland Road.

Brian wouldn't have said something like that as a joke. He was definite. I believe, knowing Brian pretty well, that he thought, 'I'm working my ticket here and Manny Cousins will get rid of me.' I'm sure he would never have resigned – he'd have wanted the pay-off.

He never should have gone to Leeds – he hated them, how they played, and he hated Don Revie. He even went on TV to say that. I think he took the job for the publicity. He was at Brighton, who were nonentities, and he knew if he went to Elland Road he'd be back in the spotlight, which is what he wanted, what he always craved and needed.

He'd have preferred to succeed with Leeds, but I am not certain he lost a great deal of sleep when he didn't. He knew he'd do all right financially and by raising his profile again he could hope to get another job. I wouldn't say he was laughing at Leeds, but either way you look at it he was certain to do all right. There is a feeling that Brian did badly at Leeds; I am not so sure of that.

Of course he became manager at Nottingham Forest and proved what a genius he was. Having taken Derby from the Second Division to champions of the First Division in less than five years he did the same with Forest. He did so without any real stars. Peter Shilton in goal was an exceptional talent but he knitted together the likes of Archie Gemmill, Kenny Burns, Larry Lloyd, John McGovern, Tony Woodcock, Martin O'Neill, Viv Anderson and John Robertson into a fine team that, with the addition of Trevor Francis, football's first £1,000,000 player, twice captured the European Cup.

I don't think many people gave us much of a chance at Preston North End in the third round of the FA Cup without Brian. But we turned in a great Sunderland performance. The icy conditions made the ground tricky and we went a goal down in the first five minutes.

Alan Brown had shocked the players beforehand by announcing we were going to play 4-2-4 – Brazil had shown how successful this could be at the 1962 World Cup, and although we might not have been as good as the World Cup holders it made a refreshing change to be trying something new.

The side played brilliantly, and I mean brilliantly. We moved the ball quickly over the ground. Wingers Jimmy Davison and George Mulhall were plied with the ball and destroyed Preston's full backs. With most of the other games called off because of the wintry conditions the BBC cameras had been rushed to the ground – they missed Preston's goal as they set up their equipment but they didn't miss the four we scored. Viewers saw some marvellous football; Nick Sharkey scored twice and Jimmy and Ambrose Fogarty added the others. This was brilliant. Even without Brian Clough it seemed that if we stuck with 4-2-4 we could go back up.

Surely, I thought, having seen us play so well Alan Brown would at least give us the chance to continue in the same way. For once, as I climbed the stairs at Roker Park to Alan Brown's office on the Monday morning I was looking forward to our discussion. He took only a few minutes to make me aware that it was a one-off. The tactics had been adapted for a difficult surface, he said, and were unlikely to be repeated. I was devastated, but Alan Brown ignored my pleas and we were back to 3-2-2-3 the following match. It was ridiculous. Yet I should have thought more carefully, because after the game when Charlie said 'That's how we should play every week', I couldn't help notice that the manager gave him a withering look.

But even had Alan Brown decided to stick with 4-2-4 it would have made little immediate difference. This was one of the coldest winters in living memory and as the country ground to a halt we played no league games for nearly two months. We did manage the first leg of the League Cup semi-final against Aston Villa a week after Deepdale but that was it for a month until we met Gravesend in the FA Cup. This was the first time the League Cup had been staged, and although in those days the final was a two-legged affair and not played at Wembley, I was naturally still keen to win it. We had equalised on sixty minutes through Nick Sharkey, just minutes after Monty had been led from the pitch with concussion, but Villa, with their centre-forward Derek Dougan in fine form, were soon back in the lead and ended up winning 3-1. The second leg in early April was a goalless draw. Villa lost to neighbours Birmingham City in the final.

In March we'd drawn 0-0 in the Roker Park Wear–Tyne derby before a massive crowd of 62,240. After missing a penalty when I fired the ball too close to the body of Dave Hollins, I decided to pass the responsibility to Johnny Crossan and the following week he scored one, as part of a hat-trick, as we won 3-2 at Walsall.

We then beat Norwich 7-1 with Nicky Sharkey, who'd replaced Brian, scoring a magnificent five – thus equalling the achievements of Charlie Buchan against Liverpool in 1912 and Bobby Gurney against Bolton in 1935. The result was greeted with something approaching ecstasy by the senior players. It meant we were sure of being in the top two after thirty matches and that gave us each a bonus of £900. Sadly Nick's contract didn't include a similar clause and he got nothing – although he did take home the match ball. I gather it remains one of his most prized possessions.

Nick, of course, wasn't as good a goalscorer as Brian Clough – few were – but he was a very fine player and a natural scorer. By the time he moved to Leicester City he'd scored sixty-two times in just 117 appearances. I felt that with him in such form there was no reason we couldn't go up and my confidence went even higher when we won at Grimsby and drew at home to Plymouth to move to the top of the league with eleven matches remaining. Newcastle were fourth but it was two from us, Chelsea and Stoke. We still had both clubs to face at Roker Park, where only Bury had beaten us.

Alan Brown decided, however, that Nick wasn't up to the task and he bought Andy Kerr from Kilmarnock at the start of April, throwing him straight in. It was by no means his fault, but with Andy we won only one of our next seven matches, during which he scored twice. Having said that, it should have been two wins as I am still convinced we were robbed away at Stoke City on Easter Monday.

The great Stanley Matthews had returned to Stoke in 1962 after fifteen successful years at Blackpool, and his presence, plus the arrival of my old friend Dennis Viollet from Manchester United, as well as the ex-Wolves and Arsenal man Eddie Clamp, had revitalised them. When we travelled there we were third and they were top with two more points.

The score was level at 1-1 with only a few minutes left when Andy Kerr went down under a heavy challenge. Andy was an honest player who never made a meal of any foul and I was certain it was a penalty. It was even more frustrating because we'd gone a goal down in the game when Stoke had been awarded a spot kick for an innocuous tackle on Viollet. I couldn't believe it and I went to the referee – in an age when you didn't tend to complain too much to them – to argue. Of course, it didn't do any good and then when I went to line up outside the box Stanley Matthews walked over and in the nicest possible way said it was definitely a penalty. My only response was 'Bollocks. Shut up you silly old bugger.' Not surprisingly we didn't speak afterwards and I've always regretted saying that. It was like writing graffiti on an official monument.

Andy Kerr played his final match of the season when we beat Southampton 4-0 in early May, Johnny Crossan again scoring a hat-trick, thrilling the crowd with his subsequent somersault celebrations. Unlike Kenwyne Jones he didn't injure himself!

Nick Sharkey was brought back for the last three matches and grabbed a couple at Luton. We recorded back-to-back victories, beating Swansea at the Vetch Field 4-3, where Crossan was again among the scorers with two. That meant we needed only to draw with Chelsea at Roker Park on the last day of the season to go up. To deny us Chelsea had to win and then beat Portsmouth in midweek. With Chelsea having lost all seven of their away games in 1963 and also thrown away an eight-point lead since Christmas it meant we were big favourites to clinch promotion.

Someone thought it was in the bag and agreed to allow Tyne Tees Television to make a programme about us winning promotion – no problem. But technology wasn't what it is today and as they wanted it to be broadcast on the Monday night they decided to interview the players beforehand as if we'd already gone up. It was ludicrous and I was dead against the idea – if we won promotion there was nothing stopping them interviewing us an hour or so after the game. Yet the club agreed and the players were asked to go through the farce of pretending we were already up.

The programme was never aired because Chelsea beat us 1-0. Their manager, Tommy Docherty, was clever that day, pushing big Frank Upton up front where he unsettled Charlie Hurley. They also got lucky when the ball hit Tommy Harmer in his 'middle leg' for the only goal in the first half. Peter Bonetti in the Chelsea goal played well, but having said that we really had only ourselves to blame as we fashioned and missed a number of gilt-edged chances – the sort I am sure Brian Clough would have gobbled up. It was a sad day all round as we walked off the Roker Park pitch with only the sound of the cheering Chelsea fans to accompany us.

I had no doubt that Chelsea would beat Portsmouth in midweek and was not surprised when I heard they'd won 7-0. I feared I might not make it back into the First Division with Sunderland before hanging up my boots. That was to prove to be the case, but not quite as I imagined!

Chapter 11

Moving on

Having spent heavily in the two previous close seasons, Alan Brown was quiet in the transfer market in the summer of 1963: there were no serious additions to the squad. A number of pundits used this to suggest that at the end of the previous season Sunderland might have blown their chances of going back up for some time.

Yet, although we suffered a shock defeat to Northampton Town in our second home match we won six and drew one of the opening nine games. I felt I was playing well and had featured in every match.

The tenth was against Cardiff City at Roker Park. John Charles, the Welsh legend, had just returned to English football and there was a healthy crowd of close to 38,000, many drawn by the chance of seeing a superstar in the flesh. But it was his colleague Ivor Allchurch who was their star, scoring a hat-trick to overturn a two-goal deficit before Charlie Hurley soared above Charles to head an equaliser. Although we should have won the game I was not too disappointed. I felt that if we continued to play that well we would soon roar up the table. I also felt I had played reasonably well.

I remember thinking that there was always next week. Little did I know there wasn't. Well, not for me, because that was my final game for Sunderland. I only wish I had realised that at the time.

Martin Harvey was twenty-two, had made his debut in 1959 and was already a full international with Northern Ireland. Although he was left-footed he'd acted mostly as my understudy at right half and had made only about twenty first-team appearances. He was naturally ambitious and couldn't be expected to sit around waiting for ever. The ending of transfer regulations tying players to clubs made it easier for the disgruntled to move on. Martin was young and improving. I was eight years older and age, as they say, waits for no man.

But I was more than a little shocked when I took a look at the team-sheet pinned to the notice board on the Monday before the Wednesday midweek game at Plymouth Argyle. Listed at number 4 – Martin Harvey. Fair enough, I reckoned, that's football and you have to take the rough with the smooth.

When I looked a little bit further down the sheet I was very disappointed. Listed at number 12 was – Anderson. I couldn't understand this – it was as big a shock as when, as an eleven-year-old, I had glanced up at the school's notice board to discover an 'Anderson S.' listed in a school team composed of fourteen- and fifteen-year olds. I was being asked to travel all the way down to Plymouth knowing I wouldn't be playing. I could understand taking a young player, who had never played, such a distance; it would give them the experience of mixing with the first team – but I had made more than 400 first-team appearances for Sunderland. What was going on?

I went to see the manager and explained my case as patiently as I could. I said the sight of the club captain as twelfth man would embarrass the players. I said I would prefer to play in the reserves. Alan Brown was intractable. I was talking to myself and faced with the possibility of being disciplined. I had no option other than to make an 800-mile round trip and sit twiddling my thumbs as the two teams battled out a 1-1 draw.

I don't really know why Alan Brown was so difficult with me. When he'd arrived I thought he'd be a good influence. Yes, he was strict and wanted his own way. But unlike Bill Murray he came to training and told us the way he wanted us to play. I can only think that he wanted to fashion a team of his own. He'd bought several players and brought others through. But I was there as an established figure. I didn't agree with him that I should be more defensive, and I thought we should play differently.

But he was in charge; I went to Plymouth and as the team started to win matches he kept faith with the players. I had no other option than to bide my time. But I wanted to play, only to find my requests to turn out for the reserves being turned down.

So, increasingly frustrated, I decided it might be the time to move on. I didn't want to, especially as I was due a testimonial match at the end of the season. I knew I was likely to have a reduced gate if I was playing for another club. Yet I felt that the manager was not going to drop Martin Harvey and I wanted to play – for me that was everything. It was great to be paid for playing and I wish we had been paid more, but first and foremost I enjoyed playing the game. I wish I could still play today!

I plucked up the courage to see the manager one Tuesday and told him I wanted to leave Roker Park. I thought he'd appreciate the situation but he was adamant I was going nowhere, asking me to battle on. He said that even if I did ask for a transfer the board would refuse it and I would therefore be wasting my time. I knew that might happen but I wanted them to know I was after a move. Finally, Brown agreed he would place my request before the directors at the next meeting. This was due to take place as usual on the Thursday.

Hours after seeing Brown I received a phone call from Syd Collings. He said he wouldn't think of letting me go and that the manager would go before I did – an obvious piece of nonsense which brought a wry smile. I told him that my relationship with Alan Brown wasn't great and that I felt it would be in the best interests of the club and me to allow me to go. 'No way, Stan,' Collings said as he put down the phone.

I didn't find it unusual that Alan Brown did not tell me on the Friday what had been decided the previous day, and so when I found Len Shackleton standing on my doorstep asking if I had handed in a transfer request I invited him in as usual. He was a regular visitor, coming to see me at least once a month after he became a football reporter, and we'd chat about things. The club knew this and never tried to stop it. And why should they? We talked about the usual football stuff, discussing how a game had gone or about my appearances for the Football League or England at various levels.

I told him it was true and that I was awaiting the board's decision. Come the Sunday and the story appeared under Shack's name in the *Sunday People*. I thought little of it but when I went to work on the Monday Arthur Wright told me the manager wanted to see me urgently.

When I entered his office he was absolutely furious. And it soon became clear why he was in such a bad mood. He asked whether I had spoken to Shack and as I felt I had nothing to hide I told him I had. I pointed out that there was nothing in the article that was untrue. Then Alan Brown revealed he had not, as agreed, placed the request before the board. It meant that the majority of the directors would have got to know about it only through the press.

As far as I was concerned that had nothing to do with me and, realising where the conversation was going, I told him straight: 'That's your problem.' He reacted angrily. He leapt from behind his desk with his arms outstretched as if he was going to strangle me. I jumped out of my seat, telling him 'Don't you touch me.' This seemed to calm him down and instead of attacking me he barked at me to get out of his room. I had already made up my mind to do that anyway! I decided in the circumstances to stay out of his way for a few days and wait and see what happened.

Two days later I was sitting at home at about 10pm, watching television, when there was a knock on the front door. I was amazed to find Alan Brown asking to come in. It was late, and he wasn't exactly great company at the best of times so I couldn't help thinking that what he wanted had better be good. It even crossed my mind, although only very briefly, that he might be there to apologise for his behaviour. It soon became clear that wasn't going to happen.

He sat down and started talking about football in general but as it was obvious that wasn't the reason for his visit I asked him why he'd decided to call round at my house not long before I was due to go to bed.

'We've received an offer for you and have accepted it,' was his reply.

So much for what had been said by Syd Collings. Now it was up to me. I hadn't even been given the courtesy of being told which club was involved before they'd accepted their offer.

What if it was some side halfway down Division Three – or worse, Newcastle? I couldn't accept either of those possibilities. I wanted to continue playing in Division Two at least and as a Sunderland fan I couldn't go to St James' Park.

Yet when I asked which club it was Brown was deliberately evasive. I couldn't understand how this man, normally so blunt and often rude, wouldn't answer the obvious question. What on earth was it all about, I thought, as he waffled on endlessly about what a good servant I had been for Sunderland and how they'd be unhappy to see me move.

Had he forgotten that it was me who asked for a transfer? I needed to move because I wanted to play first-team football. After about an hour he said finally that the manager of the club wanting to sign me was sitting outside in the car!

'You what? You've left him outside for an hour? What the hell for?' was all I could think to say, and my anxiety wasn't soothed when I suggested he should go and get him and Brown told me that whoever it was wouldn't mind. I was speechless at this behaviour but that was nothing as to what was to follow – which was the biggest shock of my life.

I had absolutely no idea who would come through my front door with Alan Brown but when it was Newcastle manager Joe Harvey I was totally flabbergasted. At first I thought this was some sort of joke, but Alan Brown didn't have a sense of humour.

I'd known Joe from having played golf with him, Bobby Mitchell, Bob Stokoe and Ronnie Simpson and had always got on well with him; but this was different. It took some time but I calmed myself down and we must have spoken for an hour or so. It was all very amicable as he told me he felt I could help knit together a young Newcastle team as part of his drive to help them regain their place in Division One.

Yet in the back of my mind all I was thinking was 'No way am I going there, no way am I going there, no way, no way, never, never, never and never again'; and when they both left nothing had been agreed.

The following day, when I called at Roker Park to see Brown he was forthright, making it clear that my Sunderland career was over and that I should leave as quickly as possible. The club had accepted the offer and the quicker things were resolved the better.

I needed to sort a few things out and while doing that Alan Brown robbed me of a fair amount of money. I asked him if I would still be given a testimonial at the end of the season. I knew the gate would be reduced by any Newcastle connection but I felt I had earned it. 'Yes,' he told me. Also I was entitled to a second five-year service payment which amounted to £750. Would I get this if I had the testimonial, I asked? Brown said he didn't know but would phone the League secretary Alan Hardaker. Later Brown told me I could have one or the other – the £750 or the testimonial. It left me in a quandary, but I thought I'd stick with having the match; it would mean one last game at Roker Park and with Sunderland likely to get promoted I might do well on the back of their success.

A year later I found out there was no need to make such a decision. Alan Hardaker told me Brown had never phoned him and that I was entitled to the long-service money even if I had had a testimonial. I never got the money. Len Ashurst has said that Brownie was an honest bastard. One of those words was correct.

Faced with little real option other than to transfer from red and white stripes to black and white ones I left Roker Park for the last time as a Sunderland player, putting behind me more than eleven years in the first team and close to 450 first-team appearances.

Funnily enough, as I left to go and meet Joe Harvey, one of the fans who could often be seen standing around outside the main entrance at Roker Park, no doubt in an attempt to cheer me up, said, 'Hi Stan, you'll be back in the side shortly.' It brought a smile to my lips as by the end of the day I was a Newcastle player. I have to say it proved the best move of my life. I enjoyed two fabulous years there and I still keep in touch with many of the players.

A few months later, in March 1964, I had the 'pleasure' of playing against Sunderland at St James' Park as captain of Newcastle United. Before the match I told Joe Harvey that if he wanted to leave me out it was fine by me. He said he didn't know what I was on about. When I said it could be embarrassing he simply laughed off the idea and told me I was playing.

It's very difficult playing against an old team and I hated the prospect of it. Obviously I wanted Newcastle to win, but I wanted Sunderland to win promotion.

On the day itself the weather was terrible. Marjorie and I took the train and as I was walking to the ground it seemed clear the match was off as fans were coming away from the city. Newcastle never had the best of pitches and I was certain it would be postponed. So I was shocked when Joe said the referee had declared the pitch playable. There were only 27,341 there because many had gone home convinced it was off. Newcastle won 1-0 after Charlie Hurley handled the ball on the line and Ron McGarry scored the penalty. Sunderland hadn't played well but they would have got a draw if Nicky Sharkey hadn't screwed their one chance wide of goal. Once again there was a possibility of Sunderland, who earlier that week had lost a second replay FA Cup quarter-final match against Manchester United, being denied promotion at the death.

Shack, who hated Alan Brown, added petrol to the fire by writing about how my 'fine' performance proved he'd been wrong to get rid of me. The article had nothing to do with me. In fact, I could well have done without my name being mentioned at all because the next week I was due to carry out a task I had performed regularly over the years.

Donald Bee was the brother of a school friend of mine, Bryan. For many years he'd arranged for me to present the prizes at the darts and dominoes night at Southwick Social Club. It had always been a good evening, but when I'd gone to Newcastle I wasn't too sure about doing it and as it was scheduled for the Wednesday after the St James' Park match I asked if he might consider getting someone else. I wasn't keen as I thought they'd boo me.

Donald said I wasn't to be daft as people would be fine, and he finally persuaded me. I was behind the curtain on the stage when he did the introductions and when he said my name and I emerged there was deadly silence followed by a few boos. People were soothed when I said that despite the result there was nothing to worry about as Sunderland were certainties to be promoted. The crowd still wasn't that happy and funnily enough someone else presented the prizes the following year.

Of course Sunderland did get promoted. I was really pleased. After all, I'd played in almost a quarter of the matches and was delighted for ex-colleagues such as Len Ashurst, George Mulhall, Monty and Charlie Hurley; Martin Harvey as well. I never had anything against him.

The club was good enough to invite me to a number of events, including the celebratory dinner, which I appreciated. The success also proved a massive bonus for me personally. My testimonial took place only two days after Sunderland had grabbed a 0-0 draw at Southampton to as good as seal promotion.

A crowd of 27,802 was at Roker Park to see Sunderland take on an all-star international side, captained by me. It included Jackie Milburn, Bobby Mitchell, Bryan Douglas, George Eastham, Alan Hopkinson and Tom Finney among others. Great players all of them.

I received a marvellous reception and after the expenses were paid I was left with close to £4,000 – a fortune in those days.

Chapter 12

The mighty Magpies

Newcastle United were in the bottom half of Division Two when I joined, in Joe Harvey's second season in charge. He had been a big part of the 1947–48 team which gained promotion to Division One and had captained the successful FA Cup final sides of 1951 and 1952. After managing Barrow and Workington he had replaced Charlie Mitten at St James' Park in June 1962.

Joe was a larger-than-life character and in 1989 when he died suddenly of a heart attack the funeral cortege went to, of all places, Sunderland crematorium and there was a considerable crowd outside, including a good number of Sunderland fans.

In the prelude to my signing he'd made it clear he was looking to use my experience to bring on what he'd described as a talented bunch of youngsters. He was honest enough to admit that he didn't think they were ready to go up that season, but he felt a push the following year was certainly possible. He immediately appointed me captain as the current skipper, Jim Iley, had indicated he'd be happy to give up.

I consider the role of captain to be vital in football. A good one needs to possess a number of qualities, including commanding respect for what he says. He must also be able to show by example that he is determined to lead the side to victory. He doesn't have to be the team's best player; that's not always possible anyway because it's not a good policy to have a forward as captain, certainly never a centre-forward. They are often isolated from the action and a captain needs to be in the thick of things. I am also not too keen on goalkeepers as captains. It's best left to a midfield player as they are a link between defence and attack.

Newcastle had lost their previous four league games and had gone down at Bournemouth in a midweek league cup tie before I made my debut, along with David Craig, against Cardiff City at St James' Park. Despite my Sunderland connections there was warm applause from seemingly most of the 38,495 crowd when my name was announced. Sadly that was as good as it got because the match was a disaster, with John Charles and Ivor Allchurch inspiring their team to a 4-0 victory.

I struggled, having not played for more than a month, although I did manage a powerful, rising drive from twenty-five yards that the Cardiff 'keeper Dilwyn John tipped over and I was shocked that a number of papers selected me as the team's best player. I was also surprised at how resigned the crowd was; if we'd lost 4-0 at Sunderland the Roker Park faithful would have been outraged. At St James', where they were now in their third season in Division Two, it was as if they didn't really believe the team could do any better.

If that was the way they thought, they were wrong. In training, taken by Jimmy Greenhalgh, I had been impressed by a number of the players, including George Dalton, Jim Iley, Ron McGarry and Alan Suddick. But I had to find out if Joe Harvey would be any different to Alan Brown when I put forward suggestions.

The atmosphere when I went to see Joe on the Monday morning was entirely different from those often embarrassing discussions with Brown. Joe was keen to know my opinions and that was always the case during my time as his captain. That did not mean he always agreed or even acted upon my views, but at least I was being listened to. In time the players were happy to talk to me about ideas they had to improve the team, knowing I would raise them with Joe. Mind you, sometimes I didn't know if he was pulling my leg or not; he'd say things like 'So you reckon Robson's playing well? I'm not so certain and I might leave him out.' Come the Saturday Bryan 'Pop' Robson would be in the team.

I fell out with Joe Harvey just once. It was at half-time during the game at Cardiff City in my first season. We were losing and Joe was really angry. But what upset me was that he was singling out the younger players for particular criticism. I decided to say that it was the team that was playing badly and not just one or two individuals. He told me in no uncertain terms to shut my 'fucking mouth'. I was livid.

In fact, we came back to force a 2-2 draw, so perhaps the dressing room tirade worked. I'm still not sure. Going home on the train we were close to the bar and he kept asking me if I wanted a drink, but I made clear I didn't want him to get me one.

Come the Monday morning Jimmy Greenhalgh said I was to go straight up to see the manager. I expected the worst; I felt I would be stripped of the captaincy. Yet when I got to his office he said to sit, asking if I wanted a cup of tea.

'How are you today?' he asked with a great big smile on his face.

Joe was never a soft touch but on the other hand he could appreciate the point of view of others.

My debut convinced me that one of our problems was that we were leaving too many gaps at the back; that the full backs needed to get tighter to the halfbacks. I suggested that we play a little more defensively in my second game and although it wasn't the best of matches we managed to bring back a point from a goalless draw with Swindon. With a little more luck we might have won.

That was the start of a good run. We won five of our next six matches, drawing the other, to move into the top half of the Second Division, nine points below second-placed Sunderland.

Joe Harvey had signed Trevor Hockey from Nottingham Forest at the same time as me. He was a robust player and the crowd loved him, yet off the field Trevor was very quiet, hardly saying a word. Out wide we had Alan Suddick, very talented and clever although I felt he never fulfilled his potential. He would have been better playing at inside forward but we had Willie Penman and Dave Hilley and they were good players so Alan was forced to play on the wing.

Despite our league form we were embarrassed to be knocked out of the third round of the FA Cup by non-league Bedford Town at St James' Park. They deserved it too, winning 2-1, with my goal being of no value. When we got back to the dressing room at the end Joe Harvey was shouting and cursing at us, and after he slammed the door behind him chairman Stan Seymour opened it again to tell us 'You're all bloody rubbish.' He certainly wasn't joking.

Fortunately that shock did not knock us out of our stride in the league and we won seven, losing just one, of the next ten matches. One of the victories was the one against Sunderland. Had we started the run earlier we would have been in with a shout of going up. Nevertheless, we moved to fifth but our poor start meant we were still a long way behind my former club, who at Easter were in the promotion frame with Leeds. We faced Leeds twice in four days, losing both games by a single goal. The matches could have gone either way, and we would have earned at least a point in the second game at Elland Road had George Dalton's match, and ultimately his career, not been brought to a premature end by a very poor challenge from Johnny Giles. It was that tackle that led to me putting down the phone on Don Revie when he called to discuss the match a few days later.

Ironically, those two games put me into the spotlight years later when the *Sunday Mirror* began an investigation into Revie's reign at Leeds. Evidence, of a sort, was produced to show that Revie was involved in bribing opposition players to throw matches. And Gary Sprake, his one-time 'keeper at Elland Road, said he'd been persuaded by him to fake injuries so as not to play for Wales.

I suddenly found that the newspaper wanted to know about a conversation I'd had with Don before the games. Don and I had spoken regularly on the 'phone after he left Roker Park so I was not in the slightest bit surprised to take a call from him. We had a good chat, during which he mentioned that Leeds had so many injuries he hoped we'd take it easy against them. It was all good-natured, and I thought nothing more of it. I even told Jimmy Greenhalgh the following morning. Nothing more was said about it, and I never raised the subject with Don because I couldn't accept his explanation for the injury to George and he never rang me again.

Despite our efforts it got back to me that one or two of the Sunderland players felt Newcastle had been more than happy to lose the two games. Nothing could be further from the truth and I was very upset about the whole incident.

Then in 1977, when I was manager of Fourth Division Doncaster Rovers, I was sitting in the manager's room at Belle Vue when two reporters from the *Daily Mirror* turned up saying they wanted to do a piece on the club. I was pleased because teams in Division Four do not often get coverage in the national press. I politely answered questions about how it was a struggle to keep the club afloat, but explaining we still had ambition to move up the leagues. I had no idea what was coming when one of them asked if I had anything to say on Don Revie and began asking me about the telephone conversations thirteen years earlier.

I explained clearly that Don had not suggested he would pay Newcastle's players to throw the game. It didn't seem to do the trick, though. I found myself being photographed in the dugout at subsequent games and was reported as being worried. The paper stated they weren't suggesting I was involved in any suspect activities, but I still wasn't happy about being dragged into something that had nothing to do with me. If others wanted to make allegations against Don that was up to them, and as there were so many it's clear he had been up to no good on a number of occasions. But I didn't want to add to them, and the claims that appeared in the *Sunday Mirror* that he had offered £10 a player were ridiculous – not least because in 1964 most of those at St James' were on at least £25 a week.

The following year, when I went to Bolton Wanderers as assistant manager, I bumped into Vince Wilson from the *Mirror*. I knew him very well but couldn't bring myself to speak. Then when he rang to ask me about going to a PFA dinner in London I felt it was time to put things to rest, so I agreed. On the way down he asked me if I would be prepared to visit the *Mirror's* offices in Fleet Street and reluctantly I said I would. Once there I was introduced to the sports editor, Tony Smith, who said he was really sorry I had been upset by the paper's coverage. I told him I didn't believe him, that I had denied the allegations when the journalists had arrived at Doncaster and there was nothing in the story. I also pointed out that following the piece no one from the Football Association had ever approached me about it and as far as I was concerned it was journalism of the lowest kind.

We eventually finished eighth in 1963–64 with forty-five points. Leeds were promoted as champions with Sunderland second.

Despite my new club's modest achievements I felt optimistic that the 1964–65 season might take Newcastle back into Division One: we had beaten many of the clubs who had finished above us.

We gained three points from two home games before our first away game, which was at The Valley. We won a hard fought game after 'Pop' Robson beat my ex-Sunderland colleague Peter Wakeham in the Charlton nets for the only goal of his debut. Going home on the train the feeling was that this could be our year; winning breeds confidence and ours was high.

Pop was destined for a very successful career. He was always curious and keen to find new ways to improve his game. Just as importantly, he recognised early on that to do well you have to be willing to give up some of the pleasures in life. To be a professional footballer you have to be exactly that – professional. Even with all the talent in the world you have to work at your trade. So one night when he and Geoff Allen were having a sing-song and a few beers, and I said that I felt it was time for them to go up to bed and get a good night's sleep before a match, there was no argument.

I think it says a lot that even now, more than forty years later, Pop is still involved in the game as a scout for Chelsea. Pop, who notched more than 250 goals and was top scorer in Division One in 1972–73 with twenty-eight goals, is a credit to himself and his profession. Younger players would do well to look at him as an example of how to behave. Why he didn't get at least one cap for England is a mystery.

I formed a good partnership down the right with Pop and behind us was David Craig at right back. He was quick, a good tackler and in fine form, which allowed me the freedom to develop goal-scoring opportunities for others and also to get one or two goals myself. David's left full back partner Frank Clark had signed from the famous non-league side Crook Town, winners of the Amateur Cup on four occasions.

Frank was a thinking man's footballer. He made up for the fact that he was not the fastest with a fine positional sense. He rarely got the runaround from a winger and his use of the ball was excellent. I tried to sign him for Doncaster when I was manager. Foolishly he decided to sign for Brian Clough instead at Nottingham Forest, where he won League Championship and European Cup medals!

Frank and Dave were the regular full back pairing for Newcastle for many years, which allowed Joe Harvey to concentrate on improving other areas of the team.

I began to really take pleasure in my football, and as the side improved on the pitch the atmosphere off it became really enjoyable, even if a major part of it was our big centre-half John McGrath taking the mickey out of me. On his retirement he became a well-known after-dinner speaker. I know who he practised on between 1963 and 1965 – me!

When we beat Coventry City 2-0 in early September Ron McGarry was one of six players dismissed in Football League matches that weekend, a record. Today few weekends go by with fewer than six players sent off in the four leagues. Of course what doesn't help nowadays is the willingness of players to fall over at the slightest challenge and feign injury. Diving, especially in the box, is also much more prevalent. There were some players from the past who dived: Charlie Fleming at Sunderland in the '50s was one, and Harry Potts in the '40s was good at getting penalties for Burnley. But they were few and far between and the game would be better today if the diving stopped.

We beat Preston North End 5-2 at home in our ninth game and went top. In October we also scored five at St James' Park when we hammered Leyton Orient without reply. During that game I hit one of the two best goals I ever scored: Colin Taylor swung over a corner and, standing on the edge of the area, I hit the ball on the volley and it flew into the net. Orient seemed to bring out the best in me because my other favourite goal was the one I'd scored against them in 1960.

The following Saturday I came across Bob Stokoe again. We travelled to Gigg Lane to face Bury. Winning 2-1, with just a couple of minutes left, I received the ball around thirty yards from goal. Rather than take a shot I dallied to waste a few precious seconds and then, when no one pressed me, I wasted a few more. Suddenly I heard the sound of the approaching Bury player-manager and ex-Newcastle favourite Stokoe. I soon got rid of the ball, but not quick enough. He flattened me and as I lay there screamed: 'Don't you take the piss out of my team!'

When we trooped off after collecting both points Bob still hadn't calmed down. He was still shouting at the top of his voice at me as we made our way down the tunnel. Joe Harvey asked me what was going on, but I couldn't really tell him. Later we suffered our only home defeat of the season against Bury, losing 3-2. I have never seen anyone so happy as we came off – Bob was a big Newcastle fan but he was ecstatic about his side's victory. Mind you, it was their fourth in a row at St James' Park.

Bob was the most competitive person I have ever met – and I have met a few in my time. When Joe Harvey and I used to play against him and Bobby Mitchell in golf foursomes you have never heard swearing like it. Bob and Joe would be at each other like hammer and tongs. In other games you'd often let the other side pick up the ball when it was three or four feet from the hole, but none of that took place with this foursome. 'No fucking chance, you might fucking miss that,' Bob would say.

Mind you, Bob could be as soft as a brush about some things – I remember going to a Sunderland reunion dinner when he was manager there. I expressed my condolences that he'd recently lost his beloved black collie dog. He was in tears; I don't know who was more embarrassed – me for asking or him for showing such emotion.

Newcastle's match at Swindon Town in late November was one of the strangest of the many hundreds of games I played in. We didn't play that well, yet the scoreline at the end read Swindon Town 1 Newcastle United 6.

For the first twenty minutes I am not sure we even got into their half, and I'd guess that by the end we had at most eight shots – six of course, including two of mine, went in. As we were coming off Mike Summerbee, playing at right wing for the Wiltshire side, said to me 'How the bloody hell have we lost 6-1, we were the better side!'

Nevertheless, the result was exactly what we needed and was the first of seven straight victories. One of these was against the team that went up with us, Northampton Town. We played brilliantly that November day at St James' Park, roaring into the lead just after kick-off courtesy of Trevor Hockey. That's how it remained until just two minutes before half-time, when we scored three times to make it 4-0 with Ron McGarry grabbing a couple.

At the end it was 5-0 with Ron getting a hat-trick. He must have been a bit disappointed to see all the papers picking yours truly as the man of the match the following day! I must admit I really did enjoy playing in that game. I seemed to have acres of space in which to pass the ball and on one occasion, as I ran through the middle of the park, Terry Branston, the Cobblers centre-half, was screaming at his fellow defenders to 'put an end to that fella'.

We played Middlesbrough twice over Christmas. There was an inch of snow on the Ayresome Park pitch for the first match, where my shot from a free kick took a deflection to beat Eddie Connachan in the 'Boro goal with Dave Hilley adding the second. Arthur Kaye scored for 'Boro in the return but another two from Dave in front of a crowd of more than 54,000 saw us leave the pitch with a five-point gap over third-placed Norwich.

We extended the lead and although our run came to end in a remarkable game at Highfield Road, where Coventry beat us 5-4, we were now seven points clear of Norwich. It was obvious that if we maintained this form we would go up. Northampton Town, managed by the ex-Arsenal captain and fine wing-half Dave Bowen, were second, four points below us.

Like many sides in such a situation we stuttered. We gained only a single point from four February matches, but a determined all-round team performance at Portsmouth garnered two vital points, which set us up for a key home game against Norwich. At that stage we were second with forty-three points from thirty-three games, a point behind Northampton who had a game in hand. Norwich were third, just a point behind us.

St James' Park wasn't packed – there were 41,441 there and they saw one of my best performances in a Newcastle strip, especially as I had been hardly able to train during the week leading up to it because of a very heavy cold. After thirty-nine minutes of a tight game I threaded my way past two defenders and managed to curl the ball to the back post, where Bobby Cummings headed home with great power. This gave us a two-goal lead because Pop had settled any tension by putting us ahead in the tenth minute and Norwich never seriously threatened in the second half. We followed this with three victories and a draw, which meant that with four games left we were beautifully poised to win promotion.

We achieved this before a passionate St James' Park on Good Friday 1965. Victory over Bolton Wanderers would guarantee at least second spot. Bolton had been unlucky to be relegated the previous season from Division One and had two emerging talents in Wyn Davies at centre-forward and, out right, Francis Lee, the man who provided the ammunition for Wyn's aerial abilities. Wyn was to go on to become a star at St James' Park but I am convinced he was too terrified to even play that day. Our centre-half John McGrath played like a man possessed; no one would have got past him.

I didn't know John before I signed for Newcastle but we became great friends until his untimely death in 1998 at the age of sixty. When I signed he was in competition with Bill Thompson for the centre-half's role, and it didn't take me too long to realise that John wasn't playing to anything like his full potential; he was making far too many elementary mistakes. So we'd go for a cup of coffee after training and chat about all things football. Joe Harvey had been a big help when it came to team meetings. He would start them off and then say 'and now over to Stan'.

Initially this was a shock, but I'd make it my job to read out match reports, discuss what had happened and try to work out how we could eradicate mistakes and so improve as a team. It also meant the other players were more than happy to talk to me. John and I had some great conversations and I know they were a big help to him. He became a tower of strength at the back for Newcastle for a number of years.

John's performance against Bolton was the perfect platform for a famous victory. Willie Penman grabbed a first-half opener and then Jim Iley hit a great shot from well outside the area to put us 2-0 up and I knew we were promoted. The huge crowd, forty short of 60,000, was fantastic in its support, cheering us all the way to the vital two points. But they had been great all season and I was ever so pleased to win promotion for them.

When the referee sounded the final whistle they went ballistic, pouring on to the pitch to celebrate. We were persuaded to go back out to greet the cheering, and, unable to get back down the tunnel on to the pitch the players clambered up through the paddock and into the directors' box. This was when I started what is now a common sight. I took off my shirt and threw it to the crowd below. The rest of the team followed suit. I am not so sure Stan Seymour thought it was the best thing to do but I was ecstatic. I very much doubt that a supporter got a whole shirt.

Throughout the celebrations, which had to be cut short because of the match the following day at Crystal Palace, I couldn't help thinking back to the night in Sunderland when Joe Harvey had emerged from the darkness and I had been left speechless. I hadn't wanted to go to Newcastle but it had turned out to the best decision I ever took in my football life.

I was disappointed, though, when Joe left me out for the Selhurst Park game. I was feeling fresh but Joe felt a rest would do me good. Unfortunately, it meant I missed playing every game that season, something achieved by Gordon Marshall in goal, Frank Clark and John McGrath. I had never been an ever-present when at Sunderland, so was especially keen to play against Palace, but there was no altering Joe's mind.

Our final match was at home to Manchester City. We were a point clear of Northampton Town, who were also promoted; a club which had risen from the Fourth to the First Division in just four seasons. It was a fantastic achievement, especially for such a small club. We had a superior goal difference so a draw was all we needed. I'd gone through my long career without winning a major medal and I was determined I'd get at least that.

The match was not the greatest; we could never really get going but it was a goalless draw and we'd done what we needed. It was our first goalless draw that season.

We were the Division Two champions and after four seasons out of the top flight Newcastle had returned to resume derbies against Sunderland.

Sadly, because of the uncertainty about who would win the title the trophy was not at St James' Park. I would have enjoyed being handed it in front of our fans.

Instead its presentation was a bit of a damp squib. Joe Harvey, returning from a Football League Management Committee meeting, asked me to meet him at Newcastle Central Station as he stepped down off the train. I had to take the train from Sunderland to Newcastle, be handed the trophy, have my picture taken by the press and then go back home to Sunderland. It all felt a bit daft.

Now, you would have thought that having taken the club back to the top division the directors would have been delighted. But when we went on a tour of West Germany and Denmark we found ourselves staying in terrible accommodation. As captain I took stick from the players and as I wholeheartedly agreed with them I didn't need any real pushing to take their complaints to Joe Harvey. He was fine but said we'd need to go and see the directors. To my surprise we had to jump into a taxi. After a short ride we pulled into a palatial hotel. It was where the directors were staying!

I duly explained to Stan Seymour that the food was poor and the hotel stunk of garlic. I asked if it was possible to move somewhere better. Fenton Braithwaite, another director, was listening to our conversation and almost floored me when he said to Stan Seymour 'They're only players.' Catching my breath I managed through gritted teeth to splutter: 'Mr Braithwaite, if it wasn't for those players you wouldn't be here.' The maximum wage may have ended a few years previously but some of the attitudes that kept it in place for so long clearly still needed changing. Not that my intervention did any good; we didn't get our move.

I was confident we'd more than hold our own in the top flight and I was looking forward to once again playing at top grounds such as Old Trafford, Highbury and Roker Park. That didn't mean that I felt we should start with the same side, and when Joe Harvey asked me who I felt we should sign my reply was instantaneous: 'Davies and Lee from Bolton.' Joe did eventually sign Wyn but that wasn't until long after I had left the club.

He should have signed those two in 1965, although I know that he didn't have the biggest of transfer budgets. Francis Lee was an arrogant player. At the time he was a right winger but when he moved to centre-forward he became top class and went on to win all three major domestic trophies with Manchester City as well as a European Cup Winners' Cup winners medal in 1970.

We started the 1965–66 season by winning two and losing two of the first five. In our fourth match we earned our first victory, at The Hawthorns, which was especially satisfying. It was a week after we'd lost at home to West Brom, who had let it be known they felt we would be relegated!

The following match, at home to Northampton, was my first experience of substitutes in league matches. At the start of the season the Football League had decided to experiment by allowing replacements for injured players. There was little doubt that one of the main reasons a twelfth man was introduced had been the high number of injuries in FA Cup finals during the '50s and '60s. It was felt that the premier match of the season was being ruined, as most teams left with only ten fit men had crumpled to defeat.

Ollie Burton was Newcastle's first substitute and he replaced Trevor Hockey during the 2-0 win. Of course, nowadays teams have seven players on the bench – in my day there wouldn't even have been space for that many! – with three allowed as replacements. I still feel that the original rule of allowing substitutes only when a player is injured was the correct one but I can't see that being brought back.

I managed my first goal as we beat Burnley 3-2 at home, which left us fourteenth with eight points from nine games. Fifty-yard runs weren't my forte but with just twenty minutes remaining Dave Hilley passed the ball to me and from just over the halfway line I moved forward. The shock of seeing me running so far might have been why the Burnley defence preferred to back-pedal rather than try to take the ball off me. I just kept on running; I could see Gordon Harris shaping to tackle so I hit the ball from the edge of the area. It flew past Harry Thomson to make it 2-1. Dave made it 3-1 soon after and ours was a really happy dressing room at the end.

Seven games later, after we beat Burnley's near neighbours, Blackpool, at home we had accumulated fourteen points from sixteen matches. We might not have had the players to challenge the best but we could look to get into the top half of the table.

I was looking forward to the rest of the season. I was playing well, and had received praise from the press and the St James' Park crowd. I recognised that I had lost a little bit of pace but I was never the quickest so didn't feel this was holding me back from playing a full part.

So I didn't know what to say when, following defeat at Blackburn Rovers, we were in Joe's office as usual to discuss the match. Only this time he had news, saying he'd received an offer for me. It was from Middlesbrough. They wanted me to become first-team player-coach under ex-Sunderland and Derby legend Raich Carter. Trevor Hockey was also being moved on, signing for Birmingham City for £25,000, where he was later turned into a fierce, combative midfielder with long hair and a beard.

I didn't want to go to Ayresome Park, and it was a very sad day for me when I left Newcastle United in mid-November 1965 to sign for a fee of £11,500. My sudden departure meant I was also unable to say a big thank you to the Newcastle fans, who were great to me. So it was a great thrill the following season to return to St James'

Park for an FA Cup second replay between Middlesbrough and York City. It was estimated there were around 10,000 Newcastle fans in the crowd of just over 21,000. I was given a great reception before the match started.

I still go back to St James' Park now and then and any fans who recognise me are always very encouraging. I was very happy to see them make it back to the Premier League in 2010. Chris Hughton did a magnificent job in turning them around after such a disastrous relegation season. I am a big fan of Andy Carroll and reckon that with him in the side Newcastle can at least hold their own in the top flight.

I am proud to have played and captained the club and the Division Two champions medal is one of my most prized possessions. I still remain in close contact with a good number of players from that period, including Pop Robson and Frank Clark. It was a good period for me. Many of the team I played with went on to win the Inter-Cities Fairs Cup by beating the Hungarian side Ujpesti Dozsa over two legs in 1969 and naturally I was thrilled for them.

It might seem a strange ending a chapter on Newcastle United with a mention of Colin Bell, a man rated by many as Manchester City's finest ever player. However, he could so easily have played for Newcastle.

Not long after I signed I was asked back to Horden to present medals to local league players. I got into conversation with a committee member and he was adamant that one of the younger players had it in him to become a professional at the highest level. His name was Colin Bell. I had never seen him play but I let Joe Harvey know and he promised he would get someone to look at him. A few weeks later I asked what the report was like and was told he was a decent player but wasn't what the club was after.

It was hardly any time at all before Colin signed for Bury, making his debut at Maine Road against Manchester City aged sixteen. He scored, and when he moved to Maine Road three years later he was the pivot around which Joe Mercer and Malcolm Allison built a side that went on to win all three domestic trophies and the now defunct European Cup Winners' Cup. He also won forty-eight England caps before injury cut short his career. Colin Bell was my sort of player, constantly wanting the ball, rarely ruffled and using it to open up defences. Francis Lee was just one of those to benefit from his talents. And to think Newcastle could have had him for nothing!

Chapter 13

Dropping down

When Joe Harvey said that Middlesbrough had made an offer for me I was more than convinced I could continue to play First Division football for at least another eighteen months. But Joe said that I should consider it very carefully because the deal involved me going as a player-coach. 'Boro were also offering to match my wages at St James' Park, so there were no problems financially.

What I wanted to know, however, from Joe was whether he really wanted me to stay and I asked him a number of times. But I never did get an answer and I felt that the very least I should do was go home and consider the chance to get involved with Middlesbrough. There was an added bonus, I thought, in that they were managed by one of the game's greatest footballers, Raich Carter.

I'd always been interested in the coaching side of the game, and Alan Brown had encouraged me to take an FA coaching badge during the 1962–63 season. This consisted of a week at the FA school at Lilleshall under the direction of George Ainsley, later to become manager at Workington. George was a good communicator and I enjoyed the schooling I received from him, although I felt too much emphasis was placed on written aspects of the course, culminating in exams at the end. I felt this gave an advantage to the many teachers involved but downplayed the skills of professional footballers who could show young people how to trap and pass the ball.

On my return to the north-east I completed the certificate over the following three weeks by running a series of sessions at Hartlepool schools. The experience had whetted my appetite for staying in the game after I finished playing. At the same time I was also a firm believer that playing and coaching didn't go together.

Sitting at home mulling over the offer I thought that I could learn a lot from Raich Carter. I'd never played against him but had seen him play as a young lad in October 1948 in a Third Division North match at the Victoria Ground, Hartlepool, when he was player-manager at Hull City. Although I was only fourteen I could see he had been a cracking player and even though he was thirty-five and did hardly any running he dictated the pace of the game. All Hull's moves went through or were set up by him.

I particularly remember when the Tigers got a free kick just outside the box. He wandered to a couple of yards away from the ball and began pointing at the various Hull players to go 'over there' and 'over there'. This went on for a while and the crowd started telling him to 'get on with it'. Suddenly he moved forward the two yards and curled a shot over the bewildered Hartlepool defensive wall and past an off-guard 'keeper for a fine goal. He'd kidded everyone. Hull won 2-0 and went on to secure promotion.

Everyone who'd seen Raich Carter play said he was brilliant. He'd won the League and Cup as Sunderland's captain in the 1930s and later the FA Cup with Derby. And, in a career truncated by the war, he'd played thirteen times for England. He'd been manager at Hull City and Leeds United before taking over at Middlesbrough in 1963. I was certain his experience would be invaluable if I was to become a coach. I had to agree with Joe that it was a good opportunity, although I was aware that the Ayresome Park side weren't exactly setting the Second Division alight that season, having lost 5-0 at Derby the previous Saturday, and faced a struggle to stay up.

Middlesbrough also had Harold Shepherdson, the England coach, as Carter's assistant. Surely two such experienced football men could teach me a lot. So the more I thought about it the greater the appeal. I was persuaded I should sign, knowing that I would be only the second player after Tommy Urwin between the wars to play for all three north-eastern clubs. As I was also made captain, taking over from Ian Gibson, I became the first, and so far only, player to captain all three. Alan Foggon later became the third, and to date only other player, to play for the north-east's big three. I'd be very surprised if anyone is ever the fourth, although players these days do play for a lot more clubs than back in my day.

So I met Raich Carter, Eric Thomas, the 'Boro chairman and Eric Varley, another director, to accept their offer to become player-coach. That was on the Thursday and the following day I turned up for training and went straight in to see 'The Boss'. I asked him what he wanted me to do. His reply was a shock. 'Just do what you think is right,' he said.

I thought it might be a trick to see how I'd make out, but I went to see Harold and told him that as I was due to play the following day I thought he should take the training. Normally training on the Friday was very light. In those pre-Premiership and Sky Sports times every match kicked off on Saturday at 3pm, although some clubs were allowed to start at 3.15 pm. The aim was to keep muscles supple and the heart moving while avoiding doing anything too strenuous in order to preserve the players' energy for the match. I was amazed when all the players, including me, were put through a fierce training session that involved a lot of running.

I didn't say much. I couldn't; I hadn't even had time to properly introduce myself to the players and while I knew Dickie Rooks, who had joined 'Boro from Sunderland in August 1965, and one or two others to say hello to, I didn't know them well enough to strike up a conversation. However, when I found myself resting next to Gordon

Dropping down

Jones I had to ask him whether this was normal for a Friday. If it was then I wasn't surprised that 'Boro weren't doing that well.

'Not really, I think that was for your benefit,' he said. Needless to say, when I started organising the training, we didn't repeat that particular exercise.

My first match was at home to Jimmy Scoular's Cardiff City, who were two points and six places higher than us in twelfth. The team was at sixes-and-sevens and although I managed to score the game was already lost and finished 4-3. It was of no consolation to hear that Newcastle had also lost, 5-1 at home against Leicester City.

I thought after the display against Cardiff that the manager would be the first one out at training in his tracksuit but Raich was not like that. He stayed mainly in his office, which was, oddly I felt, decorated with pictures of him from his playing days. It was as if he was saying 'Look, I was a good player so I know what I'm doing.'

Raich left me to organise the training and I tried my best to get things going, to encourage the players and convince them that together we could pull away from the relegation zone. But after a few days I had the distinct feeling that some of them had given up on the season.

When I at last got up the courage to speak openly with Raich Carter I explained to him that, although the players were prepared to listen to me, it was the manager they wanted to hear from. 'I'll think about it,' he said, making clear that was the end of the conversation.

He did not even watch the players train. His attitude seemed to be that if you could play then you could play, but if you couldn't then you couldn't and no amount of training or coaching could do anything about it.

He would say something to the team before games but it was not exactly heart-warming material. Once we were playing at Norwich and we'd gone by coach.

'That was a great trip,' he said. 'Notice how good the coach driver was; how he kept the coach on the road and drove smoothly. Now that's the way I want you to play.'

He remained an aloof character and I didn't know him any better at the end of our short spell working together than I did at the start.

Performances were poor. When we lost to Huddersfield at home in early February we were only just outside the relegation zone and, under pressure from a disgruntled crowd, the directors sacked Raich.

Harold and I were asked to take control and we agreed to work together. In his office I told Harold that as the older, more experienced man he should be in overall charge but he quickly made clear he didn't want the responsibility. We always got on well but Harold was content to take a back seat, which surprised me.

What also took me aback was the reaction of a couple of the players, who shall remain anonymous, who made it blatantly clear to me that they did not want to play for the first team. These same players had listened to Eric Thomas appeal for one hundred per cent effort but told me they didn't want to play and there was nothing I could do about it. I couldn't afford to waste time dealing with them as I needed to spend every bit of energy trying to keep the club in Division Two – although I made up my mind that they would not be getting new contracts come the season's end.

There were sixteen games left and we were in the relegation zone, twentieth and two points above Charlton Athletic. Ten of the games were away, giving a lopsided and difficult end to the season, especially as 'Boro had not won away that season.

As we had failed to score many goals I pushed Dickie Rooks up from centre-half to centre-forward for my first game, away to Crystal Palace. Dickie always gave his all and he had a decent match. Jim Irvine's goal ensured we returned north with a valuable point.

Dropping down

We captured all the points on offer from two home games with Preston North End and Bristol City. At half-time against Bristol we were three ahead, but two goals by John Atyeo, arguably the best player ever to represent the club, threatened to undo all our hard work. However, Dickie Rooks rose to flash a header past Mike Gibson to ensure we ran off 4-2 winners. Despite the result we were by no means safe, especially with four of the next five away. When we lost the first three, as well as the home game against Plymouth Argyle, we were back in the bottom three, one place above the relegation zone. Jim Irvine gave us the lead at The Dell but three goals in the second half saw Southampton win 3-1.

There was relief when a seventy-fifth-minute winner by Bobby Braithwaite gave us a three-point gap over our defeated opponents Bury. We were slaughtered at Burnden Park – Bolton winning 6-0 – but in our next game we won for the first time away from Ayresome Park. Orient were bottom and only 2,286 witnessed a close game in which two Irvine goals and a Rooks penalty saw us scrape home 3-2.

Our fourth-to-last game of the season was at home to Carlisle United and injury meant it turned out to be my last game as a player. We lost 2-0, so only a last-minute surge could have kept us up. We managed to beat Norwich City but after losing away to Coventry we knew that even if we won at Cardiff they could still leapfrog above us as they had a game in hand. It didn't matter because we lost 5-3 at Ninian Park, despite Dickie Rooks scoring a hat-trick.

It meant Middlesbrough and I were relegated for the first time ever to Division Three. Six short months before I had been running out at Old Trafford and Anfield; now I was facing the prospect of games at Feethams and Borough Park against Darlington and Workington. To make matters worse I was at least partly responsible.

Naturally the supporters weren't happy and there was widespread condemnation of the board, with the local press going as far as printing their photographs under the banner headline of 'The Guilty Men'. It led Eric Thomas to remark that they looked like the great train robbers – Ronnie Biggs et al. It wasn't pleasant and the directors didn't like it.

Middlesbrough supporters can be a hard lot to please and to be sure they have had to put up with a lot over the years. Their club has always been classed in the papers as the third team in the north-east behind Sunderland and Newcastle, and with this relegation they would become the fourth if they finished below Darlington the following season.

Just before the end of the season Eric Thomas asked if I was prepared to take the manager's job permanently. I agreed and Harold Shepherdson became assistant manager with full control of scouting. As I didn't believe in combining playing with managing I decided to retire. It was a hard choice. It's an odd manager who doesn't think that playing is better than managing. I loved playing and felt that I could have done a good job in the Third Division but I didn't want to find myself having a go at players after a defeat with the danger of them thinking 'What's he talking about, he played worse than me.'

Gordon Jones was designated to take over as captain and I knew I could depend on the former England Under-23 international to turn in consistently good performances. For a full back Gordon had a beautiful left foot and rarely misplaced a pass. His experience would also be invaluable in the new team I intended building.

My next task was to make out a retained list and I let sixteen players go in the summer. They included some I really liked as people but in football management there's little room for sentiment. Your job depends on putting out your best side to win matches. Good people don't count on a football field; good players do. So I had to be ruthless.

Dropping down

That summer saw England win the World Cup. Like all other Englishmen I was delighted, especially as under Alf Ramsey England had come a long way since I had sat and watched Brazil tear us apart in Chile four years before.

I didn't manage to get a ticket for the final but I was at Ayresome Park when North Korea beat Italy 1-0 in a group game. Virtually all the 'Boro fans were rooting for Korea. Many of their players seemed no bigger than schoolboys, but they ran and chased the Italians and never gave them time to settle. The Italians, one of the favourites, just didn't know what to do and they got more and more frustrated as they found it impossible to score the opening goal.

When Korea scored the only goal through Pak Doo Ik the ground erupted, and did so again when the final whistle sounded. Italian agent Gigi Peronace simply couldn't believe that Italy had lost.

In the quarter-finals North Korea even went as far as leading Portugal 3-0 before one of the players of the 1960s, Eusebio, scored four times in a 5-3 victory. That set up a semi-final with England, and although the Portuguese striker scored his eighth goal of nine in the tournament to finish as its top scorer, it was Bobby Charlton who was the star, scoring twice from the central midfield position he should have occupied in Chile. Bobby Charlton, Bobby Moore and Eusebio were the stars of the competition.

Chapter 14

Going up with the 'Boro

During the summer of 1966 I was trying very hard to sign players but we suffered a blow when Ian Gibson made it apparent that he did not want to play in the Third Division and Coventry City paid £60,000 for his services.

It meant that we were short of experienced players, and although that didn't seem to matter when the season kicked off with a 3-2 win against Colchester United at Layer Road we were soon in trouble. We lost four and drew just one of the next five. We were second bottom but I was cheered when John Hickton agreed to join us from Sheffield Wednesday.

My old sparring partner Alan Brown had taken them to the FA Cup final the previous season and told me that John could play in a number of positions. So I felt the £20,000 fee would be a worthwhile investment. It turned out to be the best £20,000 any manager could have spent, as any 'Boro fan from that period would surely agree.

John's first match, at home to Workington, started badly when we went two goals down. Luckily, just before half-time we were awarded a penalty and John, playing full back, struck it home neatly. After the break we somehow managed to scrape home to win 3-2 courtesy of two Arthur Horsfield goals.

I was quickly learning the pressures involved in management. You always stress to players that the first five or ten minutes of any game are the most important – even the very best teams find it difficult to recover if they start a game poorly. You want a good, quick pace and for your players to get at the other team, whoever they are. Before one match, against Gillingham, I had urged the players to get off to a good start as they ran out of the dressing room.

As there were a few minutes before kick-off Jimmy Headridge, the physiotherapist, asked if I wanted a quick cup of tea. When I finished it two minutes later we set off for the touchline. What I didn't know was that this meant a walk along the back of the stand to the far end before going out of the tunnel on to the side of the pitch and then back along to the dugout. When we were halfway down the back of the stand there was huge roar – Gillingham had obviously opened the scoring. I couldn't believe it. One-nil down already. Jim and I were cursing our luck when, less than thirty seconds later, as we turned to see the pitch for the first time, another roar went up. Gillingham had scored their second. We were 2-0 down in the first couple of minutes and I hadn't even seen the goals! We lost 5-1.

Thankfully, I was boosted shortly after by being able to persuade Airdrie's goalkeeper Willie Whigham to join us. He was to play a big part in the club's climb back and he might have given Jim Platt a more challenging time for the 'keeper's jersey later on if he hadn't been such a big drinker. One of Willie's sessions sticks in my mind. We'd played AS Roma away in the Anglo-Italian Cup in the summer of 1970. Willie's drinking partner, Hugh McIlmoyle, had been given permission to miss the second game away to Lanerossi Vicenza a week later to fly home because his marriage was in trouble, and before he went he and Willie got totally wrecked. When Jimmy Greenhalgh went to wake Willie he had no luck. Hours later he finally managed to rouse himself and I told him to put on his training gear. Jimmy and I worked him as hard as any player I've been associated with. To his credit he never said a word and when we played Lanerossi Vicenza he had an excellent game. He was particularly skilled in getting down to save shots and he was a great handler of the ball.

The previous season Willie had flattened Jimmy with a 'Scots kiss'. I wasn't bothered about the reasons; football is a passionate game and people fall out all the time. Sometimes there's violence involved. I told Willie he had to apologise, he refused and so I dropped him for the game at Blackpool. His deputy, Maurice Short, was a seventeen-year-old who benefited by making his debut in a 1-1 draw. Willie played the rest of the games that season. He was never fazed by who we were playing and sometimes in the days leading up to the game didn't even know who we faced.

'Who are we playing on Saturday?'

'Bury.'

'Oh great, where at?'

A few weeks later.

'Who are we playing on Saturday?'

'Manchester United in the FA Cup.'

'Oh great, where at?'

Once, at Norwich, Willie made a sprawling save from the ex-Newcastle man Albert Bennett, whose momentum was such that he stopped just in front of Willie. Next thing I know our 'keeper is chasing Albert across the pitch and I have no idea why. Willie and running were never suited so Albert had no problems keeping his distance before the referee's whistle brought Willie to his senses.

Gordon Jones ran over to explain that the Norwich man had looked down at Willie after he made the save and said, 'You must be the ugliest 'keeper I have ever seen.' Albert was lucky Willie didn't catch him as he would not have looked a pretty sight himself afterwards.

In 1966 we were having problems scoring goals. The possible solution occurred to me after watching John Hickton enjoying himself smashing them home in training. I toyed with the idea of playing him up front. I was reluctant to move him forward because he had settled down well in defence. But as our form improved and we had more of the ball it was difficult not to notice how he was forever moving forward to join in attacks, and I knew he'd occasionally played in attack for Sheffield Wednesday.

So I decided to push John alongside John O'Rourke, whom I'd bought from Luton Town. I didn't bother changing his shirt number and he played with number two on his back. I doubt any number two has scored as many goals in a season! Whether his number confused defences I don't know, but turning him into a centre-forward certainly worked for us.

We started on a decent run, winning four from five, including a 5-4 victory at Mansfield. Afterwards their manager Bill McKinney, the ex-Newcastle player, joked that defences were on top. This was followed in the next away game by a 4-4 draw against Swansea Town. Fancy conceding eight goals in two games and not losing either! We moved slowly up the table, beating Darlington away and at home over Christmas by 3-0 and 4-0 respectively. The first game attracted one of Feethams' largest crowds ever – 18,144 – and I particularly remember the dressing room as it had a big stove in the middle. This must have been a thing among the lower league clubs in the north-east as Hartlepools also had one. Great on a cold day but not so good in hot weather.

Alec Stock's Queens Park Rangers, who thrilled everyone in football that season when they won the first League Cup final to be staged at Wembley after Rodney Marsh inspired them from 2-0 down to beat West Brom 3-2, were a long way out in front and they went on to win the league by twelve points, losing only five games all season.

However, Watford and others, including Reading, were dropping points and we just hung on in there. I kept telling the players to believe in themselves and that certainly paid off against Shrewsbury Town when John Hickton grabbed the winner with less than two minutes remaining. The crowds were also increasing and confidence was growing that we could perhaps sneak up.

However, after we lost three in a row over Easter, even I thought we'd be playing at least one more season in the Third – although I consoled myself with the knowledge that with a full pre-season training behind me and a team of my own players we'd go up the following year.

In the penultimate match of a season that started late because of the World Cup and ended in mid-May we were up against Peterborough United. More than 32,000 were in Ayresome Park. We were sixth before kick-off and had to win. In the first half we hit the woodwork three times and in my anxiety I must have smoked two full packets of cigarettes.

John Hickton put us in the lead after sixty-two minutes but Peterborough scored a quick equaliser and I felt that we might blow it. But we didn't and the winner was a great goal – Eric McMordie slipped the ball beyond their defence and with three defenders closing in John Hickton hit a shot that Tony Millington could never have saved.

When the players ran off we were a point behind second-placed Watford with a game in hand. Their 1-1 draw at Oldham had finished their season and presented us with an opportunity. Watford had a better goal average – just 0.0089 of a goal – so we had to win our last game. Standing in our way were Oxford United. Nearly 40,000 crammed into the ground, with another 10,000 turned away. On twenty-nine minutes the anxiety was lifted when John O'Rourke headed home David Chadwick's corner. Fourteen minutes later, in a repeat, it was 2-0 and when John Hickton headed in another Chadwick cross ten minutes into the second half I knew we were up. John O'Rourke got his hat-trick and we won 4-1. The crowd invaded the pitch at the end and the scenes were amazing. Within hours I had received a telegram from the

Watford manager Ken Furphy congratulating us. Despite his obvious disappointment he was gracious enough to say: 'I think 'Boro have deserved promotion after such a disastrous start to the season.'

In a complete reversal of the previous season the *Middlesbrough Gazette* printed a picture of the directors with a banner headline congratulating them on their efforts!

Whenever I go back to the 'Boro there is always someone who will come up to me and say that 1966–67 was one of the most exciting seasons for them. They may be just being nice now that 'Boro have played in the Premiership, at Wembley and Cardiff in the League Cup final and in Europe, but I understand their feelings. I will always be grateful to the players of that team, the vast majority of whom could play the ball.

As a manager my philosophy was 'pass and move' and I always had the players working with the ball in training. What I tried to instil in them was that once they'd won or received the ball they needed to keep it. It was about making yourself available and being able to control the ball when you got it. Even today I get frustrated watching British players who haven't mastered the ability to control the ball. I still think that players from Europe have better control than those brought up here. It frustrates the hell out of me.

At Middlesbrough my philosophy was helped enormously by our groundsman Wilf Atkinson, who treated the pitch as if it was his own lawn and produced a fabulous surface on which to play. When we were in the Second Division there were a couple of occasions when we lost only once at home in a season, and one of them was the final match when there was little to play for.

Chapter 15

Missing out on the promised land

There was, of course, still a big job to do at Ayresome Park. We had the basis of a good side with Willie Whigham in goal, Gordon Jones at the back, David Chadwick and Derek Downing on the wings and up front a powerful strike force of John Hickton and John O'Rourke.

I signed my ex-Sunderland teammate Johnny Crossan at start of 1967–68. He'd done a fine job in helping Manchester City to promotion to Division One and then to establish themselves there. I was hoping he might be able to do the same for me. I spent a lot of money on him but it didn't work out.

I also had high hopes for Don Masson, but he wanted to play up front whereas I saw him as a midfield player. No matter how hard I tried to persuade Don he wouldn't listen – as a youngster he was very aggressive on and off the field. He didn't have the pace to play at inside forward but he did have the vision to see the game from halfback and to influence it because he was a tremendous passer of the ball. I l left him out and Jimmy Sirrell, the Notts County manager, rang with an offer of £3,000. I said he'd have to come up with another £4,000 and when he agreed I told Don that it was up him. I was keen to keep him and, looking back, I should have. It would have meant being a bit harder on him, insisting he play midfield. Letting him go was the worst mistake I made as a manager.

I have heard it said that I was too soft to be a manager. It was later suggested that my successor at Middlesbrough, Jack Charlton, got more out of the players by being much harder with them. That might well be true, but we all have our different styles and I think it's fair to say that Jack's style was much more defensive than mine. It's a beautiful game, football, when played properly and I didn't want to intimidate players. I needed them to use their skills to express themselves. Clearly such an approach didn't fully work out for me at Middlesbrough, but I don't regret trying to get the side to play the way I like to see football played.

Far too much English football in the '70s and through the years has revolved around the long-ball game; which is why I love watching Arsenal play these days. While the current side are not as good as the invincibles of 2003–04, when they went through the season unbeaten, I love to see them get the ball down and pass it from one end of the field to the other.

Don Masson decided to take up Jimmy Sirrell's offer and while I don't know what changed, he settled down eventually to play in midfield where he had a great career, earning international honours with Scotland. I still see Don and we laugh about what happened.

Geoff Butler was also an up-and-coming right back, but after we had beaten Chelsea in the League Cup at the start of the 1967–68 season their manager Tommy Docherty asked if he was available.

I was duty bound to put the request to the board and although Eric Thomas knew I wanted to keep Geoff, the club needed the money. In such situations the game is to ask for a fee you think the other club will be unwilling to pay, in the hope that they'll settle for paying a bit more than you actually think the player's really worth. Geoff was a young lad with no First Division experience and so I told Tommy that the fee was £60,000.

'OK, Stan it's a deal,' he said.

'Oh, really, that's great,' I said, cursing that I hadn't asked for more but not daring to then of course! I was sad to see Geoff go, but it was a good move for him.

The situation with John O'Rourke was different, however. I left him out, feeling that he hadn't made the jump in standard needed to play in a higher league. It wasn't that he wasn't working hard in training or playing his heart out on the pitch. I just felt I needed to get someone else in to play alongside John Hickton, by now wearing the number nine shirt. Ipswich Town made an offer and I let John go. Local lad Arthur Horsfield came into the side and did fine.

I thought we did well enough in the first season back in the Second Division. We didn't win until the eighth game but later, when we beat Carlisle United 4-0 just before Christmas, any doubts that we could hold our own had been dispelled as we leapt into eighth.

In the second half of the season we maintained our form and performances, finishing in some style by winning six and losing only one of the last nine. This gave me the confidence to believe we could push for promotion to Division One in 1968–69.

Over the summer I made a few enquiries about players but couldn't get the ones I wanted. They included Carlisle's Hugh McIlmoyle, because I was convinced he and John Hickton would be effective together up front. When I did manage to sign Hugh halfway through the following season he proved a very complex character who always had problems off the field. On it he was superb in the air, held the ball up well and was very cool in front of goal. Although he had a good career I think he underachieved.

At the start of the season Brian Clough pulled a masterstroke by managing to persuade Dave Mackay to move from Spurs to Derby County, where he was immediately installed as captain. Not surprisingly, with such a classy as well as combative player in their side Derby started the season in good form. But we did, too, and when the teams drew 0-0 at Ayresome Park in October we stayed in second place, two places above them. We were still second even when they came from behind to beat us 3-2 at the Baseball Ground on Boxing Day. We had played more times away than at home after twenty-five matches – fourteen against eleven – and things were stacked on our side. With six of our next eight at home we grabbed thirteen points in an unbeaten run to consolidate our second place at the start of March.

John Hickton hit four in our next home game, a 5-3 win against Hull City, and with seven games left it was now a three-way fight between Crystal Palace, Cardiff City and us to finish second. Derby County had established a four-point lead at the top and were favourites to be champions. We still had to meet Palace and Cardiff so our fate was in our own hands.

We shared the points at Blackburn before drawing 0-0 at Ayresome Park against Cardiff. This left us third, level on points with our next opponents, Palace, who had a game in hand. There were nearly 44,000 at Selhurst Park for the Good Friday fixture and the match was a no-holds-barred contest with few thrills. It also ended goalless. The following day we travelled the short distance to The Valley to play fifth-placed Charlton Athletic. It was always going to be a difficult fixture; they had lost only once at home in the league that season and still had an outside chance of going up. We were two down at half-time and in the second period never looked like getting back into the game. With Palace winning we left London as outsiders, having played a game more and with two fewer points.

Over the next few days I contemplated making wholesale changes. We hadn't scored in three games but in the end the only alteration I decided on for the match against Norwich was Johnny Crossan for Derek Downing. That game also ended 0-0, and although Palace couldn't score either at Huddersfield, they now had a two-point lead with three games to play against our two. To make matters worse they also had a better goal average.

In the circumstances it was no surprise that our last home game attracted the lowest Ayresome Park crowd of the season – just 10,417. The opposition, Bury, were in the relegation zone but we lost for the first time at home that season, going down 3-2. With Palace drawing 0-0 at Preston it meant the South Londoners would play in the First Division for the first time. Brian Clough's Derby were runaway leaders.

We finished fourth. Even now there's nothing I can put my finger on to explain why we didn't go up. The players and I just got a little bit frustrated; we tried to remain calm but it's very difficult. Towards the end we weren't creating or scoring enough goals. Then the crowd gets frustrated, they take it out on the players and it becomes even more difficult. Pressure can do different things to people.

We finished fourth again in 1969–70. We started slowly and at the beginning of October were fourteenth. I finally managed to sign Hugh McIlmoyle and his arrival gave the side a big boost. He and John Hickton each notched a couple in a 4-0 romp at home to Bolton Wanderers, a game which marked the start of a ten-match unbeaten run which included eight victories and carried us to within four points of second-placed Sheffield United.

In January we went to Upton Park and beat West Ham 2-1 in the third round of the FA Cup, with Hugh McIlmoyle opening the scoring and Derek Downing hitting the winner with just eight minutes remaining. Derek was a great player to work with; he had tremendous enthusiasm and a beaming smile. He worked extremely hard in training, hardly ever complained and could be expected to chip in with a good number of goals from his outside left position.

Missing out on the promised land

At the end of the month we moved within three points of second place after beating QPR courtesy of another goal from Downing. The following week, by beating York in the fifth round of the FA Cup, with another late winner from Derek, we found ourselves just 180 minutes away from Wembley. Our quarter-final opponents, before a 40,000 Ayresome Park crowd, were Manchester United. John Hickton scored but Carlo Sartori equalised and the game finished 1-1, although we really should have won. In the replay four days later John's goal was not enough to prevent our exit from the competition. Goals from Willie Morgan and Bobby Charlton meant United won 2-1 in front of 63,418, of which 15,000 were from Middlesbrough.

In mid-March we welcomed second-placed Sheffield United to Ayresome Park and when John hit a late winner we were third, just a single point behind them.

After we snatched another late goal, this time through Eric McMordie, to give us victory at Watford on Good Friday, we travelled north to face Hull City at Boothferry Park the following day in second place with just five matches to play. Huddersfield Town were well in front at the top and as the teams below us had games in hand we knew we had to keep on winning.

Joe Laidlaw scored our first and John Hickton managed another but we were defeated 3-2 and Blackpool went above us. We really needed to beat Huddersfield at home on Easter Tuesday. John scored again but the match ended disappointingly in a 1-1 draw. We did beat fifth-placed Cardiff City 2-1 to leave ourselves with a slight chance but Blackpool were two points ahead with three games to play and had a game in hand. Defeat at already relegated Aston Villa put paid to our hopes. It was another case of so near, yet so far.

John finished as the division's top scorer for the second year running, matching his total of twenty-four of the previous season. He repeated the feat the next season, ending up level with Luton Town's Malcolm Macdonald. John was particularly brilliant at taking penalties. He'd blast one, then place the next one in the right corner and the one after that in the left. He had such a low backlift before he struck the ball that no 'keeper could possibly judge in which direction he was going to send the kick.

Our form in 1970–71 wasn't nearly as impressive as the two previous campaigns. We did beat QPR 6–2 early on, with Hugh McIlmoyle playing his best game for me, scoring twice and helping John Hickton to a hat-trick. I also had the personal pleasure of returning as a manager to Roker Park on Boxing Day, where I was given a great reception before what turned out to be a thrilling 2-2 draw. I had been slightly worried about how the fans would react as in October a newspaper had misquoted me about Sunderland.

After the midweek game at Carlisle – we were beaten 1-0 – the *Mirror's* Charlie Summerbell had pointed out that the hosts were due to play Sunderland on the Saturday. I said jokingly: 'They'll beat them as well.' I never expected to see this in the paper but it was on the back page the following day in bold type saying 'Carlisle will murder Sunderland.'

I received a letter from my ex-boss Alan Brown, who had returned to the club, and after Sunderland drew with Carlisle the captain Colin Todd attacked me verbally, drawing further headlines. When I next saw Charlie Summerbell I told him I would never give him a quote again. Over my years in the game I'd always had a good relationship with members of the press. I never prevented any of the players I managed from speaking to reporters, provided they didn't openly criticise their teammates or coaching staff.

When I was with Sunderland and travelling to away games by coach or train I'd often play a bridge foursome which included the *Sunderland Echo's* Billy Butterfield, who was popularly known by his byline of 'Argus', and naturally we'd chat about all things football. None of these conversations would appear in his paper.

I was extremely angry at what Charlie Summerbell had done and I never did give him another quote.

I'd be a liar if I said I didn't always harbour an ambition to manage Sunderland, where I played for twelve fabulous years. At various times in my career I'd hear rumours that they were thinking of asking me to manage them but nothing ever materialised, although in January 1968, in the days leading up to the sacking of Ian McColl, I found myself indirectly caught up in events behind the scenes.

A well-known Sheffield journalist rang to ask if was interested in the Sheffield Wednesday job. Wednesday were in the First Division and the manager was none other than Alan Brown. I said I was more than happy at Middlesbrough. A few days later McColl was sacked and Brown went back as manager to Roker Park. I have no doubt that the telephone call was made on behalf of the board at Hillsborough.

One of the highlights of my time as a 'Boro manager came ten days after our draw at Roker Park – we put Manchester United out of the FA Cup. We drew 0-0 at Old Trafford and then, despite a goal from George Best, won 2-1 at Ayresome Park. Unfortunately we lost 3-0 at Everton in the next round, but that didn't take away from the United result. Matt Busby said he couldn't believe we were a Division Two side. I told him it wasn't that easy to get up to Division One, and at the end of the season we finished in a disappointing sixth with Leicester City and Sheffield United at the top.

With hindsight I should have moved on then. I'd had four attempts at gaining promotion to the top flight and the last had been the worst. Jack Charlton, who followed me at the start of the 1973–74 season, stayed only four years and when I asked him why he was quite forthright. He said that after four years it gets too friendly and that it's always best to keep things on a professional rather than personal level.

I can see what he meant. After a time you find the directors, most of whom are fans of the club, starting to share their thoughts with you. After a while they start to share with you the thoughts of people they've spoken to! On a couple of occasions I told them that if their confidant knew so much about football why not ask him to manage the side.

I also started receiving telephone calls from players' wives. Now I might be many things but a marriage guidance counsellor I am certainly not. I have to say I was not that happy about getting such calls.

Neither was I ever happy to receive a call from one of the club's landladies. Not that I ever had any complaints about the job they did in looking after the apprentices. So when I did get a call it was generally to report that one or two youngsters had been up to something. Usually this involved staying out late and returning home the worse for beer. It can be difficult for any young person who moves away from home to settle down, and many have found it difficult. George Best returned to Belfast suffering from homesickness and had to be persuaded to return to Manchester. Being an apprentice footballer is especially difficult; it requires real discipline to miss out on the usual pleasures of being young. But if a young player wants to make it in the game it's vital they get a good night's sleep, drink modestly and put one hundred per cent effort into their training. If they don't, especially these days, they won't make it and they will have wasted their talent. To become a professional footballer means making real sacrifices at a young age, something fans occasionally forget.

We were, in truth, never in with a chance of winning promotion in 1971–72 although we played well at home, winning sixteen, drawing four and losing just one. One victory was against Sunderland, when John Hickton scored twice in a 2-0 win. Away it was a different story and we won only three and lost fourteen, including getting well beaten 4-1 at Roker Park. Despite our impressive home record the crowds, as you'd expect, fell away and there were fewer than 10,000 for the final match against Hull City, which we won comfortably 3-0, including a goal from a young David Mills.

Coincidentally we were again drawn against Manchester United in the FA Cup and again we drew 0-0 at Old Trafford. But this time they beat us heavily in the replay 3-0. In our side was the England World Cup winner Nobby Stiles, part of the fabulous Manchester United team that won the European Cup in 1968.

I had bought Nobby at the start of the season along with Johnny Vincent from Birmingham City. I hoped Nobby would bring more strength to the midfield while Vincent would add additional flair and grab a few goals on top. It didn't work out – Nobby was a loveable character, he still is, and was fantastic in the dressing room but I had to tell him constantly that his job was to win the ball and supply passes to the front men.

He took too much on to himself and desperately wanted success but as a result he was overdoing the things he was good at. I think he got too angry with himself and this did not help him. He was a super player to have at the club; I just wish we could have done better.

Vincent was a class player who never really reached the heights of the game. He didn't work hard enough and he faded out of football far too early. The Ayresome Park crowd warmed to him, though, and when I took him off just after half-time during the game with Cardiff in September 1971 they booed his replacement, Eric McMordie.

I would be constantly urging John to make space for himself to receive the ball; once he had it then he could do real damage. I'd try to persuade him to work harder and then I'd try to motivate him by getting angry with him. But all he would ever say was 'Yes, boss.' After a while I just had to realise enough was enough and move him on. You can motivate some players by persuasion; others by annoying them. With John I have no idea what, if anything, motivated him.

I bought John Craggs from Newcastle United and he was a very solid right back performer who very rarely had a poor game. The £60,000 I spent on him was a bargain and he went on to make more than 400 first-team appearances for Middlesbrough.

Stuart Boam was purchased from Mansfield Town for £50,000. We'd been on the lookout for a centre-half for some time when I saw him play for the Stags and was immediately impressed. Bill Gates was moved from number five to partner him in the middle of the back four. Willie Maddren was playing at centre-forward at the start of the 1971–72 season and had a fine game at The Valley when he scored both goals in a 2-0 win. Early in his career, when he was in the reserves, I'd seen enough to know he was going to be a good player so I was surprised when Harold Shepherdson told me Willie was playing terribly and couldn't even pass the ball accurately.

I asked Willie to come and see me. It was a while before he told me he had a bad knee and when I looked it was swollen. He'd worried about telling anyone. We sent him for an operation and although he always had a bit of trouble with it it was not enough to stop him doing well and he and Stuart eventually formed a formidable partnership at the back.

Willie was bit like Bobby Moore in that he was a very good reader of the game and made up for a lack of pace with his positional sense. He was also a powerful header of the ball and would probably have scored more goals from corners or attacking free kicks except that Stuart was more of a threat and consequently was the one who went forward for set pieces.

The young striker David Mills was starting to show real promise that season and he worked extremely hard in training to improve his game. His work rate on the pitch was fantastic; he would run all day and never give up, no matter what the scoreline was. He also had a more than decent goal-scoring record, but despite this he lacked composure in front of goal and it was this that prevented him becoming a really top-class striker. I used to tell him to take a leaf out of Hugh McIlmoyle's book – well, on the pitch at least. Hugh scored a good number of the chances he got.

'Just take your time in front of goal, calm down and take your time,' I'd say to David. He would listen, he'd do his best to do as he was told but it just didn't work. Despite this he had a very good career and in 1979 Ron Atkinson paid a British record fee of £500,000 to take him to West Bromwich Albion.

The 1972–73 season was to prove to be my last at 'Boro. I'd been in charge for seven years and it was long enough. We started the season by beating Sunderland at home 2-1 with Malcolm Smith grabbing both, and ironically that was the final north-east derby match for both Alan Brown at Sunderland and me at Middlesbrough. By the time of the next one I had quit, Alan had been sacked and Bob Stokoe was leading Sunderland's charge towards Wembley. In November we did rise to fifth in the table courtesy of a single John Hickton goal away at Preston North End. The previous weekend we had drawn 3-3 with leaders Burnley at Ayresome Park in a thrilling game, and if we had played as well in the other games we would have been up at the top of the league.

When we lost 2-1 in the first match of 1973 away to Fulham, a game in which Graeme Souness made his debut,

I knew it was time to quit. Only three games in twelve had been won and we were eleventh.

I was convinced that I wasn't motivating the players any longer and they needed someone else. I would have quit anyway but I had also taken a phone call from the Liverpool secretary Peter Robinson. He wondered if I knew anyone who might be interested in taking a job in Greece at a top club who wanted an English coach/manager. I promised to ask around and get back to him. I found myself thinking that it might be a good idea for me to take the post, and when I found out it was with AEK Athens I phoned Peter to arrange a meeting. After 'Boro crashed out of the FA Cup at Plymouth Argyle in a dire game I quit the manager's job and took charge at AEK.

I don't think my departure had too great an impact on the players. In fact by the season's end they had risen to fourth when Jack Charlton came in as manager and took them up as runaway champions the following season.

I don't blame anyone other than myself for the failure to get promotion to the First Division for Middlesbrough. Many observers said I left the club in a stronger position than when I went there, but I am still disappointed that we didn't go up.

Despite this I enjoyed my time there and I still manage to see quite a few of the players from that era. Most of them will have their own opinions of me as a manager, but I feel I treated them as fairly as I could and have no regrets on that score.

Nobody was more pleased than me when 'Boro gained promotion under Jack Charlton in 1974. Jack did a fantastic job; he's a man I've always liked and he was kind enough to say that I'd left him with a decent side. But no one should take away from him what a great job he did.

One bit of business I did in my final few weeks at Middlesbrough proved extremely valuable for the club. We had been looking for a strong midfield player for some time when we got news that a young Tottenham player by the name of Graeme Souness was looking for a move nearer to his native Scotland.

I duly despatched Harold Shepherdson and a director to a Tottenham reserve match, hoping that this youngster would fit the bill at Ayresome Park. It was therefore a bit of a surprise when Harold returned none too enthusiastic. However, I made a few enquiries and decided buying Graeme was a gamble well worth making. I rang Bill Nicholson, who I knew well from my playing days with the England Under-23s and the Football League, and was told the fee was £35,000. It was clear that Bill wanted to hang on to Graeme, but he understood the player's wishes and also his desire to play regular first-team football, which he couldn't guarantee at Tottenham.

At the next board meeting I told the directors what I wanted and the fee it would take. All I got was silence and it was only after the chairman asked if I was prepared to see if I could get the fee reduced that they even decided to discuss the situation.

One or two were keen to support me, but only on the understanding the fee was smaller. One director was adamant that it was a waste of money to spend even £25,000 on a Tottenham reserve player, but after a long and tedious meeting it was agreed I could approach Bill Nicholson to offer a smaller amount.

When I rang him the following day I asked him to consider £27,500. 'Christ, Stan, you'll get me sacked,' was all he could say but he agreed to ask his chairman. I wasn't too confident it would be enough but Bill, bless him, finally called back and said it was OK.

Souness turned out to be a gem of a player for Middlesbrough; not in my last few weeks as the manager before I left for Greece but over the next few seasons. First he helped the club to win promotion and then establish themselves in the top flight before he moved on to glory at

Liverpool, who signed him for £350,000. Not a bad return for a Tottenham reserve player, as I later pointed out to the director who had been the most vocal in opposition to buying him. By this time I was at Doncaster and attended a match at 'Boro. I heard the director was bragging to people about how much the club had made as if he'd been the person responsible. He wasn't too happy when I spoke up.

Before I agreed to join AEK Athens I was asked if I would be interested in the assistant manager's post at Southampton. I'd never before applied for any manager's job but was persuaded to put my name forward and I got a letter in return asking me to meet the directors.

After travelling to the interview the first man I spoke to was Ted Bates, who was looking to move upstairs after almost two decades in charge at The Dell, during which he'd taken the south coast side from the Third to the First Division and even into Europe.

Ted accompanied me to see the directors and I spent about an hour and a half in the boardroom answering questions, gaining the distinct impression that Ted thought I'd done enough to be offered the job.

'Well done, Stan, we have one more man to see before we make a decision,' he said.

'Who might that be?' I enquired.

'A chap called Lawrie McMenemy,' he said.

'I won't get the job, Ted,' I said and thanked him for his help. I knew Lawrie could charm the birds off the trees – he was a big, strong, strapping lad who when you met him gave you the impression he would go on to be a decent manager. He'd done well at Grimsby Town, not the easiest of places as it's off the beaten track, and he went on to do a great job at Southampton, the highlight of which was winning the FA Cup in 1976.

Talking of the FA Cup, I also have my own memories of the final that took place three years before Southampton beat Manchester United, the one that finished Sunderland 1 Leeds United 0.

I was invited to the Tyne Tees studios a few days before the match where the other studio guest was Jack Charlton, newly appointed as manager of Middlesbrough.

The programme's presenter was George Taylor and my role was to put forward a case for why Sunderland might do the unexpected and win the final. Jack can be opinionated (to put it mildly!) and he was adamant that Sunderland had absolutely no chance and even went as far as to call it a mismatch. I wasn't sure Sunderland were going to win; I felt it was unlikely, but I didn't feel they had no chance.

I pointed out that they had good players who were in fine form, men such as Ian Porterfield, Bobby Kerr and Billy Hughes. I also argued that they had one of the best goalkeepers in the country in my good friend Jimmy Montgomery. They had also beaten two top First Division sides en route to Wembley in Manchester City and Arsenal, not to mention Luton Town from Division Two.

Of course Sunderland won, and they deserved their triumph. Marjorie and I were at the game; Sunderland had provided us with seats. Apart from Monty's double save he didn't have much to do; Leeds created very little. Ron Guthrie had a tremendous day, Ian Porterfield controlled parts of the game and Johnny Giles never got a shot or a pass away because he was closed down quickly by the Sunderland midfield.

I was absolutely thrilled, especially for Jimmy and Bob Stokoe. As I've described, I knew Bob very well and admired him for having even agreed to take on the job at Sunderland having been a Newcastle player. It was a great day and weekend and one I will never forget.

Chapter 16

It's all Greek to me

In the early 1970s British managers were the fashionable thing for a Greek club to have; even the national team was managed by my ex-Sunderland colleague Billy Bingham between 1971 and 1973.

The big three clubs in Greece were AEK – formed on April 13 1924 by Greek refugees from Istanbul who fled in the wake of the Greco-Turkish war – Olympiakos and Panathinaikos, and AEK had taken its fifth Greek league title in 1971.

Peter Robinson of Liverpool set up a meeting with the reporter acting on behalf of the club and we agreed I would visit Greece to talk about the job on offer, which followed Branko Stankovic's departure.

The chairman was a charming man called Ioannis Theodorakopoulos. His son Taki is today the well-known correspondent for *The Spectator*.

At £10,000 a year the wages on offer were double what I'd been paid at Middlesbrough, so it didn't take me too long to decide that I would welcome the chance to try my luck abroad. Of course Marjorie, who had not been in the best of health, had to find it acceptable. By now Sherley was at university and after a long discussion it was agreed I would go to Greece on my own to work and decide after a few months whether Marjorie would follow me.

So I became the third English manager, or coach as the Greeks styled the position, in AEK's history following Jack Bimby between 1948 and 1951 and Ted Crawford in

1953–54. John Barnwell later made it four when he was there for the 1983–84 season.

I arrived in Switzerland, where AEK were playing three friendlies, and was met by the trainer and ex-player Alexis and the players. I was delighted to find out that one of them, Tassos, a winger, spoke very good English and so initially I was able to speak to the players through him.

The squad included Mimis Papaioannou, who had joined the club ten years before. He had proved an instant success by helping AEK win their first post-war title, scoring twice in the final play-off game against Panathinaikos. The following year he was the top scorer in the Greek league and in all he helped AEK win four more championships. By the time he retired he was the all-time record goalscorer in the Greek First Division. He also won sixty-one international caps, scoring twenty-one goals. During the 1960s many clubs, most notably Real Madrid, tried to buy him.

I found him to be a very nice lad. He was not at all conceited. He was very good in the air, and could rise and seemingly hang there to beat players much bigger than him. He was particularly skilled with his left foot and during my time in Greece I chose to play him at inside right because I felt he could cut inside to shoot. When he played at inside left I considered he had a tendency to drift out wide and not threaten as much. If I had one criticism of him it's that he insisted he had to be one hundred per cent fit before he played. That might seem a bit daft, but if everyone who ran out on a football field was completely fit every club would need a squad of fifty or so players. I am not talking about limping on to the pitch but being able to overcome a sore thigh muscle or a bruise on the ankle. Mimis wouldn't play if he was unsure. He had set high standards and didn't want to turn out if he felt he might not reach them in every match. Still, it was a pleasure to work with him.

The opposition in Switzerland wasn't that good and we were undefeated in three games, with two victories. This was a great introduction and then I had my first taste of just how fanatical Greek fans can be. When we returned home we were met at the airport by around a thousand supporters treating us like conquering heroes. It was obvious expectations were high and 35,000 turned up to watch a friendly with Hamburg.

However, the players were mostly part-time. The hot climate meant training didn't start till around three in the afternoon and that games were played at a slower pace than in England. The players were happy to train with the ball but had low fitness levels. At the beginning I decided to fall in line with this way of thinking, especially as the results were not too bad.

I hadn't been in charge too long when I heard rumours that Greek football was none too clean; referees were supposedly easy targets where cash was concerned. Of course, we later learned that the progress of Panathinaikos to the European Cup final in 1971, which they lost to Ajax at Wembley, had been at least partly based on bribery. But I didn't know this when I went to Greece.

So I had no specific reason to suspect anything might be afoot when early in the 1973–74 season, after winning the first three league games, we played Panathinaikos. They were managed by the great Ferenc Puskas, who'd played so magnificently for Honved, Hungary and Real Madrid in the 1950s and 1960s.

I'd been lucky enough to see him play in a friendly during a summer holiday I'd enjoyed in Madrid with Marjorie in the late '50s. He was then at Real Madrid and I was mesmerised by the ability on the ball of him and his teammates. He, Alfredo di Stefano and Francisco Gento pulled their opponents apart to win 9-1. It was a great thrill to be pitting my wits as a manager against the great man.

We were drawing 0-0, which I regarded as a good result. I showed my watch to the trainer Alexis and indicated there was a minute to go. I duly waited, and waited, and waited for the referee to blow the final whistle, but it didn't happen and more than four minutes later, when one of our players clearly won the ball in a tackle, Panathinaikos were awarded the softest penalty I have ever seen. I was absolutely furious and my rage intensified when Demelo duly struck home the penalty. We'd lost 1-0.

When we were in the dressing room, in a futile attempt to pacify me, Tassos said that I shouldn't get too upset as there was nothing I could have done because the referee had been bribed. I was not having that; I wasn't going to be cheated in such a fashion and when the local reporter asked for my reaction I said I thought we were cheated out of the game. This seemed to cause all sorts of problems for the Greek authorities. They must have known what was going on but didn't want to admit they had a problem because they didn't know how to tackle it. The Greek press had a right go at me, but I was prepared to stand my ground.

Instead of investigating my complaint the Greek FA charged me with bringing the game into disrepute. I attended the hearing, where I was told that I could not accuse referees, and by implication the clubs who offered them bribes, of cheating. I was told to apologise but I had done my homework before I went in and was able to produce a number of newspaper cuttings on incidents that had occurred during the previous twelve months pointing to bribery of referees. I also argued that Panathinaikos had been allowed to choose a German referee for our match when Greek officials officiated at all the other league matches.

They got no apology from me and I never heard another thing about it. But if I thought that my high-profile complaints would stop the dubious decisions I was wrong.

With the score at 1-1 in an away match against Larissa in December, a ball was played over the top of our defence to a player who I can say honestly was around twenty-five yards offside at least. The linesman clearly thought so too. His flag shot up and even though the Larissa player, Rakintzoglu, whacked the ball into the net past Erea, our 'keeper, who had his hands on his hips, I wasn't too concerned and I told the coaching staff who were getting agitated to calm down.

Even when the referee, Mr Papavasileou pointed to the centre circle I wasn't concerned as I could see the linesman still had his flag raised. My players were now getting very angry. I was trying to pacify them; I didn't want anyone sent off and I could see the referee had run over to speak to the linesman, who still had his flag up.

I was certain the 'goal' would be cancelled, but suddenly after speaking to the referee the linesman lowered his flag and they both ran to the halfway line. I was going mental, bawling and shouting. It was a disgrace but there was little I could do about it. Afterwards one of the AEK directors said there was no point in getting angry, it was a situation you had to accept if you wanted to manage in Greece. Such incidents were one of the reasons I decided towards the end of the first season I didn't!

To be fair to AEK, they would have been happy for me to stay even though results hadn't been that great. They paid me to the end of my two years less tax, which was marvellous of them. I wanted to come home chiefly because I was missing my family a lot and while Marjorie and Sherley had visited a couple of times it was for short holidays only. In addition, not being a drinker and there being no such thing as cable or satellite TV in those days to keep me entertained, all I was left with during most evenings was reading – which I enjoy but not all the time.

Another reason I decided to quit was the level of violence that would occur among the fans. This eventually got so bad in Greek football, with constant pitch invasions, that points were later awarded to teams just for completing matches!

AEK were always disliked by the followers of other clubs because of their history; they were viewed as not being proper Greeks.

At one match at another Athens club, Egaleo, it was 2-2 with four minutes to go after we had twice come from behind. There was then a scuffle between our centre-forward Psymoyannos and their centre-half, which saw both players sent off. Our player had seriously insulted the other lad's mother, the worst kind of insult you can make in Greece.

The situation got so out of hand that soldiers went onto the pitch to get them off it. Psymoyannos was still shouting as he walked off, so the soldiers pointed their weapons at him. He was directly in front of the bench so I wasn't that comfortable, to put it mildly.

I was looking forward to the game ending when, of all things, the ball went over their defence and Tassos, standing about five yards offside, cracked it home. There was pandemonium as the referee allowed the goal and almost immediately ended the game. We had won 3-2 in, let's be honest, controversial circumstances.

As the crowd rushed on to the pitch we all ran to the dressing room. We could hear an almighty commotion as the crowd began to riot. The police told us to stay in the dressing room – not that we intended going anywhere, I could assure them. We could hear stones and rocks crashing off the walls and we could hear chanting. What they were saying I couldn't make out but I knew it wasn't favourable!

After a while Alexis suggested it might be best for us to leave the stadium. It would mean jumping on the bus, ensuring the gates were opened and hurtling up a street for a few hundred yards before turning left onto a motorway.

A police escort would protect us, we were told – so we crept onto the bus – but the moment the gates opened and we set off a crowd of between eighty and a hundred appeared and threw everything they could find at us.

You have to give credit to the driver; he got us on to the motorway although every window in the bus was smashed. I spent the whole time on the floor and amazingly no one was badly injured. I then learned that such incidents were not uncommon and that turned out to be true as twice more in my time the bus was wrecked coming from an away game.

Violence, it seemed, was an everyday event in Athens, as I discovered when I witnessed an act of police brutality the like of which I have never seen before or since. I was driving into Athens using the back route and there was a policeman directing traffic. The person in a car in front of me tooted his horn at him – I guess he was getting tired of waiting. The policeman jumped down from his podium, walked over, opened the car door and pulled out the driver. He then beat the living daylights out of the man, leaving him lying on the pavement before getting back up and starting to sort out the traffic again.

During my time in Athens students occupied the polytechnic and the authorities took a very hard line. There were twenty-four deaths outside the building and the army used a tank to smash their way through barricades. Everyone was talking about it but you couldn't see what was happening as the area was cordoned off.

My final game in charge came on April 15 1974. This was away to Olympiakos. At half-time we were drawing 0-0 but conceded a quick goal when Delikaris fired home shortly after the interval. We were pushing forward and I was fairly confident we would get an equaliser. So I was left stunned when the referee sent off our centre-back Slathopolos after an innocuous challenge. It's possible the referee just made a mistake, although I doubted it. My misery was complete when the home side knocked home three more goals in the next five minutes to make the result 4-0. There were still seven games of the season left but I was determined that enough was enough and I was getting out of Greece.

I left behind a team which finished fifth, with Olympiakos winning the league. My record was: won twelve, lost seven and drew eight in the league, and won two and lost one in the Greek cup.

Of course since then many things have changed and I was pleased when Greece won the European Championships in Portugal in 2004. They have talented players who, given the chance, will make an impact on the world stage.

Chapter 17

A right mess you've got me into, Gordon

Not long after I quit Middlesbrough I received a telephone call from Brian Clough insisting I visit him at the Baseball Ground and watch a game. He simply wouldn't take no for an answer and so I took the opportunity to watch a fifth round FA Cup tie against Queens Park Rangers. The Londoners were making a strong bid for promotion to Division One and gave the First Division champions a good game before going out 4-2.

In the boardroom afterwards the QPR manager Gordon Jago asked me what I intended now I had left Middlesbrough. I explained that I was thinking of going abroad.

I didn't know Gordon that well. We'd chatted before and after games when our teams met and in my final season at Ayresome Park he had tried to buy John Hickton for £125,000. It took all my powers of persuasion to convince the board to turn it down; Eric Varley was particularly keen to take what was at the time a considerable fee.

It never occurred to me at the Baseball Ground that Gordon was being anything other than friendly. I thought nothing more about the conversation until just after I returned from Greece. I picked up the phone and was surprised to find him on the line. QPR had been promoted at the end of the 1972–73 season and had done well in their first season back in Division One, finishing eighth. Gordon talked about how optimistic he was for the future.

A right mess you've got me into, Gordon

When he asked me about my plans I told him I wanted a break as I had received a good pay-off from AEK Athens and hadn't seen a lot of my wife and daughter recently. But Gordon was keen to know whether I would be interested in the vacant coaching job at Loftus Road. I think it was the fact that they were in the top flight that persuaded me to travel to London to talk to Gordon. London was never a place that I particularly enjoyed visiting and I could never see myself living and working there.

When we met I was very impressed with Gordon and his ideas about how he liked to see football played, and it didn't take me long to agree to become coach. When we agreed my salary and shook hands I thought it was settled. But Gordon then said Jim Gregory, QPR's chairman, would also have to agree. This was a surprise and it should have caused me to wonder whether I was making the right move.

We spent the next couple of hours arguing with Jim about the amount I was to be paid, but I wouldn't budge on what I'd agreed with Gordon. Sat next to Jim was a chap I could only imagine was his bodyguard. He was a frightening man and when I was speaking all he would do was look at Jim and shake his head. I was very uncomfortable and told Gordon Jago this. Eventually Jim agreed with Gordon about my wages and we shook hands. If I thought that was the end of the matter I was soon to find out how wrong that was.

Pre-season training was due to start in a couple of weeks, so with Gordon and Frank Sibley, another coach, we started to map out the training routines. Frank, who had retired from playing at just twenty-three following a knee injury, was a super bloke to work with, so that was not going to be a problem. The training went well: the players worked hard and appeared keen to get the season off to a good start.

But then there was an episode that should have set alarm bells ringing in my head. The press photographs for the new season were to be taken but the captain Gerry Francis asked to see me and said the players refused to have a team photo taken unless they were paid. They had been promised payment for other photos but had not received a single penny. I rang Gordon and he rushed to the training ground only to be told the same story; he was wasting his time unless he could come up with some money.

Gordon was in a panic and rang Jim Gregory but got no joy from the chairman so the press photographers had a wasted day.

QPR had some top-class players, men such as goalkeeper Phil Parkes, Frank McLintock, captain of Arsenal when they did the double in 1970–71, Terry Venables, Gerry Francis, Don Givens, a very good striker and Dave Thomas, an excellent winger. And, of course, there was the great Stan Bowles. Stan was a complex character, but on the pitch he had wonderful control and would play quick, short passes to open up defences.

QPR could compete with any side in the country and in 1975–76 they were to finish second, somewhat unluckily, to Liverpool, although I'd gone by then. However, when I was there, it seemed there was a reason they were not reaching the heights of which they were capable.

Gordon had spells when he was full of beans and then, for no obvious reason, bouts of depression. This impacted on his relationship with the players and I don't feel he used his authority too well. For example, early in the season we played at Luton Town and en route we were to pick up Stan Bowles. We waited, but when it was clear he wasn't going to turn up Gordon said he was sure Stan would make his own way to the hotel for the pre-match meal.

Stan finally arrived twenty minutes late and I let him know I wasn't too pleased at his attitude. Before I knew it Gordon was having a go at me and I was forced to defend myself, saying 'It's Stan Bowles you should be speaking to and not me.' Gordon should have tackled him because had he done so Stan would not have got into trouble by making the V-sign at the Kenilworth Road crowd. Not that his behaviour prevented him playing well; he was marvellous.

Naturally, being made a fool of in front of the players left me feeling insecure, although once I did persuade Gordon that Bowles should be disciplined. I said I would take him for an extra training session and I worked him as hard as I could. I would hit cross-field passes at him and he would pull the ball out of the air and shoot instantly. Then I told two apprentices to mark him as tightly as they could. But again he would control the ball immediately and shimmy away from them. As he came off he said it was the best training session he'd ever had and I have wondered since if players as gifted as Stan Bowles get bored with normal training and need one-to-one sessions.

There were other problems at QPR. I am sure Jim Gregory had a lot to do with Gordon's moods and I'm certain the players knew this better than I did; too many things were happening off the field which influenced the playing side.

For instance, I didn't think the club was treating me as an important member of the staff. I stayed at a hotel for the first couple of weeks until the manager told me QPR were no longer prepared to pay the bill. I saw Gordon about it but he did nothing. I was forced to find alternative accommodation and I finished up in a bed and breakfast, which made it very hard to concentrate on the job.

I'm sure the players knew something was going on. I was fast losing their respect and getting little help when working with them. I spoke to Gordon about this on a few occasions but he seemed unconcerned and then suddenly, without telling me, he resigned after the home match with Everton.

It was true we weren't doing well – we had only won once, at Leeds, in nine games. But we had looked like beating Everton only for Jim Pearson to make it 2-2 in the final minute. The game was on a Tuesday evening and we were missing Stan Bowles, who had returned late from an England get-together with Don Revie the previous weekend. Gordon had banned Stan for two weeks and had also transferred Terry Venables to Crystal Palace – again without telling me. Gordon was under pressure to improve results yet he never said anything about quitting and I had no idea he was about to.

It put me in a very difficult position. Press reports indicated I was being considered for Gordon's old job, along with Leicester's Jimmy Bloomfield, Orient's George Petchey, Sheffield Wednesday's Steve Burtenshaw and ex-skipper Venables, but I knew Gregory was not going to offer it to me. I was Gordon's appointment, not his; and any new manager would more than likely bring in his own staff.

But I decided not to resign. I was caretaker manager for four matches, one of which was an excellent game at Highbury where Frank McLintock was outstanding although he was overshadowed by a marvellous display from Stan Bowles, who scored both our goals in the 2-2 draw.

A week later we were at home to table-topping Ipswich Town, managed by Bobby Robson. Ipswich probably deserved a point but we won 1-0 thanks to a Gerry Francis volley.

It wasn't our two points that made the headlines, though. Arsenal had made a bid for QPR centre-half Terry Mancini and whether it was Terry's way of making sure the directors, especially the chairman, knew he wanted to go I will never know but at the end of the game he ran over in front of the directors' area and dropped his pants to reveal his backside. Gregory was furious, convinced that Terry had directed his arse solely at him! I had to try to persuade him that wasn't the case because I didn't want him doing anything daft.

A right mess you've got me into, Gordon

Not that it mattered. The FA got involved and charged Terry with bringing the game into disrepute, and although I'd left by the time he appeared before the panel he persuaded me to support him – little good it did; he was suspended for a month. But Terry eventually moved to Arsenal where he did a good job.

Terry was always very serious about his football and he hated losing. Off the pitch he was totally different, telling jokes all day long and constantly thinking of pranks to play on his unfortunate teammates.

The end came when Jim Gregory sent his son to tell me I was sacked. It wasn't a great surprise, and although it was the first time I'd ever been fired in some ways it was a relief. I didn't settle well in London and as a consequence I did not do a great job. Dave Sexton, who'd just been dismissed by Chelsea, took over and QPR moved quickly up the league, proving my point at least that they were equipped to do better.

QPR played at Ayresome Park the November after I left and Jim Gregory phoned to invite me to the ground, where he at least had the guts to say he was very sorry at the way things had turned out and that I was just unfortunate to be at QPR at the wrong time.

Chapter 18

Managing at the bottom

About four months after leaving QPR I got a call from Doncaster Rovers asking if I would consider taking over from Maurice Setters. With the club struggling near the foot of Division Four there was every chance they would be forced to apply for re-election and if unsuccessful go out of the Football League, especially as they had finished in the bottom four the previous season.

I didn't think the job would interest me but I was prepared to listen to what was on offer and met Ben Rayner and Tony Phillips, the chairman and vice-chairman, at the Scotch Corner Hotel on the A1. It was Saturday February 1 1975 and Doncaster had earlier that day played at Gay Meadow, where they had lost 7-4. The defeat left them twenty-third; only Scunthorpe were below them and they had two matches in hand!

After a couple of hours, during which Ben and Tony did their level best to persuade me that things weren't that bad – there were after all sixteen games in which to pull things round, they pointed out – I agreed to go to Doncaster on the Monday morning and have a look around. I wasn't that convinced I was doing the right thing but, after a year away in Greece and my time in the unfamiliar territory of London, at least it was work in northern England.

Arriving at Belle Vue, I met the coach, ex-Nottingham Forest player John Quigley, who was just about to take training. The first thing I noticed was how poor the kit was, and I thought it wasn't perhaps too surprising the team was struggling. The dressing rooms and ground were also a shambles, but when I went out to examine the pitch I was delighted to find it was first class, as good as anything I had ever seen. The groundsman, who I learned was George Foster, clearly cared a great deal about his trade and I hoped that in time I could produce a side to do justice to it.

After more discussions with Ben and Tony I decided to take the job. I knew, however, that to save the club I needed to get off on a good footing with the players straight away and raise their morale. The club had won only one of the previous fifteen league games, nine of which had been lost.

So I began by asking who had supplied the training kit and was told it had come from a director called Hubert Bates who ran a sports shop. I asked that new kit be obtained by the following Monday, if not sooner. Mr Bates wasn't happy but we eventually got on well enough, and I ended up admiring him after he told me of his experiences as a Japanese prisoner of war.

My first match was at home to Torquay United and we played much better than I had dreamed was possible, winning 3-0. We then travelled the short distance to Oakwell and thrilled our small band of travellers by beating Barnsley 1-0.

Mansfield Town were top of the league, yet before a crowd of 7,278 we beat them 4-3 in a cracking game. They had lost only twice in twenty-nine league games and Colin Foster and Terry Eccles had them two up just before half-time. Steve Uzelac got us back in the game by whipping home a loose ball and at half-time I urged the players to double their efforts.

Then Brendan O'Callaghan nodded on a free kick and Peter Kitchen turned and shot at the same time to pull the teams level. Terry Curran made it 3-2 but Eccles grabbed his second and a draw seemed certain. I would have been happy with that but with just two minutes left Peter got his second, pushing the ball past Rod Arnold from close range. It sparked wild scenes among the previously goal-starved Doncaster fans. Three matches, three wins. It then became four, then five in a row. Rotherham put an end to the sequence but two further victories made it seven from eight and from looking certainties to apply for re-election we rocketed up to fifteenth, eventually ending seventeenth on forty points.

Despite the run in which we took twenty-one out of a possible thirty-two points I was under no illusions that the team needed improving if we were to look to compete at the top rather than just staying away from the bottom four. The problem was that there was very little money for transfer fees to bring in better players – £5,000, equivalent to around £50,000 in today's terms I'd guess, was a lot of money for the club to be spending on one player. That I soon realised would at best buy a player only ten per cent better than what I already had – so it would be a huge gamble.

I decided to concentrate on trying to improve the players already at the club. I hadn't seen much Fourth Division football. In fact, after I agreed to go to Doncaster I'd taken the opportunity to watch a game with journalist Vince Wilson and been shocked at how poor it was – some of the passing was terrible. I realised quickly that I had to set my sights a little lower with some of the players, most of whom with the right encouragement would give you everything.

When I did buy players I concentrated on getting those I already knew, men such as the ex-Huddersfield and Carlisle United midfield player Chris Balderstone. I felt his experience and ability on the ball would prove useful. In fact, Chris came six months too late, during the summer of 1975 and his lack of pace proved a real handicap.

In addition, he was now more committed to cricket, which had taken a back seat in the 1960s when he concentrated on football. Chris had been the star man at the Benson and Hedges Cup final at Lord's in 1972, helping Leicester to their first-ever trophy. As his cricketing standards rose, the possibility of his playing for England was being mentioned when he came to Doncaster – something he achieved only months after we mutually agreed not to renew his contract at the end of his first season.

In the summer of 1975 Leicestershire were competing at the top of the County Championship, hoping to win it for the first time. It had been agreed when Chris signed that football would take priority but he was naturally desperate to play in the last game. This was against Derbyshire at Chesterfield, but the problem was we had a game with Brentford on the evening of September 15.

I arranged to go with Phil Day, an employee of the chairman, and collect him at close of play. When I arrived Chris was batting, and continued to do so right up until stumps, finishing on 51 not out in a game that helped his side win the championship.

As soon as play ended we packed him, still in his whites, into the car. It is about thirty miles from Chesterfield to Doncaster and we were making good time until we approached the ground and the traffic was so congested it seemed we would miss the kick-off. Ordering Chris to take off his clothes I told Phil to drive down the outside lane, shouting out of the window that Chris Balderstone was in the car and needed to get through. Thankfully the policeman directing the traffic saw the funny side of things and waved us through, helping us to arrive in the nick of time.

When Chris ran out to play in the 1-1 draw he became the only man to have played first-class cricket and League football on the same day. He was back batting the following morning and made 116 before taking three for 28 as Derbyshire were bowled out for 140 with just five minutes remaining.

I also bought Joe Laidlaw, ex-'Boro and Carlisle, who did a competent job when I was hoping for a bit more. Mickey French came from QPR, scored a few goals at the start but soon faded and I had to let him go.

It was a matter of constantly looking for bargain buys, and that meant watching two, if not three, games a week. On a Monday it might be Mansfield, Tuesday Barnsley and Friday Stockport. Then our own game and Monday back to Chesterfield. I am sure some months during the football season I hardly slept more than four or five hours a night. By the time I'd got home, watched a bit of television or chatted with Marjorie, if she was still up, it was usually well after midnight when I went to bed.

Even then I often didn't sleep, particularly after a bad performance. I'd find myself going over formations, thinking how to motivate certain players and generally being unable to switch off. When the team were doing better the pressure was different – supporters would get excited, such as at Middlesbrough when we were third or fourth at Easter. Then I'd lie awake working out how to win the vital games to snatch promotion.

No matter how well or badly I slept I was almost always back in for training at 9.00am the following morning. Training at Doncaster then was held on municipal pitches not far from Belle Vue because the club didn't have its own training ground. You'd get cars going past with fans, even some of our own, winding down the window to have a go at certain players.

We lost Terry Curran before the start of the following season. He was an attacking midfielder who also played on the wing. My old mate Brian Clough had rung to say he fancied one of my players and I wasn't surprised when he said it was Terry – along with our combined strike force of Brendan O'Callaghan and Peter Kitchen he was the best of the bunch I inherited. The offer was £65,000 and, as you always did in those situations, I said I didn't think it was enough but I would put the offer in front of the board and get back to him.

Quite naturally the board was keen to sell, and it was a good move for him. However, as I was keen to bring in a couple of players I got them to agree to me negotiating with Brian about taking Dennis Peacock, a 'keeper, and Ian Miller, a right winger and natural replacement for Terry, as part of the deal. I wanted to do the negotiating but in the event it was agreed that the chairman Ben Rayner would accompany me to the Baseball Ground and sort out the deal.

When we arrived Brian was all charm. I had it in my mind that we wanted £40,000 plus the two players, valued at £10,000 and £15,000 respectively – a total of £65,000. Brian, however, was playing hardball and suggested that the two players were worth £35,000, which I wasn't having, and he knew it. Next thing he suggested he would pay £70,000 for Terry but that we then pay £35,000 for the two players.

I was just about to start laughing at his audacity as that meant Doncaster would get only £35,000 rather than the £40,000 cash I knew he would have paid for Terry alone when Ben jumped in and said it was a deal. It was only afterwards when I told him what he'd done he realised he'd just lost the club £5,000. There was, at least, some consolation in that Miller was later sold to Blackburn for £200,000 and Dennis Peacock subsequently joined me at Bolton for £60,000. I couldn't help but think of Len Shackleton's views on directors as we drove away from Derby!

We began the 1975–76 season in decent form and in the second round of the League Cup we entertained Crystal Palace, then managed by Malcolm Allison. After we beat them Malcolm said he was sick of the sight of me, recalling no doubt that when he'd been manager of Manchester City I'd helped Middlesbrough knock them out of the FA

Cup in January 1972, winning 2-1 at Ayresome Park after the first match finished 1-1.

When we beat Newport County in mid-November we were only a point outside the top four promotion spots. We had also fought our way through to the League Cup quarter-finals, in which we were to meet Tottenham Hotspur at White Hart Lane.

The last time I'd been involved with a cup match at the Lane it had been with Sunderland and we'd lost by five goals. History was about to repeat itself. Backed by a decent following we started really well, taking the lead on nine minutes when Brendan O'Callaghan outjumped Willie Young and nodded the ball forward for Alan Murray to score with a diving header. We then had further chances to stretch the lead before goals from John Pratt and John Duncan put Spurs in front at half-time.

I said to the players during the interval that they had played well enough to be at least level, which is exactly what we were after fifty-one minutes when Pat Jennings pushed away Brendan's header and Peter Kitchen, following up, made it 2-2.

Not long after this match Peter was invited to train with Bobby Robson's Ipswich but sadly Bobby decided Peter wasn't for him. He lacked a yard of pace but later moved on to Orient, where he did pretty well, especially during 1977–78 when he scored seven FA Cup goals as the O's made it to the semi-final where they lost to Arsenal.

Spurs restored their lead with a poor goal, Les Chappell knocking the ball into his own net. Things went from bad to worse as Duncan hit a hat-trick to make it 7-2. I had again lost by five at Spurs, but the score flattered the home side.

The heavy defeat took the stuffing out of the team and we won only two and lost six of the next eight to lie eleventh after twenty-six matches. We ended up tenth with forty-nine points, nine behind Tranmere Rovers in the fourth promotion spot. Considering the previous two seasons it was a fine achievement but I knew it would still need a big improvement if we were to win promotion.

Sorting out the retained list is always one of the most unpleasant parts of a manager's job. It's never the easiest thing to tell a player, especially in the lower leagues, that you're letting them go on a free transfer. You call them in, tell them your decision and then they get an official letter. You hope to get a fee for some so they are in the awkward situation of not knowing where they'll be moving.

One of the most difficult situations I ever faced was having to tell Stan Brookes I wasn't renewing his contract at Doncaster. He'd done well for me, was only in his mid-twenties and was totally dedicated to the club. He also had a good rapport with the fans. But I felt he needed to go somewhere else as he'd only ever played in a struggling team and this had affected his confidence and self-belief. I hoped he'd find a club where he'd do better. He was deeply upset.

I also gave Steve Uzelac a free transfer because he, too, deserved to better himself.

Those two brought me problems with the directors. After talking to them I established that, although they had each been at Belle Vue for more than five years they had not received the £750 they were due. I told the board they were duty bound to pay it and they had to part with £1,500. To a struggling club that was a significant amount.

In 1976–77 Doncaster finished eighth with fifty-one points, eight behind fourth-placed Bradford City. We'd been fairly successful in parts, enjoying a fabulous unbeaten run in January and February, when he won eight games out of ten, including six in a row. We'd lost Peter Kitchen to Orient but I had managed to hang on to Brendan O'Callaghan, who eventually went to Stoke in March 1978 after knocking home sixty-five goals in 184 starts, a good record. He left behind a club that finished twelfth in the Fourth Division at the end of the 1977–78 season, eleven points off a promotion place.

I had said when I joined that I intended staying only two years, but by the end of May 1978 I'd been there for three-and-a-half seasons. I wasn't convinced, with the resources at my disposal, that I could get Doncaster promoted. Neither did I feel we would be required to apply for re-election. I wasn't sure what my future might hold that summer.

I was frustrated. The side started poorly the following season and in November 1978 we fell into the bottom four after losing 2-1 to York City. I hadn't managed to sign the players I'd wanted and the loss of O'Callaghan was starting to show up the gaps in attack. I was convinced we could get out of trouble and had no thoughts of quitting at such a difficult time. But without warning Ian Greaves, the Bolton manager, rang to ask me to join him at Burnden Park as his assistant. The post had become vacant after my ex-Sunderland colleague George Mulhall had moved to Bradford City to replace John Napier as manager.

Bolton had been promoted to the First Division the previous season but were struggling near the bottom. It meant we would have to leave Doncaster, so Marjorie had to agree. Fortunately she did because I was really keen to get back to the top level.

After almost four years in charge I left Doncaster Rovers having played 174 games, winning sixty-seven, drawing forty-seven and losing sixty – not a bad record considering the lack of financial backing.

I eventually moved back to Doncaster and still live there and I'm thrilled they are now in the division I knew as the second in my playing days.

Chapter 19

Badsworth Boy

One of the by-products of my time at Doncaster was a wonderful surprise that gave me an insight into a sport I knew little about – horse racing. I know many players are fascinated by the sport but I'd never been very interested in it until vice-chairman Tony Phillips asked me if I would like a share in a racehorse.

He told me there two horses for sale at Snowy Wainwright's, a trainer at Malton, and that he and three friends – Doug Armitage, Ron Howe and Maurice Gibson – were going to the stables the following Sunday. Did I want to go with them? It turned out to be one of the luckiest decisions I ever made.

The four of them were agreed on the choice of horse although, of course, I didn't have a clue. As the horse was led from the stable he was pulling too hard and jumped a fence into a field. It took ages to get him back. It was not the best of starts.

The horse was named without discussion by Maurice Gibson as Badsworth Boy, Badsworth being a small village where he lived not far from Doncaster. For a couple of seasons Badsworth Boy ran on the flat with limited success, so we had a meeting and decided he might be better at chasing. We remembered what had happened when we first saw the horse! We got in touch with top National Hunt trainer Tony Dickinson and he said he would have a look at the horse at his stables at Harewood. After doing so he would take on Badsworth with his son, Michael, as trainer.

Badsworth started his new career under the Dickinsons' tutelage with some success over hurdles. But Tony and Michael were convinced he would become a top-class chaser. And after two years it was decided the time was ripe for him to go over fences and apart from falling a couple of times he won on a regular basis.

The holy grail in the steeplechase world is the Cheltenham Festival meeting. Just to get a horse there is an achievement and in 1983 Badsworth ran in the Queen Mother Champion Chase. We were all extremely excited, thinking he had a chance of winning.

He started well and was jumping brilliantly and it looked all over when he led easily coming into the last fence. I still don't know how he managed to stay on his feet that day – he was never the best of jumpers and hit a few fences during his career – but somehow jockey Bob Earnshaw kept him upright and he went on to win by thirty lengths, an astonishing distance.

Badsworth Boy won the Queen Mother in the two following years as well, finishing ten lengths in front of the runner-up on both occasions and so far is the only horse to win the race three years in a row in its fifty-one-year history. By the time Badsworth retired he had won eight times over hurdles and eighteen over fences.

'His speed was his greatest asset,' recalled Bob Earnshaw. 'I think he was the fastest horse that I ever rode. I would just sit there on the bridle and he would float along while the others struggled. He was a joy to ride. The worry was that, because he used to hurdle his fences, he would jump low and there was no room for error. Occasionally we came to grief but never at Cheltenham. Perhaps he saw one of the big fences early and realised that he had to jump them. He seemed to respect Cheltenham more than the average "park" course.'

I used to bet on him each time. Before the first win at Cheltenham one of my golfing colleagues said he didn't want me to put any money on for him. I didn't and when he romped home my friend wasn't best pleased when I told him I'd followed his instructions. We made some good money; not an enormous amount as it costs a lot to keep and look after a horse, but enough to enjoy a few treats.

Badsworth went on to live to the good old age of twenty-seven before dying in October 2002. He was huge, had plenty of character and would bite if you got too close. He had a never say die attitude, vital for a chaser.

There is no better feeling in sport than being involved in horse racing as an owner and I will remember the pleasure I got from it for years to come!

Chapter 20

Back in the top flight

The weekend before I moved to Bolton Wanderers they had lost 1-0 to West Bromwich Albion, leaving them nineteenth, just above the relegation zone occupied by Chelsea, Wolves and Birmingham.

Bolton had been promoted at the end of the previous season as Second Division champions. Tottenham Hotspur had finished third to join them in the top flight and then created a sensation by signing Osvaldo Ardiles, a member of the Argentinian team which had won the World Cup, and Ricky Villa, who was also in the squad. Ardiles at his peak was a quick, intelligent midfield player who could bring other players into the game and, of course, Villa scored one of greatest goals ever seen in an FA Cup final.

It was a bold move, one that, along with Bobby Robson at Ipswich Town signing Dutchman Arnold Muhren at the same time, changed the face of English football for ever. Nowadays our top clubs scour the globe for talent, but then it was very unusual. All three went on to do well; Ardiles and Villa picked up FA Cup winners' medals and Muhren won the UEFA Cup with Ipswich before twice winning the FA Cup with Manchester United.

Muhren was a fantastic player, always composed with the ball at his feet. He had the Dutch mentality of not wanting to waste the ball by giving it away cheaply and his passing was superb.

I have always been impressed by the way Holland play football but I must say that after watching the 2010 World Cup final I was delighted that Spain won. The way the Dutch played in the final was a complete contrast to the way the wonderful way they've played in the past. I couldn't believe the brutality shown by the Dutch and I really felt sorry for the referee, Howard Webb. I doubt whether the change of tactics was introduced to make them harder to beat and I hope it was a one-off. I doubt it though.

It was going to be a struggle at Burnden Park but I was confident that the quality of players in the squad was enough to maintain top-flight status. There was a young Peter Reid, Jim McDonagh, Roy Greaves, Brian Nicholson, Tony Dunne, Alan Gowling and his strike partner, the inimitable Frank Worthington. I was looking forward to working with them, because, along with acting as go-between for the players and the manager, one of the main roles of an assistant manager is coaching. Ian Greaves had been a defender and so with my experience as a midfield player it looked an effective pairing on paper.

I was surprised by Ian's call. I didn't know him that well and I think the recommendation must have come from Bolton's physiotherapist, Jimmy Headridge. Jimmy had worked under me at Middlesbrough. He was very skilled with great attention to detail.

A good physiotherapist is a vital part of a football club and Jimmy was great because he was able to tell you almost exactly when a player would be fit. This meant you could plan your team. Some years later Alex Ferguson persuaded him to work for Manchester United but sadly he died prematurely when taking a player on some exercises.

One player who I found wasn't that fussed about doing his exercises was Frank Worthington. Give him a ball and he'd train all day; anybody lucky enough to see him on a good day would see what a master of it he was. But vital as skill on the ball is, it has to be backed up by fitness and effort. Skills can only be fully employed after you've worked hard on running and exercising in order to improve your stamina so as to be able to perform for the whole ninety minutes.

Frank would take it a little bit easy in training. He wouldn't miss any sessions because he loved playing, but if he'd put in extra effort he would have been remembered as a great rather than a very good player. In many respects it was the same with Stan Bowles, although I don't think Frank ever had as many off-the-field problems to worry about as Stan – probably nobody did!

One of Frank's goals was among the best I have ever seen, and as the match featured on *Match of the Day* it is the goal with which Frank has become associated.

At home to Ipswich Town in April Frank was on the edge of the area with his back to goal. The Ipswich defence moved out to play an offside trap so Frank controlled the ball with his knee, then kept it up twice with his foot before flicking it over his head to wrong-foot the defenders. Then he turned and volleyed it past Paul Cooper. It was absolutely brilliant; a once in a lifetime goal – except it wasn't. I'd seen him do similar things in training – as I said he really did love playing with the ball. Despite that goal we still ended up losing 3-2, although it was our first defeat at home in nine games, and the other eight included seven victories, one a 3-0 hammering of local rivals Manchester United.

At times in football it's the little things that count. When I arrived at Bolton it soon became apparent that Ian spent very little time with the players. He wasn't as bad as Raich Carter had been at Middlesbrough, but I still felt events on the field would be improved if he worked more closely with the team. I know from experience that players want to see the manager. I was his assistant and although they listened to me they knew, ultimately, that I didn't pick the team.

We were coming back in the car from a scouting trip one night and I brought up the subject. I was a little anxious about how he might take it – would he see it as being helpful or merely critical? I needn't have worried – he listened carefully, asked one or two questions and then said he'd sort things out. Afterwards he spent a lot more time with the players and this contributed to our improved performances.

Burnden Park became a difficult place for any team to visit – but we struggled away from home. We won away only twice, although once was at Old Trafford, which gave us the double over our near neighbours. On a Wednesday night before close to 50,000 we went a goal down through Martin Buchan in the first half before Frank Worthington equalised soon after the restart. Manchester United had a golden opportunity to retake the lead when they were awarded a penalty in the fifty-eighth minute. Gordon McQueen stroked it home but Joe Jordan had encroached into the box. When it was retaken McQueen hit the post. Ian and myself would have been happy with a draw but deep into injury time Frank hit the winner.

I was then thrilled for Brian Clough when he took Nottingham Forest, with my ex-Newcastle colleague Frank Clark at left back, to European Championship success, overcoming Malmo in the final. I'd gone as Cloughie's guest to the earlier home leg of the AEK Athens tie (they won 7-2 on aggregate). It was then that I saw for the first time signs that Brian was becoming dependent on alcohol. He insisted I drink a large whisky before the game – I didn't, incidentally – and then I saw him drinking with the directors afterwards.

Despite the fact that Bolton had finished seventeenth, which meant that Ian and I had done what every club has to do in their first season in a new division, namely stay up, we were under no illusions that the following year would be any easier. The side was getting old; Ian had taken charge in 1974 and had gambled by going for experience to help get back into Division One for the first time since 1964. They'd been cruelly denied in 1975–76 and 1976–77, finishing fourth each year when three teams were promoted, before finally going up.

When we sat down to discuss how to move things forward we knew we needed fresh blood. The club had some good youngsters but we could not rely on them to keep us in the top flight. One or two might be able to get a game the following season but the side couldn't be built around them. The only option was to go with what we already had and ask the board for funds to buy new players. When Ian did that he came away very disappointed; the directors felt that the youngsters should be given a chance.

This meant that Bolton finished well below the rest at the end of the 1979–80 season. We managed a decent start, including taking a point at Anfield from a goalless draw in our first game. Joe Fagan, the Liverpool assistant manager, unhappy at how defensively we'd played, gave us a right mouthful afterwards, saying we'd go down if we played like that all season. Ian and I were simply glad to have secured a point against the team which had won the league the previous season. If we'd attacked them we would have got hammered.

The game was historic because Liverpool became the first team to run out for a league game wearing the name of a sponsor on their shirts, in this case Hitachi. Previously only non-league Kettering Town had done this. It was a far cry from my playing days, when the thought of advertising on shirts would have never been considered. The quality of those shirts had also changed significantly, becoming much more lightweight, which meant they were a lot less heavy when wet.

The same, of course, was true with the balls. When I had started out balls were brown and the leather would absorb moisture, becoming heavier as the game progressed. This made it much harder to kick, and goalkeepers certainly couldn't get it over the halfway line back in the 1950s.

And too much heading could leave you with a headache. Stan Cullis, the iconic manager of Wolves, had to retire at twenty-nine after repeated concussion from heading the ball. By the late '70s new technology meant a by now white ball didn't become heavier on wet days, which meant it became easier to kick and control.

After four matches of the 1979–80 season we had won one and drawn three and so had five points on the board. Sadly in our next thirty-eight games we collected only twenty more and so finished bottom. We had to make do without Frank Worthington for the majority of the season. He had returned from a summer spell in America, where he had clearly enjoyed himself at the expense of his fitness, and failed to produce anything like his previous season's form. In November, when Second Division Birmingham City made an offer of £150,000, Ian and I agreed it would be best to let him go.

Frank was at the club for only a short time when I was there, but in 1978–79 he was top scorer in Division One with twenty-four league goals. This was a remarkable achievement considering Bolton's finishing position.

We had high hopes that one player we did sign, QPR full-back Dave Clement, would prove valuable. He'd played five times for England but he failed to produce the sort of form of which I knew he was capable. After I dropped him later in the season he appeared to be unconcerned. I telephoned Terry Venables, who had become QPR manager, but he was unable to tell me much. Dave was sold to Wimbledon at the end of the season and I was really upset two years later when I learned that depression had led him to commit suicide.

Two months after we'd sold Frank and just after we'd beaten Halifax Town in the FA Cup to reach round five the board sacked Ian.

When Ian told me I offered to support him by resigning as well. He was firmly against this, pointing out that I'd end up with nothing while he at least had the consolation of a payout.

I was glad of his advice and I guess that with no one else in mind, and money tight, the board were glad to offer me the job. I quickly persuaded Tony Dunne, with his vast experience at full back for Manchester United and the Republic of Ireland, to become coach although we both knew we stood absolutely no chance of keeping Bolton up. At the time we were bottom, eight points adrift of nineteenth-placed Stoke.

Things did get a little better. We won our first game, beating the European champions Nottingham Forest courtesy of a Neil Whatmore goal, and we managed to win four out of the last eighteen matches. Neil also put us ahead against Manchester United at Burnden Park at Easter but we failed to build on it and lost 3-1.

We failed to win a single away game that season. We played well enough at Maine Road to draw 2-2 with a last-minute Peter Reid effort giving us a point we deserved, but that was one of only a few reasonable away performances that year. Derby County and Bristol City accompanied us back down to Division Two.

With the board happy to let me stay on as manager I was hoping to gather together a side good enough to get Bolton straight back up. I allowed Willie Morgan and Roy Greaves to leave, and I was fortunate enough to be able to persuade Everton's Brian Kidd to move to Burnden Park. However, without the luxury of today's 'parachute payments', paid to sides following their relegation from the top flight of English football, I didn't have a great deal to spend on trying to replace an ageing squad.

I had hoped to be able to hold on to some key players but when centre-half Sam Allardyce and 'keeper Jim McDonagh indicated they wanted to stay in Division One I had no alternative but to let them go to Sunderland and Everton respectively for fees of £150,000 and £300,000.

This was bad enough, but then began one of the most disappointing episodes I experienced during my long career. I had hoped Peter Reid, a fine, combative young midfield player with England potential, would be prepared to play at least one season in the second tier but he was adamant he wanted to return to the First Division as soon as possible. I was determined to get the best price for him, and use the money generated to purchase the number of players I needed.

The first enquiry was from Everton. Great, I thought, especially as they seemed happy to pay the asking price of £450,000. I knew Peter was a big Liverpool fan, still is as far as I know, but I never thought he'd refuse to even consider moving to their rivals. I was wrong: he made it clear there was no chance he would go to Goodison Park.

The next thing I heard, from Peter himself, was that John Barnwell was interested in taking him to Wolves. I hadn't heard anything from the Wolves manager so I rang Molineux. Yes, Barnwell said, they were interested and I told him the fee we expected. He said he'd be back in touch with an offer. Meanwhile Peter declared he wasn't prepared to play while the transfer was being sorted. The problem was that there was no transfer being sorted. John Barnwell didn't come back with an offer, and although I kept telling Peter, he was insistent he wouldn't play, even though the season had started. Meanwhile he was continuing to pick up his wages because we'd been advised that if we stopped paying him he could consider himself out of contract and free to move on without Bolton receiving a fee. I felt, and still feel, this was wrong.

The whole affair dragged on for weeks and it was becoming deeply unsettling to the rest of the players. The fans were up in arms and wanted to know what was going on – like me they thought he should be playing until he moved.

Eventually I was able to persuade the Bolton chairman Derek Warburton to complain to the Football League, and when an enquiry under secretary Alan Hardaker and chairman Bob Lord was held in October it became clear that John Barnwell had not gone to his board to ask for the money to buy Peter Reid. Derek was livid and when Henry Marshall, the Wolves chairman, attempted to apologise he told him where to go.

The following week I told Peter he was playing on the Saturday against Bristol City. Despite creating Alan Gowling's goal in a 1-1 draw he got terrible stick off the Bolton fans and he was knackered, not having played that season. He wanted to come off at half-time but I was not having that and made him see out the ninety minutes.

In fact Peter stayed at Bolton until after I left. Then in 1982 he did move to Everton, where he did really well. By then, though, the fee was a fraction of what they originally offered. Bolton received little more than £60,000 and I'd spent that much taking Red Star Belgrade and Yugoslavian international Dusan Nikolic to Burnden Park. His agent had contacted me and after a fortnight's trial I signed him. He did reasonably well. He was a good passer of the ball, and although it was difficult communicating with him he developed a working relationship with the rest of the players. Unlike Peter, though, he was not a great tackler or battler for the ball.

In the circumstances it was not too surprising we had a poor season in Division Two. The highlights were beating Newcastle United 4-0 in our first home game – Brian Kidd scored a hat-trick – and a 6-1 victory over Cambridge United, also at home. But we lost far too many games by a single goal. We were never really in danger of being relegated but our final-day 3-2 defeat at home to Luton Town left us eighteenth with just thirty-eight points.

I have no way of knowing if the board had already decided to let me go but my eventual departure came after an unpleasant affair following an end-of-season benefit match at Rotherham. The players had showered, grabbed a bite to eat at the after-match buffet and were sitting on the bus. For some reason one of the directors, Brian Turnbull, hadn't turned up. With the bus revving up I went back inside to the buffet area and politely informed him that everyone was waiting. I'd never had bad words with Brian before but that night he spoke to me like a child, telling me not to forget he was a director of the club.

The following morning was my last. There had been no rumours that I was to be sacked but when I received a telephone call from Turnbull asking me to go to his house nearby, I half suspected I was going to be joining the recently sacked managers' club which included Everton's Gordon Lee and Middlesbrough's John Neal.

When I got to his house Turnbull told me that things hadn't gone well and that the side had just scraped through – all of which I knew. So I asked him what was on his mind and he told me that in the circumstances it would be better if I left my post. As he wasn't the major shareholder or even the chairman he probably didn't have the authority to sack me. That should have rested with the owners of the club, the breadmakers Warburtons, specifically George Warburton, but it was obvious Brian Turnbull was not acting without their permission.

Of course I was upset. I had persuaded George Mulhall to return as coach in the March and he was offered my job. I felt he would have a difficult time and so it proved. At the end of the following year Bolton were relegated and George joined me on the list of ex-Bolton managers. Turnbull left Bolton shortly afterwards to enjoy the tax advantages of the Isle of Man.

Although my accomplishments as Bolton manager weren't great – just eighteen victories in sixty-two games

– my overall record at Bolton, Doncaster, QPR and Middlesbrough wasn't too bad: in 547 games under my direction I had won 216, lost 184 and drew 147. If you add in what happened at AEK it totals 577 games with 230 wins, 192 losses and 155 draws.

Chapter 21

Caring for Marjorie

After I was sacked Marjorie and I decided we would move back to Doncaster. My football career had always determined where we lived, but now it was time to settle down. Marjorie's health was deteriorating; she'd suffered arthritis from an early age but as she got older it got worse and eventually she ended up in a wheelchair. She had to take a lot of tablets to manage the pain and as a result she put on a lot of weight.

I became her carer, a role I undertook for almost twenty years before she died in 2001. It's not something I took to easily; it's hard and I can empathise with the millions who do it. You love someone but that doesn't mean you don't also resent having to do so much for them. You often feel that you can never do anything right. I'd had a life where I could do much as I'd wanted. I had enjoyed my life as a player and a manager and to be restricted to the house and local shops took some getting used to. Marjorie would put up with the pain to go and see our daughter most weekends in Grimsby but would be shattered when we got back. Sherley had thrilled us by gaining a 2:1 degree in psychology at Warwick University in 1977. We were ever so proud when we witnessed her graduation ceremony that summer in Coventry Cathedral.

We were not struggling for money; we'd been able to buy our house. We didn't have a lot but I had a small pension from football and we were never the biggest of spenders at the best of times so money wasn't a concern.

I was able to occasionally supplement this with some work in football. The first was coaching at the Bobby Charlton Academy, working with youngsters – Tony Dunne had asked me to get involved and I was delighted to travel to Crewe, where one day I'd work with a group of youngsters aged fourteen to sixteen and the next with a younger group. Bobby would wander around overseeing the activities.

One day I was getting a group to practise their shooting skills. I asked them to chip the ball to me and I would catch it, spin it up in the air and ask them to try and meet it either on the volley or half volley from around thirty yards. The balls were going in every direction but one or two were flying in and Bobby was watching with interest.

'I like that, can I have a go?' he asked. OK, I thought, but I am not making it easy for you – even though his days as one of England's greatest ever footballers were well behind him. So I made the ball spin a little more; but as it hit the ground he walloped it so hard that fortunately the lad in goal never had a chance to get his hands to it. The lad's mouths dropped. So up I threw another spinning ball and he did the same again, and again. Years later I saw an advert in which he does just the same thing; I can't help feeling he owes me a few quid!

When Jim Smith became manager at Newcastle United between 1988 and 1991 I was asked to do some scouting. The chief scout, Tony Collins, arranged it although I told him I couldn't do much as Marjorie had to come first.

It was agreed I'd do games only on a Saturday, which was fine. I would be given a list of matches a few weeks in advance and my role was to report on Newcastle's future opponents. This would involve noting down formations, strengths and weaknesses, whether a side played with wingers or mainly through the middle; did the 'keeper come for crosses; were there any special routines for free kicks and corners. I'd received similar reports as a manager

– some scouts would write as many as twenty pages but I felt those were much too long and I'd keep it to no more than four. I hardly ever spoke to Jim and it can be a frustrating job if you don't get any feedback; I had no idea if the reports contributed in any way to helping the manager and/or players during a match.

They must have thought I was doing a good job, though, because they asked if I might also be prepared to run the rule over players from lower league or non-league clubs who had been recommended by one route or another. I remembered Colin Bell! I discussed this with Marjorie and as long as I was certain of being home for the evening it was agreed I could go ahead.

Sometimes it would be a total waste of time – Newcastle would get a letter from a dad whose son was playing for a decent non-league side and I'd be asked to watch him play. I'd get there early and if I knew the manager, such as Terry Curran at Goole Town, I'd ask him about the player. They'd be honest; there was no point telling lies or exaggerating a player's ability as I'd be getting to watch the lad anyway. Terry, for instance, would tell you if a player was nothing special. He had played at a high level and knew a good player when he saw one.

Some games I'd know very quickly that I'd been sent on a wild goose chase, although I always stayed at least twenty minutes. I'd file a report on each player, about his style on the ball, his passing and movement, whether he was quick or slow and whether he might be worth watching again.

Occasionally I'd feel that a player I'd watched was worth signing – that was the case with Warren Barton. He was in the Maidstone United side that lost at Scunthorpe in October 1989 in a Division Four match but I was impressed enough to suggest he could play at a higher level. Newcastle would have been able to get him, I'd guess, at about £50,000 but for whatever reason my advice was ignored and Warrem moved to Wimbledon the following year for £300,000. Five years later Kevin Keegan paid £4 million for him to move to Newcastle.

Eventually, with Marjorie in poor health, I quit scouting; Newcastle were trying to get me to do matches two nights during the week and one on a Saturday. The money wasn't good enough to justify that amount of time being spent away from home. To all intents and purposes that spelled the end of my footballing career.

Not that it has meant ending all involvement, of course. Over the years I've seen a number of games. I have also, often at Lennie Ashurst's insistence, spoken at a number of Sunderland Supporters branch meetings and I have kept in touch with a good number of my ex-team mates through the ex-players' associations at Sunderland and Middlesbrough.

At Sunderland Winston Young does a marvellous job along with Jim Montgomery and Nicky Sharkey and I enjoy going to games at the Stadium of Light as a guest of honour, as well as playing in the regular golf tournaments. Until recently Alan Peacock and Jim Platt did the same roles at Middlesbrough and I still speak to Alan regularly on the telephone. It's a shame that there is no similar organisation at St James' Park; the only time I get to see Newcastle play these days is when they are on terrestrial television, as I haven't got Sky. Not that I am opposed to the involvement of the company in football. It's brought more money into the game, which isn't a bad thing, and it's helped attract some exceptionally talented overseas players whose skills I hope will be copied by our home-grown talent.

My reason for not having Sky is because I know I would sit watching it all the time. And I want, as I move into my late '70s, to keep as fit as possible. In fact, one of the joys of having been a professional sportsman all my working life is that I got paid to keep fit. Many people spend a lot of money on gyms and use their spare time working out. I never had to do that, and as I have also hardly ever drunk alcohol, I have been pretty lucky healthwise.

It means I can still play sport today in the form of golf.

It was Don Revie who first got me into golf when he arrived at Roker Park in the late '50s. I was hooked almost from the start, but it was difficult to get many games in during the season and it meant I had to make a choice between golf and playing cricket in the summer. I'd started playing for Horden Colliery Welfare cricket team when I finished national service in 1957. At first I was a bowler but over the next three summers I managed to improve my batting to the extent that I was number three for the Horden first XI in the Durham Senior League. I even managed 99 not out one afternoon at Burnmoor and would have got a hundred had the scoreboard been big enough to include the scores of individual players rather than just the team score. It meant the captain Jackie Wheatman, believing I was in my 80s, declared early to give us time to knock over the home team. Only when I got into the dressing room did we find out from the scorer that I was on 99. I never did make a century!

I wasn't the only Sunderland player playing cricket to a decent standard; Len Shackleton was a professional at Wearmouth but, of course, none of us were anywhere near as good as Willie Watson. He played four times for England at football and twenty-three at cricket. During the summer of 1953 he batted for almost six hours at Lord's to save the second Test in the Ashes series. True to form, when we returned for pre-season training Willie, one of the most unassuming men you could ever hope to meet, never even mentioned his exploits.

Because I'd moved to Sunderland in 1957 it meant a bit of a trip each Sunday for the cricket. I was already considering packing it in when the poor weather in the summer of 1960 made up my mind for me – we seemed to spend more time watching the rain than playing. The other players were happy playing cards to while away the time but that isn't my style. I found myself taking out more and more books on golf from the library and becoming increasingly fascinated by the game. I also liked it because it is really about your own skills; so when it came to a choice there was only going to be one winner.

From then on during the summer I'd play two or three times a week at South Shields and when I moved to Billingham I became a member at Seaton Carew. I found it was a great release from the pressures of football management.

I am still playing the game and my partner Sue and I are members of Doncaster Golf Club, which has a fantastic atmosphere. Among the group I play against regularly against is Bob Smith, who tends to be the organiser, Stuart Grindle, a prize-winning gardener, Harry Avill, the comedian of the group, Peter Shaw, Phil Bennett and Brian Deacon, a mad keen Doncaster fan who rarely has a good word to say about the team! We're all retired. My handicap is nine although at one time it was down at three. I am working on getting back to that but I am not sure I'll ever do so – but it won't be for lack of effort.

I'd say that I am pretty accurate off the tee, that my iron shots have improved but my shots into the green are not as good as they should be and I am a steady enough putter. My all-time favourite course is Gleneagles, both the King's and Queen's courses. One time when I was there for a game with Tony Dunne we saw Bing Crosby. In the '70s I played with a number of celebrities, including Jimmy Tarbuck and William Roache, the actor who plays Ken Barlow in *Coronation Street*, at a number of charity fund-raising events across Lancashire. That was good fun. My best ever round was in 1979 when I carded a 74 playing at Gleneagles. I might never beat that but I have promised to make it back up there in the next few years.

I also play golf with Rosie Wight, whom I got to know with her brother Jim. They are the children of Alf Wight, better known as James Herriot, the author of *All Creatures Great and Small*, who became president of Sunderland AFC.

I also like to go out fairly regularly for a meal with Sue. We also entertain people at home, which is in Bessacarr near Doncaster, where I enjoy doing the gardening. We do a lot of walking and I get to see my daughter, her husband Ian and my granddaughter Jane, visiting them regularly with our two dogs, which allows them to run around on the beach at Cleethorpes.

Of my brothers, only Jim is alive. Born in 1932, he is now seventy-eight. Frank, the youngest, died at just forty-seven in 1987, six years after Bob, and Tom died aged seventy-eight in 2002. My mother lived to the ripe old age of ninety-four, and enjoyed ballroom dancing right up until she died in 1995, more than two decades after my father died in 1974 aged seventy-three.

I consider I have been very fortunate in life. It's true that I would have liked to have won the League in 1955, gained more caps for England and been better paid. But it was still great to play hundreds of games at the highest levels of English football. There is nothing like playing in front of huge crowds, especially when you play well and your side wins. The crowds in the north-east are also incredibly passionate about the game – sometimes too passionate, as there can be a tendency for them to want the ball into the box too quickly for my liking – and it's a great place to play football. Len Shackleton once said, when asked to comment about the Liverpool fans in the '60s, that if the clubs in the north-east were as good as Bill Shankly's team the Liverpool fans wouldn't compare. I'd agree with him.

When I was forced to quit playing I enjoyed being a coach and manager and would probably have continued a bit longer had Marjorie, sadly, not been so unwell. I am lucky that today I have a fabulous partner; I am healthy for my age and can still get out and about. Not bad for a colliery lad from Horden.

Index

Index

Index

Index

Index

Index